RECONSTRUCTING MOTHERHOOD AND DISABILITY IN THE AGE OF "PERFECT" BABIES

This is a book about transformation, about the meanings mothers of "imperfect" children give to motherhood and disability in an age in which infants are commodified and new technologies hold out the promise of "perfect" babies. In an era in which specific traits of babies increasingly appear to Westerners in terms of choice, how do mothers of infants and toddlers with disabilities—the children few would actively choose—make sense of their motherhood? The book is based on anthropological field research at a site at which children were evaluated by physicians, and on in-depth interviews with mothers who received "bad news." An ideal short book for teaching courses in anthropology, sociology, disability studies, and women's studies.

Gail Heidi Landsman (Ph.D., Catholic University) is Associate Professor of Anthropology at the University at Albany, SUNY, where she teaches courses in gender, reproduction, and disability. She is the author of numerous book chapters, articles in peer-reviewed journals, and a previous book *Sovereignty and Symbol*. She is also the mother of three children, one of whom has cerebral palsy.

D1596972

RECONSTRUCTING MOTHERHOOD AND DISABILITY IN THE AGE OF "PERFECT" BABIES

Gail Heidi Landsman

Routledge
Taylor & Francis Group

NEW YORK AND LONDON

First published 2009
by Routledge
270 Madison Ave, New York, NY 10016

Simultaneously published in the UK
by Routledge
2 Park Square, Milton Park, Abingdon, Oxon OX14 4RN

Routledge is an imprint of the Taylor & Francis Group, an informa business

© 2009 Taylor & Francis

Typeset in Caslon by HWA Text and Data Management, London
Printed and bound in the United States of America on acid-free paper by
Edwards Brothers, Inc.

Library of Congress Cataloging in Publication Data
Landsman, Gail Heidi, 1951–
    Reconstructing motherhood and disability in the age of "perfect" babies /
by Gail Heidi Landsman.
        p. cm.
    Includes bibliographical references and index.
    1. Parents of children with disabilities. 2. Mothers—Psychology. I. Title.
    HQ759.913.L364 2008
    306.874'3--dc22   2008008814

ISBN10: 0-415-91788-3 (hbk)
ISBN10: 0-415-91789-1 (pbk)
ISBN10: 0-203-89190-2 (ebk)

ISBN13: 978-0-415-91788-9 (hbk)
ISBN13: 978-0-415-91789-6 (pbk)
ISBN13: 978-0-203-89190-2 (ebk)

In memory of my mother, Dorothy Jean ("Dottie") Landsman.

For my daughter, Dorothy Jean ("DJ") Reinhardt.

Contents

Acknowledgments

We all need each other to live well. If we think otherwise, we are fooling
ourselves.

(Bill Rush)

At the heart of this book are the stories told by mothers of disabled
infants and young children. These are not, as stereotypes might lead us
to expect, stories of tragedy, nor even of "triumph" over tragedy, though
tears flowed freely and often in their telling. In collecting narratives,
I imposed on women's time when most were experiencing new, often
chaotic, and incredibly busy schedules, and I asked them to reflect upon
what was for many a profound challenge to deeply held beliefs and
expectations about their lives. That women were willing to tell their
complex stories—of hope, sorrow, betrayal, challenge, transformation
and, unscientific though it sounds, of love—is a gift the full value of
which perhaps they alone can understand. I am grateful beyond measure
to these women and their children.

An anthropologist could not have hoped for a more welcoming field
site than I found at the Newborn Followup Program of the Children's
Hospital of Albany Medical Center. Its director, Dr. Anthony Malone,
M.D. and fellow physicians and nursing staff, including Dr. Deborah
Kris, M.D., Susan Hull, RN, Barbara Quinn, RN and Carol Winn,
RN, encouraged me, taught me, and tolerated my intrusions upon their

busy practice in ways as significant as allowing me to recruit participants in the waiting room and as mundane as removing an especially noisy toy from an examination room because it was affecting the quality of my tape recording. Ms. Hull once commented that they were in the business of "breaking people's hearts"; the time I spent doing participant-observation at Newborn Followup gave me some small insight into the stresses and commitments involved in such work. Though Dr. Malone might reasonably have responded with skepticism or concern over having a scholarly observer and potential critic in his midst, he instead expressed hope that the presence of an anthropologist might lead to improvements in services and particularly in professional-parent communication; I hope his faith in me was not misplaced and that he and other developmental pediatricians find something of value in this work.

I have had the honor of serving on a number of committees that brought me into contact with parents, early-intervention service providers, and administrators from throughout the state. Thanks are due to all the members of the Parent Involvement Committee of the New York State Early Intervention Coordinating Council with whom I served over many years, and to Margaret Sampson in particular; all taught me much about the system that mediates the experience of American parents of young disabled children and about the similarities and variation in that experience in diverse places and circumstances. Many also provided me with superb models of advocacy and perseverance. Donna Noyes of the New York State Department of Health has given generously of her time and expertise, and I appreciate the many opportunities she has provided for me to interact with both professionals and parents. I am grateful as well to Thea Betts Griffin, the former Early Intervention Official of Albany County with whom I shared many enjoyable and helpful conversations about this work; and to other members of the Albany County Local Early Intervention Coordinating Council with whom I had the pleasure of working on, and learning from, various projects.

Many anthropologists of reproduction, including Rayna Rapp, Faye Ginsburg, and Carole Browner, provided encouragement from the early stages of this research, and I treasure the environment of trust and mutual respect they have helped foster in the discipline. I am lucky to have had anthropologist Linda Layne at nearby Rensselaer Polytechnic

Institute; many an idea or apparent obstacle was worked through over lunch or a walk with Linda. My deep gratitude is due as well to the encouragement provided by anthropologist and pioneering disability studies scholar and activist Devva Kasnitz. Her boundless energy and relentless commitment to the highest standards of scholarship and to the pursuit of disability rights both intimidate and inspire; one simply does not want to let Devva down.

This book is in large part about mothers. My own mother, Dorothy Jean ("Dottie") Landsman, was, to put it in deceptively simple terms, a truly good person. Through everyday decisions, she modeled a life in which every human being was accorded worth and dignity. She passed away well before I began this project, but I hope her influence has found its way into this book.

For reasons I shall later explain, in all likelihood this book would not exist at all were it not for my youngest daughter, Dorothy Jean ("DJ") Reinhardt. Nurturing her constituted both the original inspiration for the book and the greatest obstacle to completing it. Throughout, DJ's approach to the world as a good place and her ability to laugh uproariously at life's little annoyances has sustained and humbled me. My husband, Bill Reinhardt, has always stood by me in my endeavors, believing in the value of my work even when my own belief faltered; his support has been invaluable to my work and to my life. During the long course of researching and writing the book, my two older children, Jessie and Seth, endured the perils and torments of teenage life to emerge beautifully into young adulthood. Though they had many complaints about their parents, they never seemed to resent my efforts and time spent on this project, and for this I am grateful. I have been blessed as well with a father whose response to any venture I proposed was always "whatever it is, I'll support ya." And so he has, in ways beyond measure.

Major funding for the research upon which this book is based came from the National Endowment for the Humanities, Humanities Studies in Technology Program. Additional funding was provided by a small grant from the Institute for Research on Women, University at Albany, State University of New York; a pilot study received funding through a Faculty Research Award of the University at Albany.

Some sections of Chapters 3 and 5 appeared in Gail Landsman (1999) Does God give special kids to special parents?: Personhood and the child with disability as gift and as giver. In: L. Layne (Ed.), *Transformative mothering: On giving and getting in a consumer culture* (pp. 133–165). New York: New York University Press.

Segments of Chapter 4 are reprinted from Gail Landsman (2003) Emplotting children's lives: Developmental delay vs. disability. *Social Science and Medicine, 56,* 1947–1960, with permission from Elsevier.

Various chapters use excerpts from my article, Reconstructing motherhood in the age of "perfect" babies: Mothers of infants and toddlers with disabilities, which appeared in *Signs.* Copyright © 1998 by The University of Chicago.

Chapter 5 includes material that originally appeared in "Too bad you got a lemon": Peter Singer, mothers of children with disabilities, and the critique of consumer culture. In: J. S. Taylor, L. Layne, & D. F. Wozniak (Eds.), *Consuming motherhood.* Copyright © 2004 by Rutgers University, The State University of New Jersey. Reprinted by permission from Rutgers University Press.

A portion of Chapter 6 appeared as an article by Gail Landsman (2005). Mothers and models of disability. *Journal of Medical Humanities, 26.* © 2005 Springer Science+Business Media, Inc. With kind permission from Springer Science and Business Media.

Picture Credits

Illustrations 2.1, 2.2, 2.3 and 2.4: Permission for use granted by March of Dimes Birth Defects Foundation.

Illustration 5.1: The artist is Mark Morris. Reprinted with kind permission from the Human Policy Press and the Center on Human Policy.

1

INTRODUCTION

Scholars and practitioners in the medical and helping professions commonly dismiss the acquired knowledge of mothers of young disabled children as a form of "denial" or as a coping mechanism for dealing with guilt or stress. The knowledge is not validated as such and is segregated, seen as intrinsic to times of crisis or to "special mothers of special children," rather than as insight to be made available to the general public. However, it has always been the anthropologist's position that though we may never have full access to the "native's" point of view, we can and should learn from the encounter. This book is an attempt to do just that.

The role of mothers' knowledge in general is, of course, embedded in specific times and places. Preparing to teach my first course on gender, I was struck by the fact that while white American feminist scholars had largely attributed women's relative lack of public power to their reproductive roles, the Mohawk Indian activists who were struggling for sovereignty and with whom I had earlier conducted research at Ganienkeh Territory in the north country of New York State, had consistently referred to motherhood as a rich resource for wise public policy. After all, I was told, no woman would carry a baby for nine months, nurse him, raise him to adulthood, and then easily or recklessly send him off to war.

Residents of Ganienkeh had come from Kahnawake, a reserve near Montreal, Quebec, and from St. Regis-Akwesasne, a reservation straddling the New York-Canadian border; in 1974 the activists had taken over a site in the Adirondack Mountains, proclaiming their actions to be the repossession of traditional Mohawk territory and the land as outside the jurisdiction of New York State. When, after a shooting incident at Ganienkeh, New York State police demanded the Mohawk activists illegally occupying the territory turn over two warriors, it was women who advised the men against it. When a state representative then reportedly gave Ganienkeh two hours to evacuate the women and children prior to state police entering the camp with violence, the women held a council to determine the community's course of action during which they weighed the potential outcomes for children. The women are said to have emerged from the council with the response, "No, we will not leave. There are worse ways to die than from State Police bullets; we won't send our children back to die from alcohol and drugs on the reservation." Based on women's traditional knowledge of and commitment to the welfare of children, the women's statement became a rallying cry not only for the group holding Ganienkeh but for the wider community of traditionalist Iroquois Indian activists (Landsman, 1988: 146–147). By comparison with the Iroquois, mothers' knowledge in mainstream American culture occupies a much more ambiguous and far less authoritative place. Yet might it not also serve goals of political and cultural change?

In spite of lessons learned from my ensuing research on the cultural meanings of motherhood and nurturance in feminist activism (Landsman, 1988; Landsman and Krasniewicz, 1990), in the American woman suffrage movement (1992), and in local and national efforts to pass family and medical leave legislation (1995), it was the experience of becoming the mother of a disabled daughter, "DJ," that ultimately brought this book into being. That this should be so is now an embarrassment to me and speaks to anthropology's general failure to engage with the rich field of disability studies (Kasnitz and Shuttleworth, 2001; Cushing, 2006). Disability now seems glaringly obvious to me as a site from which to address anthropology's central questions of similarity and difference. However, while the draw of difference may finally be luring anthropologists to the study of disability, it is the unsought, unplanned-for encounter with disability that draws American mothers into what is, I argue, a most anthropological experience.

Reproduction in North America is saturated in the discourse of choice and control. Widespread availability of prenatal screening tests, selective abortion for disability, new conceptive technologies, publicized breakthroughs in knowledge of genetics, and the broad dissemination of health information about what women should consume and how they should conduct themselves during and even before pregnancy to ensure a "good" outcome frame the contemporary American experience of procreation.[1] Most pregnant women in the United States have come to assume that it is possible to have what is defined as a perfectly "normal" child; the potential disabled baby imagined by a pregnant woman as she contemplates prenatal screening is, as Press, Browner, Tran, Morton, and LeMaster (1998) describe, "the other." However, for a *mother* of a child newly diagnosed with an impairment, the "Other" is neither hypothetical nor located in an exotic, distant land to be written about by adventuresome travelers or esoteric anthropologists; the Other is—sometimes quite suddenly—a member of the family. And like an anthropologist in a new field site seeking to make sense of profound difference within a common humanity, such a mother, too, becomes engaged in a meaning-making, interpretive process, seeking to find, and often to advocate for, the personhood of a child whose life is routinely devalued, and indeed once might have been devalued by the mother herself.

This is a book, then, about transformation, about the meanings mothers of "imperfect" children give to motherhood and to disability in an age in which infants are commodified and technology seems to hold out the promise of "perfect" babies. It is not a book about disabled people but about the experience of, and possibilities residing in, mothers' ongoing reinterpretations of disability. In an era in which motherhood is achieved rather than ascribed (Ginsburg, 1989) and specific traits of babies themselves increasingly appear to Americans in terms of choice, how do mothers of disabled infants and toddlers—the children few would actively choose—make sense of their motherhood? How do they interpret and negotiate the meaning of disability? How might their experience of nurturing a child who "departs from what is understood to be species typical" (Asch, 1998: 77) contribute to disability studies and disability activism and to our understandings of how personhood is—and could be—constructed in America?

The Study

If the women in this study had experienced their pregnancies and developed their expectations of motherhood within the context of American discourses of choice and control, they also experience mothering a disabled child in a social context of policies and practices far different from that even of the generation of parents just preceding them. In the first half of the twentieth century, parents were encouraged to institutionalize their disabled children; those who kept their children at home were likely to be told that they were depriving them of therapeutic and educational services (Leiter, 2004). A parents' movement in the 1960s and 1970s worked to obtain community-based services and was followed by a wave of activism by disabled adults and later by collaboration among adult, parent, and professional constituencies (Leiter).

Perhaps the most significant outgrowth of this activism for American families has been the establishment of state-run programs of early intervention. Such programs emerged from the federal "Individuals with Disabilities Education Act," which was passed in 1986 and established a program to assist states in implementing statewide systems for children from newborn to age three with disabilities and/or developmental delay. Early Intervention (EI) thereby extended the scope of social policy from school and preschool ages down to birth. New York State's Early Intervention Program went into effect on July 1, 1993. My research began shortly thereafter, in 1995, a time in mainstream North American culture when it was neither "normal" to have a disabled child nor any longer socially appropriate to send such a child to an institution.

The study was undertaken with the cooperation of the Newborn Followup Program of the Children's Hospital of Albany Medical Center, in Albany, New York. In addition to treating infants who had been hospitalized in the neonatal intensive care unit and those referred by pediatricians, family practitioners, child care providers, and parents themselves, the Newborn Followup Program served as an evaluation site to determine eligibility for the state's early intervention program. With a catchment area of 25 counties, it drew children from urban, suburban, and rural communities. The law requires that an early intervention evaluation as well as any therapeutic services a child deemed eligible might receive—including physical therapy, special education, occupational therapy, nursing, social work, nutritional services, speech and language therapy, psychological services, and adaptive equipment—be provided at no charge to families; the site therefore offered the opportunity to observe mothers across a broad range of economic levels.

The field site was a fortuitous choice for numerous other reasons as well. Though space and time were at a premium at the Newborn Followup Program, I was warmly received by a generous staff open to accommodating the particular needs of my research protocol. In addition, pediatric and family practice residents did month-long rotations at the Newborn Followup Program as part of their medical education. This enabled me to observe aspects of how new physicians were being trained to diagnose and understand childhood disability and to communicate with parents. As a participant observer over the course of two years at Newborn Followup, I attended monthly journal club meetings required of residents and attended by the staff and by interested medical personnel from the surrounding area; I was present in the conference area during casual conversation among staff and residents, and I observed as the developmental specialists discussed cases with residents and/or nurses before and after each evaluation. Unlike the medical staff, I did not have nor did I seek access to patient medical records.

Though prior to walking into an examination room I always introduced myself individually to a mother in the waiting room, sat down and explained my research, and received the mother's signed permission to observe her child's session with the doctor, the fact that a nurse and at least one, and usually more, residents were present during a child's evaluation also meant that rooms were already crowded with adults and my presence as an observer less likely to stand out. While it was my intent to have no effect on the evaluation, there were times when it was simply inappropriate to remain an exclusively silent or passive observer. During evaluations it was not uncommon for mothers to cry, and as a matter of courtesy and support I often would discreetly pass the box of tissues to a woman while she continued to listen (or to appear to listen) to the doctor. On occasions when a diagnosis of cerebral palsy was given and a mother seemed to the staff to be having emotional or practical difficulties, a nurse would sometimes comment toward the end of the session that "Dr. Landsman has a child with a similar diagnosis" and that the mom might want to ask me some questions later. Several such conversations took place after the formal session with the doctor.

At the Newborn Followup Program, I observed and recorded on audiotape 130 developmental evaluation sessions of infants and young children younger than the age of 5. At any one time there were as many as three physicians conducting evaluations in separate rooms. Physicians had read hospital and/or other records prior to the child's session, and these were used to judge which session I should observe. My plan was to find those women just entering upon the identity of mother of a disabled child. I had at first naively interpreted this as being the moment of a child's diagnosis. Yet such a moment was often difficult to pinpoint. A definitive diagnosis is not always made at any particular doctor's visit; instead diagnosis may involve accumulation of evidence over the course of a number of visits. Nevertheless, in the absence of a specific medical diagnosis of disability, quantitative measurement of a child's development is required for determining eligibility for early intervention services, and prognoses—general predictions about the existence, type, permanence, and extent of impairment in the future— were usually discussed. I was routed to those sessions at which doctors expected to be giving a mother "bad news."[2]

I interviewed at length 60 of the women whose children, upon evaluation, were determined to have a disability, high risk for disability, or developmental delay significant enough to qualify for early intervention services. The study included two adoptive mothers; while I had casual conversations at Newborn Followup with foster mothers of disabled children, they were not interviewed. The vast majority of interviewees were white. Most of the women interviewed were married, with 17 percent being single or divorced at the time. Mothers ranged in age from teenagers through late 30s. Levels of education varied as well; seven percent of the women had never completed high school, while an equal number had graduate degrees. One-fourth of those interviewed had completed high school or a GED only, another one-fourth had taken some college courses, and 35 percent were college graduates. Only 14 percent were living in a rural setting, with the remainder almost equally divided between urban and suburban communities. While 21 percent described themselves as atheist or currently practicing no religion, the majority of the women interviewed had been raised within some

Christian denomination. Fully half of those interviewed were full-time homemakers at the time, many describing themselves as having recently left previous employment in order to care for their child.[3] Other women worked full or part time in professional positions (17 percent) or in the service sector (12 percent), did secretarial or clerical work (9 percent), or were on public assistance (7 percent) or students.

A wide range of impairments was represented among their children, including mental retardation, cerebral palsy, spina bifida, speech disorders, autism, pervasive developmental disorder, Down syndrome and other genetic disorders, vision and hearing impairments, and malformed or missing limbs; 42 percent of the children had multiple disabilities or significant delays in more than one domain. Though I observed some evaluations of children whose impairments were thought by medical personnel to be related to child abuse or maternal drug use, the mothers of these children chose not to be interviewed.

While many mothers I interviewed commented upon the fact that alternatives to raising a disabled child at home are chosen by other women, no woman in this study took or indicated that she sought information about such options; all were raising their child or children at home and planned to continue to do so. The appendix includes brief biographical sketches of the women interviewed in the study. Names of all participants in the study, including the mothers interviewed, their children and other family members, as well as medical staff observed or mentioned in interviews, are pseudonyms.

I generally interviewed mothers within a month of the child's visit to the Newborn Followup Program. Interviews were open-ended, lasted from one to four hours, and took place in a woman's own home. Children were usually present in the home, often within sight and, not uncommonly in the case of infants, in the mother's arms. Some demographic data were collected during the interview, including age, marital status, job history, education, past and current religious affiliation, number of pregnancies and number of children, and the like. However, the preponderance of each interview consisted of women's narratives of their experience of finding out about and living with their child's disability. All interviews were recorded on audiotape and transcribed verbatim. It was thus possible to compare the recorded conversation between mother and physician at the child's evaluation with a woman's own retelling of, and reflections upon, that experience later. In addition, 22 of the women were interviewed a second time approximately one year after the initial interview. These interviews, when coded and compared with the first round of interviews, provided rich material for analyzing the impact of the experience of mothering on interpretations of disability, personhood, and motherhood.

In agreeing to my presence at a child's evaluation, women had no knowledge of my own personal family life. Going into an *interview*, however, each mother was aware that I was myself the mother of a child identified as disabled. I don't believe that the research would have been impossible had this not been the case, but it positioned me in a particular way in relation to study participants. The notion of the ethnographer's position refers both to the structural location from which one observes and to "how life experiences both enable and inhibit particular kinds of insight" (Rosaldo, 1993: 19). This project constitutes "insider research" but within a community of experience that we had each entered into relatively late in our lives, and from different backgrounds of class, geography, education, ethnicity, and religion. As I describe elsewhere in the book, regardless of the many differences between myself and mothers interviewed, interviewees often expressed their assumption that my being a mother of a disabled child predisposed me to understand their lives and feelings; for some, it was a determining factor in agreeing to be interviewed. For each participant, acknowledgment of what she and I presumably share may have required transformation of an identity that was already developed in another culture (Landsman, 1998: 76). That transformation from one's prior identity to include a newly emerging identity as a mother of a disabled child is one of the themes of the book.

Prior to fieldwork at the Newborn Followup Program, I conducted participant observation at a support group for parents of children who had been or currently were hospitalized at Albany Medical Center's neonatal intensive care unit (NICU). The group, "Parent Outreach and More," met at the hospital and was in existence for about a year. Many of the parents attending did not live in the Albany area and were living temporarily at the nearby Ronald McDonald House or in local hotels. A few mothers of "graduates" of the NICU attended more than once, and there were some repeat visits from mothers of children who had extended hospital stays; in general, however, the composition of the group varied from one week to the next, as infants were born, hospitalized, discharged, and sometimes hospitalized again, or as children died. Few fathers attended the support group meetings; when they did so it was only for a brief time and always in the company of their wives. Unlike the interviews, the support group offered a setting for parents to tell their stories while engaged in the immediate crises of life-threatening medical complications. The setting also allowed those first encountering disability or a child's catastrophic illness to react to and comment upon the stories of others.

During the support group meetings, developmental evaluations, and open-ended interviews, it was not uncommon to hear from a woman that the child's impairment was or would be "harder on my husband." That so many women think this is so is an interesting finding. I did not, however, conduct research to determine whether such perceptions are true in any measurable way. Fathers' experiences and the meanings men give to a child's disability are important for a full understanding of American reproduction, family life, and the role of parenting in changing concepts of disability; they are indeed worthy of research. However, this book remains tightly focused on mothers. In American culture it is to women, not men, that the "special" qualities necessary to raise "special" children are attributed (see Chapter 3). And though each family makes its own particular arrangements, research consistently shows that North American women bear the major responsibility for providing care for a disabled child.[4] Most significantly for this project, however, it is women who are culturally held accountable for making the choices that lead to, or, under presumably "normal" circumstances, preclude disabled children from being brought into the world. It is (pregnant) women whose bodies are tested, whose behavior is monitored, and to whom choices are presented, all in the name of ensuring the birth of "perfect" or "normal" children. This book is directed toward understanding how mothers for whom the outcome might seem to be neither "perfect" nor "normal" reconstruct their motherhood and the meanings of disability.

The collection of narratives in 60 different interviews allowed for comparison of the narratives across features the mothers brought with them to their birth experience. Collecting narratives from more than one-third of the same mothers one year later, as well as observing women in the immediacy of the hospital setting, allowed for comparison across time, revealing the impact of the experience of mothering on meanings of disability. The combination of observation at the pediatric developmental evaluations and post-evaluation interviewing enabled me to analyze the interaction of mothers' narratives with the narratives of medical personnel, that is, to examine how mothers incorporate, reject, or reconstruct elements of the physicians' narratives in their own interpretations. A narrator "not only acts or experiences but 'thinks about' his action, evaluates it, learns from it, and tells the story—not to express his values, but to build them, to create them, to remake them each time he tells his stories" (Stahl, 1983: 274). The research was designed to examine the process of remaking stories as mothers interact with reproductive technologies, medical personnel, their own children, and the society that often devalues them. "Before it becomes a story, experience is chaotic. We tell ourselves stories, at the ends of long, confusing days or after frustrating experiences, to make ourselves whole" (Johnstone, 1990: 128). In this book, I explore how mothers, first encountering and then living with their "less-than-perfect infants," rely on both their culture's shared stories and on their own construction of new stories to make themselves whole.

What Can We Learn?

Mothers of disabled children make their way within a society that devalues their children and in which their motherhood has "failed" to follow the culturally appropriate trajectory (Landsman, 1998: 77). A large body of health psychology and counseling research has focused on factors inhibiting and/or facilitating eventual parental (most often maternal) adjustment to the child's disability (Drotar, et al., 1975; Hastings, et al., 2002; McCubbin and McCubbin, 1993; Van Riper, 2007)[5]; many scholars have proposed stages of grief and of mourning the "death" of the perfect child in such situations (Solnit and Stark, 1961; Irvin, Kennell, and Klaus, 1976; Darling, 1979; Fost, 1981). Mothers' responses to a young child's disability are in these studies described by scholars and service providers in terms of "denial," "compliance," "acceptance of reality," and "coping." In contrast, this book proceeds from mothers' own understanding of themselves and their children and documents mothers' ongoing definitions and redefinitions of their experience. It ultimately suggests that what is commonly referred to as a process of "parental adjustment" may not be a matter of becoming resigned to one's misfortune in not having a "normal child" but rather of being challenged by, and redefining through experience, preexisting cultural understandings of what constitutes "normality," perfection, and personhood.

I ask the reader's indulgence here. Words such as "normal" and "perfect" carry enormous emotional weight, and their use is rightfully offensive to many people. Yet these terms represent the cultural discourses that are readily available to mothers; mothers of newly diagnosed disabled children bring these discourses with them to their experience and are presented with them by others, both in and out of the medical profession, as ways to make sense of their new situation. Mothers in the study do use these terms; they also react to them, negotiate with them, rework them, and often come to reject them. My intent is in large part to document that process.

There is currently no consensus regarding the appropriate term to use for the children to whom I refer. One's choice of terminology may reflect an author's thoughts about the relationship of disability to identity and is sometimes taken to index a scholar's political and academic stance within the field of disability studies. "Children with disabilities" is the term preferred by many U.S. disability studies scholars and activists for its "people-first" quality. It is championed by some parents as well; for instance, parent advocate Katie Snow, whose Web site "Disability is Natural" (www.disabilityisnatural.com) contains her commentary "People First Language," makes a case for eliminating stereotypes that define a child's value and potential by the child's diagnosis. The term *children with disabilities* is meant to suggest that first and foremost, a child is a child, with disability merely incidental to a child's identity. The phrase emphasizes the notion that disability is only one of many characteristics of the child. However, the phrase can also be interpreted to imply that disability, though only one of many qualities, is something that resides within the child rather than being imposed by a societal response to impairment. To some, the term *children with disabilities* is also problematic because it seems to maintain a single standard of normality that people with impairments should strive to achieve. In the words of one disability studies scholar, "the term 'person with a disability' demonstrates and is underscored by a 'normative' resemblance that we can attain if we achieve the status of being deemed 'people first'... in the eyes of an ableist-centered society" (Overboe, 1999: 24).

In this book, I use the term *disabled children*, the phrase more commonly used by British disability studies scholars. This term is not meant to deny the full personhood of a disabled child but rather to acknowledge both that a child with an impairment is primarily disabled by society rather than by a quality intrinsic to the child, and that disability may not only inform one's life but be a positive factor in it (Overboe, 1999: 24). The use of "disabled" as an adjective has indeed become common as a marker of pride in the disability rights movement. "Rather than maintaining disability as a secondary characteristic, Simi Linton (1998: 13) points out, *disabled* has become a marker of the identity that the individual and group wish to highlight and call attention to."

Mothers in the study generally engaged with disability within the contexts of their own prior experiences, their current family and social circles, and medical and rehabilitation settings; the terms to which *they* were more often exposed were "handicapped children" and "children with special needs." There was not uniformity across mothers in terms used. As we shall see, however, that they were generally unaware of the linguistic nuances and academic and political debates over terminology did not prevent mothers of disabled children from grappling with profound questions of the meaning of disability and its relation to a person's identity and self; that is, with some of the very issues that are central to analyses of terminology in disability studies and in disability rights movements.

The book broadly follows the sequential order of American women's experience of finding out about and nurturing a disabled child. Chapter 2 presents the expectations and the understandings of disability that women bring to their experience of having a disabled child; in particular, it describes the discourse of choice, control, and mother-blame within which American women find themselves held publicly accountable for the existence of an infant or young child with an impairment. The relationship between the culturally ambiguous or less-than-full personhood of her disabled child and a woman's sense of diminished motherhood is addressed in Chapter 3; also included there is discussion of the role of the medical profession in authorizing and/or denying a child's full personhood. The next two chapters reveal different ways in which mothers' narratives both attribute personhood to their disabled children and reinstate their own "real" motherhood against mainstream discourses of disability; in this vein, Chapter 4 focuses on how women use the concept of developmental delay to emplot their children's lives into a culturally acceptable trajectory, while Chapter 5 examines how, through the metaphor of the gift, women negotiate and transform culturally constructed meanings of personhood, perfection, and normality.

The development and representation of models of disability have been central to scholarship in disability studies and to disability activism; these efforts have proceeded largely apart from anthropological analyses (Kasnitz and Shuttleworth, 2001) and often under the assumption that they are at cross purposes with parental, especially maternal, desires. In Chapter 6, I seek to have disability studies, disability activism, and the anthropological analysis of mothers of disabled children mutually inform each other. In this concluding chapter, I bring mothers' experience and knowledge to bear on efforts to theorize disability, to revise the concept of "normal," and to establish a social environment in which justice and the expression of full lives would prevail for all.

At the practical level of providing early intervention services to disabled children, it is becoming increasingly clear that "understanding a family's response to their child's disability is important because it affects the kinds of support and services that can be offered" (Wayman, Lynch, and Hanson, 1990: 68). As early intervention service programs strive to make their services "family-centered," the need to understand mothers' interpretations of their children and of their own motherhood becomes ever more critical.[6] Nevertheless, this book keeps its distance from the genre of literature, much of it patronizing to both parents and disabled people, designed to assist families. The overarching question I have asked is not how do mothers cope, but rather, what have they *learned?*

In short, I did not set out to help mothers but rather to explore what women who nurture young disabled children have come to know about what it means to be a person. The book is about knowledge acquired in unsuspected and initially unwanted places. Many mothers of disabled infants have given birth to children who, given prior awareness of the disability, they might have chosen not to bring into the world. How such women give meaning to their children and create their own identities as mothers promises to teach us much about the broad but central anthropological questions of how people in particular times, places, and circumstances construct their very definitions of humanity.

2

DOING EVERYTHING RIGHT

Choice, Control, and Mother-Blame

It's funny the things people say to you. Either they assume that this is
God's wish that you had a special child, or you know, that you did drugs
and caused this to your child type of thing.

(Lisa Hart)

Recalling comments made to her, a mother of a multiply-disabled girl
here identifies the two prevalent cultural explanations for the presence
of disabled infants in a technocratic society. One explanation is meant
to flatter, the other to blame; both distance the birth of a child with
a disability from the experience of "normal" people. The concept that
some mothers are "chosen" for the task of raising "special" children will
be addressed in Chapter 3. Here I focus on the notion that mothers
bring disability into their lives through the (poor) choices they make.

Mother-blame is neither new nor specific to Euro-American culture.
There are many historical and ethnographic examples of societies
in which the birth of a disabled newborn is linked to parental, and
particularly maternal, misconduct. Scheer and Groce report that among
the Dogon, for instance, it was believed that women who have copulated
with a bush spirit give birth to disabled infants and that incestuous
sexual unions are considered the cause of disability among the Bantu
(1988: 28). Francisco Manual Tembe (2002) reports that among the
accepted causes of childhood disability in Mozambique are bad spirits
brought by the wife from her family; as a result, a wife may be separated
from her family, marginalized by neighbors, and left to care for a disabled
child alone. Many Chinese parents in Taiwan interpret obviously disabled

children as manifestations of their own wrongful deeds in this life or a previous cycle of incarnation, resulting in a strong sense of guilt and personal responsibility for disability (Kang, Lovett, and Haring, 2002). According to Tsipy Ivry, the authoritative narratives of Japanese doctors depict women "as ecosystems—literally, as the somatic... and mental... environments within which babies are encapsulated and on the quality of which their health was almost totally dependent" (Ivry, 2006: 446). And the Korean term "Tae Gyo" refers to prenatal practices and attitudes believed important to the health and intelligence of babies; a cultural emphasis on good provision of Tae Gyo, including performance of enrichment activities during pregnancy, contributes to blaming mothers in Korea for their developmentally delayed children (Cho, Singer, and Brenner, 2000). Maternal behavior before or during a woman's pregnancy has wide currency throughout the world as cause of a child's physical or cognitive impairment.

With the emergence of specialized educational and medical professions in the nineteenth-century United States, "both the causal direction and moral blame for most childhood disability were thought to begin with the parents (especially those with the poor judgment to be poor and female)"; residential schools and asylums were developed at that time for purposes of moving disabled or vulnerable children away from their parents (Ferguson, Gartner, and Lipsky, 2000: 75). By the early decades of the twentieth century, the "feebleminded" woman was the quintessential "bad mother," representing immoral procreation and the dangers of passing on "defective" genes. American women in that era of eugenics were expected to be vigilant in order to prevent feeblemindedness in their offspring "in proper procreative habits, low stress and appropriate care during pregnancy, and attentiveness to signs of idiocy postnatally" (Carlson, 2001: 133).

The current routine availability of prenatal screening for fetal abnormalities in the United States, the development of new reproductive technologies, and the widespread dissemination of expert knowledge regarding the impact of maternal behavior on pregnancy outcome have affected in new and particular ways American women's accountability for the failure to produce "perfect" babies. These technologies play out within cultural and historical contexts, however, and in themselves do not create this accountability. For instance, the extraordinary high rate of ultrasound among Israeli women is linked to both the Israeli "heightened sense of existential threat" and to a specific ethno-theory of the body that defines the destiny of a baby as predetermined by its initial body composition. Avid consumers of new reproductive technologies, pregnant women in Israel are viewed as non-relevant to the health of the fetus (Ivry, 2003). In stark contrast, the U.S. women's narratives I collected reveal that reproduction in American culture is represented as subject to individual control, with the mother held responsible for birth outcome both through her obligation to undergo prenatal screening and selective abortion of defective fetuses and through her duty to regulate the uterine environment.[1] The engendered scientific attribution of equal material (genetic) donations and unequal social burdens attributes to men "proprietary interest" but assigns to women the actual responsibility for pregnancy outcome (Rapp, 1999b: 88); thus, even with increasing geneticization, women are held accountable for the birth of disabled children in American culture.

Calculating Culpability: Compliance with Prenatal Diet

Maternal drug abuse, alcohol consumption, child abuse, and lack of prenatal care are indeed all statistically associated with childhood disability, as is poverty;[2] however, while each of these factors was implicated in some of the cases observed at the Newborn Followup Program, among the mothers *interviewed* none had children whose disabilities were attributed by medical professionals to maternal behavior. Each mother's narrative reflects her awareness during pregnancy of expert knowledge regarding the effects of maternal behavior on the health of the fetus. This awareness was not affected by the age of the mother or her level of education.[3] With few exceptions (including adoptive mothers, a mother who drank heavily during the pregnancy, and another who got pregnant while using birth control), mothers' narratives include some statement to the effect that she had done "everything right" and therefore had believed she would not have a disabled child. For most mothers, "doing everything right" involved getting regular prenatal care, including various diagnostic tests, from medical professionals; eating healthy foods; and refraining from smoking, drinking, and using over-the-counter, prescription and illegal drugs during pregnancy. Some mothers also included in "doing everything right" either waiting to have a child until they were married or having their child early when they were still young and healthy. Exercising, giving up caffeine, and gaining the "right" amount of weight were often pointed to, though just what was considered the right amount of weight varied among the women. In general, the image that had been accepted by these mothers is one in which positive pregnancy outcome is within the control of a woman who is in compliance with expert medical advice.

When first hearing a diagnosis, therefore, most mothers at least initially assumed that they personally must have done something wrong to account for the disability. It was common in both individual interviews and at the hospital's neonatal intensive care unit (NICU) support group to hear statements such as "I probably should have quit work earlier," "I should have taken the elevator instead of the stairs," or "I know it's crazy, but I keep wondering if I ate too many Big Macs or something." Thirty-three-year old Michelle White recalls seeing her premature daughter after she had been transferred from her home hospital to Albany Medical Center:

> When I got there five days later she was 1 lb. 8 oz. and she was on a flat bed with a heat lamp in the cellophane. And all she was, was skin, bones, and organs… I screamed. I went into hysterics. And they took me out. I was blaming myself. I must have done something wrong to make this poor child suffer like this.

Maria Peters is a married nineteen-year-old mother of Puerto Rican descent who, before discovering she was pregnant, had planned to go to college. She describes first hearing about the child's risk for disability.

> When I found that out, then I was thinking maybe yeah, maybe I did something, maybe it was from the shots because I had got the MMR shot to go to school. And that's when I started crying, like really bad. I'm like, "I messed him up."

Prior to bringing her child to Newborn Followup, Lucy Baker had been told by a doctor that her child's cognitive delays were due to "some sort of autosomal recessive gene"; at her visit to the Newborn Followup Program "the hardest thing" to hear was the developmental specialist's contradictory explanation that "it was something from when I was pregnant." "And obviously," she continued,

> they can tell you as many times as they want "It was nothing you did, nothing would have changed it," it doesn't make it any easier... That really was what kind of sent me over the edge, you know.

By locating causality in the uterine environment, the doctor had, in essence, confirmed her guilt.

Research on pregnant women in the United States suggests that during pregnancy a woman negotiates among the sometimes competing interests of what she believes her baby-fetus needs and what she herself wants; according to a study carried out in California, pregnant women have "internalized the norms of biomedical knowledge regarding proper nutrition" (Markens, Browner, and Press, 1997: 366), but nevertheless make accommodations in accordance with their own desires and embodied knowledge (see also Browner and Press, 1997). Findings from my study are consistent with those of Markens, Browner and Press in that regardless of whether they followed biomedical advice to the letter, women indicate that they were very aware of what biomedical practitioners advised they "should" be eating. All but one mother in the study subjected her prenatal diet to some level of conscious control. The exception was Phyllis Smith who, uninsured and despondent over problems in her marriage, drank alcohol heavily during her unwanted pregnancy. Phyllis states that while she was just too depressed at the time to care, she nevertheless knew that drinking was bad for the baby. Though doctors do not attribute her baby's disabilities, including deafness and visual impairment, to her drinking during pregnancy, Phyllis herself does.

As did the pregnant women studied in California, women I interviewed describe how *during their pregnancies* they too had relied on their own past experiences or those of their mothers or friends to reassure themselves that occasional "lapses" such as a cigarette or drink here or there would not in themselves cause damage, especially when offset by other "good" behaviors.[4] My study, however, was focused not on the period of pregnancy but on what follows. While *pregnant* women may talk in general terms about balancing good behaviors against bad for the overall health of the future baby, mothers of premature infants or of babies with birth defects recall with startling precision their failures to comply with actual or implied biomedical advice; many attempt to correlate those individual violations of dietary rules with their knowledge of fetal development. During pregnancy, women may express a belief in a causal relationship between a baby's general good health and eating habits that are simply "more-good-than-bad"; mothers of disabled infants, however, incorporate new information— their pregnancy outcome—to reinterpret this explanation and consider the possibility that even a one-time breach in recommended diet can have an immediate, specific, and direct effect on pregnancy outcome.

A striking feature of mothers' narratives thus are women's attempts to pinpoint their specific violations of the recommended prenatal diet and to relate them to their knowledge of stages of fetal development. Upon receiving her son's diagnosis of spina bifida, thirty-year-old nurse Ashley Burkart tried to recall her behavior during early pregnancy: "I know it happens by the 28th day, so I'm trying to think—I know when I got pregnant because this whole thing was very planned out—so I'm trying to think what was I doing that day?" When Judith Larson found out that one of her twin daughters had a seizure disorder and developmental delays, the first thing she thought of was the Super Bowl party she had gone to before she knew she was pregnant, at which she drank beer, ate a lot, and smoked cigarettes. "You know, like they say, that's not good," and though "it's not very likely doing that for one day is going to cause major birth defects, still… you get these guilty feelings." Tina Graham, whose son has mental retardation, similarly reviewed her pregnancy: "Did I eat the right things? I mean I went over everything. I took one Tylenol when I was pregnant. One, and it haunted me."

Upon her son's diagnosis with pervasive developmental disorder (on the autistic spectrum), Maureen Quinlan immediately thought, "Okay, I had half a glass of wine on our anniversary, so I thought, oh, gee, that's what did it." This last case is particularly ironic in that poor mothering, specifically an emotionally distant child-rearing style described by Bruno Bettleheim in his famous *The Empty Fortress* (1967), was once widely considered to be the cause of autism. Maternal responsibility for disability has not abated since that time but rather has been expanded to, and now focused upon, the gestational period. At the evaluation, Connie Brown, whose son was born missing one hand, appeared anxious to learn from the developmental pediatrician the point during a pregnancy when the fetal hands develop; during her interview, she told me she had specifically asked the doctor for the information so that she could determine whether that time coincided with the evening she drank at her sister's fortieth birthday party.

> I keep going back to that time, counting the days to when I thought I was pregnant and I didn't know at the time because it was way too early to tell. And I still keep saying maybe if I wouldn't have had those three Absolut and tonics this wouldn't have happened. And that's what I've been beating myself up about over and over and over again.

Women do not necessarily actually believe that such individual breaches of the preferred regimen caused their child's disability. However, most report having had to fight their feelings that this was so. Some women explicitly describe this sense of responsibility and guilt in gendered terms. Connie Brown commented that her husband tells her all the time, "This is ridiculous, we don't know why it happened, who cares why it happened, that's not the issue," to which she says she responds "You're absolutely right, but you don't understand; you've never carried a baby."

Except in those cases in which a woman has definitively learned through chromosomal testing or genetic counseling that her child's disability is traceable to a genetic defect inherited through the child's father, the mother's responsibility for control of the fetal environment is paramount in women's *early* reflections on the cause of the child's disability. That this sense of maternal responsibility for birth outcome is found across all types of disabilities and across class and educational lines speaks to the pervasiveness of Americans' acceptance of the validity of, if not full compliance with, biomedical advice regarding prenatal diet. This is so, however, not because of women's blind acceptance of biomedical experts as authoritative but, at least for some women, because biomedical advice regarding the importance of proper maternal nutrition appears to fit closely with women's own embodied experience of fetal development during pregnancy. Donna Leiden reflected on how much easier her son's disability has been on her husband. "He has always been like, 'he's going to be fine, it's just an arm, it's just a hand...'" "But then again," she responded to her husband, "I suppose you didn't grow him."

Abstract biomedical knowledge regarding the genetic contribution of the male is accepted but only in terms of the man's passing on a specific inherited gene or genes for a disability; the possibility of birth defects caused by the male's exposure to environmental toxins or his own prior drinking or drug use, for instance, were never entertained in mothers' narratives I collected. Instead, environmental influences on the fetus-baby are interpreted as mediated exclusively by the mother's own body and behavior.

The feminist movement may have inadvertently exacerbated women's public accountability for what are considered poor birth outcomes. "Women's claims to exclusive control over reproduction decision-making have rested heavily (if uneasily) on feminist arguments that women's gestational contribution to reproduction is unique" (Daniels, 1999: 84–85). Daniels suggests that feminists have been aware that diminishing the social and political importance of gestation could result in endorsing more male control over fetal and female bodies (1999: 85); a consequence of the current prevalence of the belief that women's contribution to procreation is greater than men's may be that responsibility for fetal harm rests more strongly with women than with men.

Linda Layne focuses her critique of feminism on the ethic of individual responsibility endorsed by the feminist health movement.

> The fundamental premise of the women's-health movement, that women must wrest back control of their bodies from physicians, *especially* during pregnancy and birth, reinforces the notion that positive birth outcomes are something women can control.
>
> (Layne, 2003: 243)

In this context, the failure to produce a positive birth outcome takes on a moral dimension.

While American women generally accept biomedical authority in issues of prenatal care, they do so critically. Browner and Press (1997) have shown that during pregnancy women implement those recommendations that are confirmed by embodied experience and reject both those that are difficult to fit into daily life and those that run counter to their own preexisting beliefs (120). There is little reason to suspect that women in this study had approached their prenatal care substantially differently. However, my research extends the time frame analyzed, demonstrating that women incorporate the experience of giving birth to a child diagnosed with or at risk for disability into their (re)assessment of authoritative biomedical recommendations. Very soon after learning of their child's diagnosis, mothers reinterpret biomedical prenatal recommendations in more restrictive terms than they had done during pregnancy, such that they postulate a *direct and immediate* causal relationship between maternal diet and pregnancy outcome. In this way, explanations for a disability can be linked by a woman directly to a specific drink, pill, or action (climbing stairs, cooking Christmas dinner) she took on a particular day. During a child's developmental evaluation, therefore, a mother will often question the doctor regarding the exact point during the pregnancy when the disability developed in the fetus, and later use that information, if given, to determine whether there is a direct match with the time she recalls having deviated from biomedical advice. Mothers in this way perform calculations of their level of culpability for what is culturally regarded as a dismal failure: a disabled child.

With the longer-term experience of mothering (rather than simply giving birth to) a disabled child, such calculations may undergo additional reassessments. As will be discussed in later chapters, the result is often the development of a critique of the dominant cultural interpretation of disability as failure and/or of the mother as a site of blame for disability. The act of mothering a disabled child is, as will become apparent later, regarded by women in this way and others as transformative. The focus of this chapter, however, is the particular temporal point that exists between a woman's expectations during pregnancy and her practice of mothering a disabled child. How do American women reconcile the attitudes they bring with them from pregnancy regarding maternal responsibility for control of fetal development with the newly acquired knowledge that their own child has a disability?

Public Health Campaigns and Mother-Blame

I did not ask women about their diets or drug use during pregnancy, yet few failed to bring the issue up on their own. Both in interviews conducted shortly after a child's diagnosis and in those conducted a year later, when women recalled their memories of first learning of their child's disability, they clearly described holding themselves accountable for the child's health in terms of compliance with prenatal dietary advice. Often, as in the cases of Judith Larson and Connie Brown, they expressed guilt and/or regret for not having adhered to dietary restrictions during the time before they even knew they were pregnant. In this way, women's narratives suggest that maternal responsibility has been expanded beyond the consciously known prenatal period to include the pre-pregnancy period of a woman's life as well.

The belief in accountability for *pre*-pregnancy behavior is consistent with current public health literature, which stresses that a woman should begin to prepare for a healthy baby well before becoming pregnant. It is also reflected in the arena of the workplace. *Auto Workers v. Johnson Controls*, for instance, raised the issue of whether women of child-bearing age should be denied higher paying jobs in a heavy industry (where they would be exposed to environmental hazards) as a means "to 'protect' fetuses that do not even exist" (Pollitt, 1998: 279).

The March of Dimes organization distributes a "Preconception Planning Information Sheet" and has produced a series of public health materials entitled "Think Ahead!" dealing with pre-pregnancy issues; recipients of fund-raising solicitations from the organization get a list of recommendations that includes advice to visit one's doctor prior to conceiving. Visitors to the Centers for Disease Control and Prevention (CDC) Web site can read "What YOU can do to Prevent Birth Defects." Noting that "so many pregnancies are unplanned or mis-timed," the CDC recommends that

> if you are having sex and you are capable of becoming pregnant, you should be taking 0.4 mg. of folic acid each day in case you become pregnant—even if you're not planning to become pregnant for a long time.[5]

For those who are thinking of getting pregnant sometime in the near future, the CDC notes that "getting ready for pregnancy is an important step to a healthy pregnancy and a healthy baby," and provides five steps, which include taking 400 mcg of "folic acid every day for at least three months before getting pregnant to help prevent birth defects," stopping smoking and drinking alcohol, making sure any medical condition is under control, consulting a health care professional about any over-the-counter and prescription medications one is taking, and avoiding contact with toxic substances that could cause infection at work and at home (http: //www.cdc.gov/ncbddd/pregnancy_gateway/before.htm).

Health professionals have supported the notion of women's responsibility for getting professional advice prior to pregnancy on the theory that it is during early pregnancy, before a woman may even be aware that she is pregnant, that a fetus or embryo is most vulnerable to harm. That a woman's body may be the site of harm to the fetus represents a relatively recent view in American life. As Laury Oaks explains, until the 1960s, health experts presented women's biology as itself *protective* of fetal health (2001: 22). This was exemplified in the notion of the placental barrier, thought to block hazardous substances from fetal circulation. The discovery in the late 1950s and early 1960s of an association between women who took the drug thalidomide during pregnancy to ease morning sickness and the birth of children with major physical deformities led to a revision of the concept of a protective placental barrier. Ironically, as Oaks (p. 24) points out, this reversal of medical thinking bolstered the authority of the medical profession to supervise prenatal care; it also shifted to women the responsibility to protect the health of the fetus, a notion that remains the dominant theme in pregnancy advice literature. "You have the chance," the authors of the popular book *What to Expect When You're Expecting* inform their pregnant readers, "to come as close as possible to guaranteeing your baby not just good health, but excellent health—with every bite of food you put in your mouth" (Eisbenberg, Murkhoff, and Hathaway, 1991: 80).

In part because of the assumption that men harmed by toxic exposure would be rendered infertile, the male role in fetal harm received little scientific attention (Daniels, 1997). It has received even less attention from the general public. Public warning labels in bars and on beer and liquor containers are reminders to mothers of low-birth-weight infants that society holds *them* accountable for their children's disabilities. Women have been the primary targets for public health campaigns on birth defects; my research suggests that such messages have been heard and for mothers of disabled children provide a reference point for their sense of guilt and/or feelings of being blamed by others. "I've had people really openly ask me if I did drugs while I was pregnant," complains Tina Graham, "and that to me is like a knife in the chest."

Posters such as one produced by the March of Dimes, displaying two dramatically different-sized baby footprints and the caption "Guess which baby's mother drank while she was pregnant" explicitly express maternal blame. The "Mommy...Don't" posters produced by March of Dimes portrayed the fetus as a subject whose interests are endangered by his/her mother's choices. Sonya Somich routinely obtained infant formula for Katrina, her third child, at the Women, Infants, and Children (WIC) office. Katrina was born prematurely at less than twenty-four weeks' gestation; for months after being discharged from the NICU, the baby still used oxygen. Sonya described the poster, which hung on the WIC office wall. The poster showed two babies. On the left, she said, was a healthy baby, with a statement reading that if you ate well, stayed off drugs and alcohol, and got regular prenatal care, you could have a child like that, fat and happy. If, however, you used drugs and alcohol and smoked, you would have, "well, there was a baby who looked just like Katrina."

A 1994 March of Dimes catalog of public health education materials did state that "more and more studies underscore the significant impact

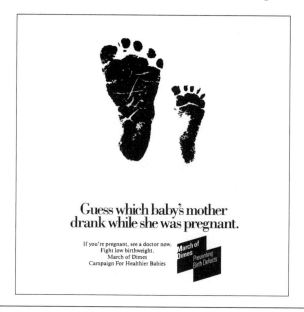

Figure 2.1 Poster from the March of Dimes Campaign for Healthier Babies, c. 1994.

Figure 2.2 The poster's caption reads: "You wouldn't give your baby a cigarette or a drink after it's born. Don't smoke or drink while you're pregnant. Smoking can stunt your baby's growth. Alcohol can cause severe birth defects. And…get early and regular prenatal care," c. 1995.

Figure 2.3 The poster's caption reads: "You wouldn't give your baby drugs after it's born. Don't take drugs while you're pregnant unless your doctor, who knows you're pregnant, prescribes them. Some drugs can cause severe birth defects. And…get early and regular prenatal care," c. 1995.

of a father's health behaviors and support of the mother on the health of his baby," and included pamphlets entitled "Dad, It's Your Baby Too" and "Men Have Babies Too" (March of Dimes, 1994). The phrasing of such titles suggests that the father's role in birth outcome had not yet been accepted by a society that nevertheless openly embraced the notion of maternal responsibility. Ten years later, the March of Dimes Web site's section on pregnancy had expanded emphasis on fathers and had a section entitled "Just for Dads"; its advice, however, was primarily related to "helping out during pregnancy," including "help her eat a lot of different foods," "help your partner stay away from alcohol," and "help your partner stay away from street drugs."[6] Societal concerns with the health behaviors of individual women, while very useful, may deflect attention not only from the role of male behavior and male health practices in reproductive outcome but from the consequences of poverty and exposure to environmental and workplace hazards for both men's and women's reproductive lives.

A current prenatal care poster produced and distributed by the March of Dimes lists "Three Ways to Have a Healthy Baby." The tips include: Take a pill with folic acid every day; don't smoke, don't drink alcohol or take drugs; and see a health care provider as soon as you think you are pregnant. While perhaps appearing less accusatory of mothers than some earlier posters and certainly offering excellent advice, the implication is still that the birth of a healthy (i.e., non-disabled) child is within the control of a woman who behaves appropriately and who seeks and complies with professional medical care during pregnancy. Yet while the belief in maternal responsibility for childhood disability is widespread and persistent, according to the Centers for Disease Control and Prevention, the causes of about 70 percent of all birth defects remain unknown (www.cdc.gov/ncbddd/bd/faq2.htm#IllegaldrugsandBD).

"Doing Everything Right" vs. The "Bad" Mother: Reflections on Choice, Consequences, and Class

Disability scholars and the memoirs of disabled people (Davis, 1995; Hockenberry, 1997; Connolly, 2007) point to the way in which a disability always produces the demand for a response. The concept of

Figure 2.4 March of Dimes poster, c. 2007.

disability is in this way comparable to our understanding of race or gender. However, as Davis notes, if one is a woman or a person of color, one's body reveals enough so that one doesn't have to explain *why* one is a woman or a person of color; conversely, "the disabled body must be explained, or at least tolerate the inquisitive gaze (or the averted glance) of the questioner. The question never has to be put because it is always actively in a default mode—it is already asked" (Davis, 1995: xvi). Photographer Kevin Connolly, who has no legs, traveled the streets throughout the world on a skateboard and captured these questions in the form of photographs of stares. In his statement for "The Rolling Exhibition," he describes the question and the varied, context-dependent stories that follow each stare:

> Was it disease? Was it a birth defect? Was it a landmine? These narratives all come from the context in which we live our lives. Illness, drugs, calamity, war—all of these might become potential stories depending upon what we are exposed to in connection with disability.
>
> (Connolly, 2007)

Mothers in the study describe their sense that indeed the question is being asked but feel it is asked not of their innocent children but of them. The context here is one in which maternal behavior is highly scrutinized. Thus, Nancy Papagallo, a young single mother whose infant son is on oxygen because of a heart defect, talked about taking her child out in public: "It's hard. I don't want them thinking—they look at my kid thinking that I've done something wrong."

The profound injustice of having done "everything right," of having followed the experts' advice, and still having a disabled child while other mothers who used drugs or alcohol during pregnancy have normal children, is a common theme in the stories of mothers of disabled infants (Landsman, 1998). Some excerpts follow:

> I did everything right before I was pregnant for her. I didn't smoke, ate right, exercised, and for two months she was fine.... I've asked God numerous times. My husband doesn't want to talk to me anymore, you know, I get angry. I did everything right to have her. Why does she have to suffer? Why do we have to suffer? We wanted her. Some people go out and have 20 million kids, and every single one of them is fine. They had six beers or whatever. It just doesn't make any sense to me. It makes you angry that you tried to do everything right.
>
> (Laura Robertson)

> You know, I never realized that that could happen, number one. And that, why me? You ever ask yourself, why my kid? Why my kid? I never smoked. I never drank. You do, you ask yourself. I barely even ate, you know? I never did anything wrong. I had a doctor from when I was four weeks on. You think there's no way.
>
> (Denise Rivers)

> It just tears at you that you worked so hard, and you ate well, and you exercised, and you did everything possible thing that you could do to make sure you had a healthy baby.... I was meticulous as to what I ate and how often I ate, and I gained eighteen pounds with him, just eighteen pounds. So I was careful not to overeat and just eat the correct foods, and take my vitamins, and I worked very hard in keeping him—knowing he would be healthy, which he wasn't. And there's hundreds of babies that their parents eat junk food and smoke cigarettes and do drugs. These babies don't seem to be born with birth defects. The anger that you feel

when you work so hard, and you still end up with a baby that's got a problem.

(Francine Hanson)

Francine Hanson's son, her second child, was born in a small, rural hospital. Compared to her daughter, he seemed to her to be weak and poor at nursing; she found she often had to shake him awake for feedings. She tells how when she called the hospital nurses to express her concerns, she was told simply that she was not feeding the baby enough. Angry at the suggestion that she was not accurately assessing her child's needs, she requested a referral to a cardiologist in Albany. On being given an appointment for one month later, Francine called the cardiologist's office herself and demanded to see the physician earlier. She was given an appointment for the following week. According to Francine, at the appointment the cardiologist ran some tests and immediately called for an ambulance to take the infant to Boston Children's Hospital for emergency surgery; the boy was about to go into congestive heart failure.

In telling her story, Francine described how indignant she was that her own knowledge as a mother had been trivialized (but was now validated in the story). What most infuriated her, however, was that she and her son had to wait an hour for an ambulance and EMT crew for the trip to the out-of-town hospital. The hugely popular rock band the Grateful Dead was performing in Albany that day, and numerous ambulances were stationed at the concert venue, presumably in anticipation of the need to treat drug overdoses of fans. Here were people *choosing* to endanger themselves, Francine maintained, while an innocent child, who had done nothing to bring on his own precarious situation, was left to suffer. This story became a commentary on innocence and responsibility for disability and a reflection on the capricious relationship between choice and consequences. Some people, it is implied, *do* deserve or earn their disabilities as, indeed, some mothers risk harm to their babies. The inequity is that those who choose to take the risk may nevertheless escape harm, while the truly innocent, both mother and child, may not.

The stories in which mothers blame themselves, identifying something that they unintentionally, perhaps, but nevertheless "did wrong," do the work of perpetuating the dominant cultural belief that outcomes can be controlled through correct choices. For the women who configure the otherwise insignificant sequence of activities and events of their pregnancies into the larger plot of individual responsibility, control, and cause-and-effect reality, preexisting knowledge of how the world works remains intact but at the expense of a woman's identity as a good mother. Mothers of disabled infants who hold themselves *innocent* of wrongdoing in pregnancy, conversely, *can* lay claim to the identity of good mother; for them, however, the irony inherent in making the right choices and still having a disabled baby is left unresolved. Life is simply, and maddeningly, unfair.

The pain inherent in confronting and seeking meaning in this unresolved irony was brought to the fore in an exchange between two women at a hospital support group meeting. Telling the story of her three-year-old who was currently hospitalized with leukemia and of her baby with Down syndrome, who had recently died during heart surgery at seven months of age, a mother commented that friends often look at her and wonder how she can do it. She explained that she responds by telling them of her belief in a poem posted on the wall at the Ronald McDonald House (housing out-of-town parents of hospitalized children) that describes how the angels choose which child will go to which parent and ensures that God gives special children to special parents. The immediate response from the mother of a child with spina bifida listening to this story was a bitter laugh.

> Yeah, right. What I want to know is, why Jessica? Why does *she* have to suffer? You do everything to be a good mom and this happens to her. And over there there's people drinking and druggin' and their kids are fine. I don't get it. I just don't get it.

Referring to the NICU, the discharge nurse sighed in response, "It's the most unfair place there is."

Of course, dominant discourse does provide an explanation for "why," and mothers of disabled children are concerned to distance themselves from it. Mothers interviewed were clearly familiar with the class-based stereotype of the irresponsible, drug-addicted "bad mother" who causes disability through her own actions; they take pains to distinguish their own lives and choices from that stereotype. There is a moral dimension mothers give to their choices here, which in turn makes the birth outcome all the greater betrayal. Middle-class mothers, for instance, often stress their access to good prenatal care and the care they personally took to ensure both a healthy pregnancy and a secure financial and family environment for their newborn. Patricia Marks describes the shock she felt when her first child was born:

> And we were like the classic, we couldn't believe this had happened to us because we had done everything right. We were married. We had our education. We were financially secure. It was a planned pregnancy. I had had excellent prenatal care. It was like, wait a minute! I'm supposed to have this eight-pound, you know, bubbling baby to bring home, you know. What do you mean, you don't know if he'll be alive tomorrow?

After comparing the choices she made to those made by other extended family members during their pregnancies, Lisa Hart, whose daughter has cerebral palsy, similarly describes her surprise:

> I'm just amazed that here I am, you know, fruits and vegetables, don't drink, don't smoke, you know, walk and get my exercise and prenatal care the whole time I was pregnant and stuff, and people treat you like, you know, you're some like little teenager who was out doing drugs and have this kid with all these problems and good for you.

In her first interview, Suzanne Dalton, a college-educated alcohol counselor, describes the impact on her deepest religious beliefs of finding herself in a setting she thought should be reserved for "bad" mothers:

> I can't really tell you how it's affected it, but my faith feels damaged. I sometimes still pray, but I don't know. My biggest thought was how come us? I waited until I was older until I had kids. I waited until I was married. You know lots of people don't but I thought that was important. And I waited until we were financially ready. We put a lot of thought into it. We weren't just like "let's get pregnant and see what happens." We really considered it. We both really wanted it... But you think of crack babies or things like that.... The only time I thought of the NICU was in relation to babies whose mothers had used alcohol or drugs or something like that.... But in my case, I mean before I got pregnant I went to the doctors and said "I'm thinking of pregnancy, what should I do?"; they put me on vitamins. There was nothing that I didn't consider.

The juxtaposition of the narrator, who planned her pregnancy and/or actively wanted her child, with the image of the reckless teenager who carelessly let herself become pregnant and then abused her fetus or child appears repeatedly in the stories of middle-class women. Such women felt that their ability to obtain good medical care and their responsible personal behaviors before and during pregnancy should have protected them from bad birth outcomes; but they also felt that a healthy baby was their moral due, the just consequences of having made the right choices.

This sense of protection is not exclusive to the middle class, however. Working-class mothers (like Francine Hanson and Jessica's mom, above) and those on public assistance express the same stereotypes of the "bad" mother who *should* be held responsible for her child's disabilities, and they articulate their own differences from that stereotype. While narratives of working-class women are less likely than those of middle-class women to include issues of financial security as a prerequisite for a pregnancy, they do tell of actively wanting their children and of making choices to live differently from many of those with whom they had grown up. Just as do middle-class mothers, working-class women describe these choices in moral terms and the birth of a disabled child as an ultimate betrayal of their efforts to live a responsible life. Maureen Quinlan, for example, explicitly compared herself to others she had known in her youth.

> I mean, I made the right choices with my life when I was a teenager… and I saw people all around me, you know, in the '70s or so, all the teenage girls, you know what I mean, pregnant; it was like why do you want to ruin your life? I've met a lot of people, you know, throughout my life that, you know—I thought of, but I didn't do drugs—but I told them, I said, "you can be anything you want to be. You just go find out how to do it, and do it." And I've always believed that. And so, here I had to come smack up in my life of I made the right choices and yet I still have to deal with stuff. So, that was why I was so mad at God. It was like, I prayed, you know. During my pregnancy, I didn't drink, I didn't smoke, I didn't do any of those things….

Maureen had told of growing up in a principled home "with no love" where she was physically abused by her father and made to work long hours in the family-run laundry. She had expected her carefully chosen survival strategy and her commitment to making the right choices regarding her pregnancies, to keep her from having to deal with disability. Now with two sons diagnosed with pervasive developmental disorder, she finds having made the "right choices" irrelevant.

> All through growing up, I knew I just had to wait it out until I was 18 and then I could go and do, have my own life. You know, like I said, I went through a lot of beatings and stuff like that. I just figured all you do is just wait. That was the answer. I would just find the answer and then move on. That's always been just something, you know, I'm very analytical, I have an analytical mind. So, there's nothing analytical about this! So it just really just threw me off track.... It went against—all of a sudden I had no answer, no control of the thing, or if I made the right choice it would change.

Denise Rivers, living in an apartment in a working-class city neighborhood, compares her choices to those of many of her neighbors, and similarly finds little justice:

> We love our kids. We knew we were having them, we chose to have them, you know.... I see all these kids running around, people don't care about them, they run the street; the thing that angers me is like why my child kind of thing, you know.... Because you did all the right things.

Denise wonders whether as a teenager, her little girl, who has hydrocephalous, will be angry with her. "Why do you think she'd be angry with you?" I asked.

> I don't know. I mean, do you ever think about how we answer their questions? 'Why did it happen to me, Mommy, or why do I have this plastic thing [shunt] in my head that makes me breathe, why am I the sick one?' I mean, why was it her? People who take drugs. There's people who don't care about their kids. Why is it somebody who cares about— you know, why?.... You can't answer it for yourself. How are you going to explain it to her?

At the time of the research, the "crack epidemic" and its implications for exposed newborns had been highly publicized in the media. The number of newborns affected by maternal drug use quadrupled in many urban hospitals between 1985 and 1990 (Roberts, 1991), and the response of state prosecutors, legislators, and judges has been punitive; women (especially black women) who use drugs during pregnancy have been jailed, deprived of the custody of their children, and prosecuted after their babies are born (Roberts). Such fetal abuse cases are not only extensions of child abuse cases but are related to abortion law as well; legal analysts have interpreted the availability of legal abortion to imply moral duties toward fetuses that justify state intervention on their behalf (Oaks, 2001: 175). Thus, in an article in the *Virginia Law Review*, John Robertson argues that

> the mother has, if she conceives and chooses not to abort, a legal and moral duty to bring the child into the world as healthy as is reasonably possible… the viable fetus acquires rights to have the mother conduct her life in ways that will not injure it.
>
> (quoted in Oaks, 2001: 175)

As Ginsburg has argued, with the availability of abortion, motherhood in American culture has become an achievement (1989: 109), and women are judged on the basis of their stance toward it. In this case, the stance in question involves a mother's choices during pregnancy.

In interviews, middle- and working-class mothers alike contrasted themselves to the image of the "bad" mother who doesn't take responsibility for her pregnancy. Women of both classes stressed the responsibility they personally had taken for making choices in life: the choice to have children (regardless of whether a pregnancy itself was planned), the choice to utilize and comply with biomedical expertise during the pregnancy, the choice to sacrifice one's own immediate desires for the health of a child. That making such choices still left one powerless to protect one's child from disability produces a range of emotions, including what mothers have variously described as "damaged faith," anger, and guilt. Rosemarie Garland Thomson suggests that the disabled figure troubles the American image of the "normate" self, which is characterized by self-government, self-determination, autonomy, and progress (1997: 42). These qualities, she notes, all depend on the body as an instrument of individual will. By being unable to control their own bodies, as "evidenced" by abnormal birth outcomes, mothers of disabled children are themselves also seen as challenges to the American norm.

The same medical professionals who often find themselves explaining to guilt-ridden parents that "sometimes these things just happen," nevertheless sometimes speak as if they also assume, as did most women during pregnancy, that compliance with expert advice affords protection. Linda Rubenstein tells a story about an encounter between her mother and a nurse caring for Linda's premature son in the NICU:

> She was talking with one of the nurses who was pregnant and my mother was like "how can you—doesn't it scare you to death, you're dealing with all these little preemie babies, ...doesn't it scare you to death that—of what can happen?"; and her answer to my mother was "oh, well, I'm getting very good prenatal care, da da da da da da da", and my mother was very taken aback by that. "My daughter didn't even drink Pepsi with caffeine in it at all or anything!"

Linda concedes that "yes, there are some families in there that maybe that is why the baby was in there because they didn't have prenatal care and there are drug babies and stuff like that," but, she claims, pointing to herself as an example, "there's a lot of people out there that are doing everything they're supposed to and this is still happening."

Aware that health care professionals make class-based judgments about mothers, women worry that the association of childhood disability with maternal irresponsibility might affect both their child's care and their own interaction with medical staff; women therefore often attempt to distinguish themselves from those "bad mothers" who doctors and nurses might assume caused their child's disability. Brenda Wilson, whose child suffered a stroke and had a lengthy hospitalization, "always felt like if I finished my education or if I was in the medical profession or something... I would have had more respect from the doctors." She felt doctors "talked down" to her "until I told them, wait a minute here. I pay my taxes, and I'm a good mother. I didn't put my child here. I didn't shake my child. I didn't neglect her to put her here." That being a taxpayer is included among the criteria for being a "good mother" worthy of doctors' attention and qualifying a child for good medical care is significant. Mothers of children at risk for disability have made their own analysis of what Ginsburg and Rapp (1995), drawing on the work of Shellee Colen, call "stratified reproduction." The term describes "power relations by which some categories of people are empowered to nurture and reproduce, while others are disempowered"; this concept, they propose, enables us to see the ways by which "some reproductive futures are valued while others are despised" (1995: 3). Recognizing these power relations *and* that their pregnancy outcomes threaten to place them in the "wrong" category, women strategize in defense of their children but also of their own motherhood. Mothers of all classes in the study strive to reposition themselves in relation to the image of the careless, dependent welfare mother whose child may be innocent but who herself is culpable.

Donna Haraway describes the distinction made in theoretical population biology between those species whose reproductive strategies rely on investing tremendous resources in each individual offspring and those whose strategy is to spew "as many offspring into the world as possible, with little physiological or biosocial investment in any individual" (Haraway, 1997: 204). She argues that this "lesson in evolutionary theory" has been translated into human reproductive politics in a way that contrasts "careful parents with solid family values versus vermin and weeds," or in other words, "intensely cultivated fetuses" versus "throwaway fetuses..." (204). Haraway's discussion refers to an imperialist imaginary in which reproductive strategies of societies of the north (the United States) are compared to those of people "down there." However, the imagery flourishes within the United States in the widely held vision of the middle-class mother dutifully complying with biomedical expertise in a carefully planned pregnancy versus the poor (usually black) teenage single mother carelessly producing an overabundance of "crack" and/or premature babies at risk for disability. Though the scientific evidence that teen childbearing, per se, has important negative consequences for children has been the subject of debate and controversy, "well-publicized conventional wisdom continues to hold teen childbearing to be, in all cases and in every aspect, an antisocial act and important public health problem, *especially* when practiced by urban African Americans" (Geronimus, 2003: 881). During their pregnancies, both working-class and middle-class mothers had shared this image of the "bad" mother whose lack of resources and/or irresponsible behavior brought on her child's disability or ill health. Upon initially learning that despite her responsible efforts to control pregnancy outcome her own child has a disability, mothers of all classes therefore felt equally miscast in the role of mother of a disabled child.

Blaming the Medical Practitioner

Though most mothers first sought accountability for the birth of a disabled child within their own behavior, the narratives collected also included stories in which mothers held medical staff responsible for the disability through mismanagement of their child's birth or subsequent health care. A mother employed as a hairdresser tells how during her second pregnancy she pleaded unsuccessfully with her obstetrician to plan a cesarean section and was denied only to have the baby asphyxiated during labor; upon delivery, the infant was revived against the mother's wishes and is now disabled with profound mental retardation as well as mobility, speech, and fine-motor impairments. Similarly, Denise Rivers, a medical transcriber, describes how, against her own wishes and those of the resident monitoring her labor, the attending physician chose not to do a C-section despite fetal heart decelerations because (Denise believes) the attending physician was busy with another delivery; as a result, Denise's daughter has hydrocephalous and mental retardation. Julie Sanders, a single mother on welfare, tells a riveting story of a panicked midwife who, during a difficult delivery, reached in and pulled her son out by his arm, permanently severing the nerves of the boy's shoulder, arm, and diaphragm and resulting in extensive hospitalization, surgery, and partial paralysis. Yet even when mothers can point convincingly to what they believe to be medical malpractice, their own sense of responsibility can remain. As Julie Sanders explains,

> It was horrifying. My son, everyday for the first two months he was in the hospital I kept crying. I just couldn't stop. Then I was thinking if I pushed harder I could have, maybe, I don't know. You know what I mean? If I really pushed harder. I could have pushed harder maybe.

When my own uterus tore during labor in a failed vaginal delivery after cesarean section, my daughter slipped through the tear and was asphyxiated, suffering brain damage. Intellectually, I blame the obstetrician who, supposedly covering for my own absent obstetrician and despite my repeated requests over a six-hour period to talk to him, failed to appear and put an end to what was planned to be a trial of labor. Yet, for some time I was haunted by an image: a full six hours before the tear occurred—15 hours after my water had broken and nowhere near delivering vaginally—I knew it was time for a C-section as I had previously discussed with my own obstetrician. What if at that point I had made myself intolerable to the medical staff? What if, instead of repeatedly asking *politely* for the attending physician so that I could discuss the matter, I had kicked over an expensive fetal monitor, or thrown an IV stand out the window, or screamed at the top of my lungs that I would sue everyone in the hospital if the doctor didn't show up *now* and perform the surgery? In other words, what if instead of complying with the (now seemingly trivial) conventions of normal social interaction, I had been willing to be seen by the staff as a lunatic? Might the nurses or residents have been successful in getting the obstetrician to appear and do the surgical delivery before it was too late? Might my daughter DJ now be "normal?"

Some mothers portray the medical staff as having undermined all the hard work they had personally done to ensure the healthy development of the fetus. However, regardless of whether a woman blames a medical practitioner or herself, in those narratives collected *shortly after a child's diagnosis*, disability is most commonly portrayed as avoidable and subject to control. At that point, there is general consensus among women in the study that compliance with biomedical knowledge regarding diet and prenatal care *should* have resulted in the birth of a normal, healthy child. Denise Rivers, for instance, feels the standard medical indicators for a C-section were apparent during her labor but believes the doctor, for purposes of his own convenience, selfishly chose not to act on them. Julie Sanders feels the attending physician took it for granted that her third pregnancy would be an easy delivery that could be left in the hands of a midwife rather than a physician who she believes would have recognized the baby was too large for a vaginal delivery and would have performed a C-section, avoiding the outcome of Erb's palsy from severed nerves at delivery. Nancy Papagallo believes that in spite of five or six ultrasounds, staff at her local hospital failed to detect a problem that, if known, might have been treated effectively at the larger Albany

Medical Center. In these narratives, particular medical practitioners failed to carry out its tenets, just as in other narratives pregnant women failed to adhere to all the demands of the recommended prenatal diet; but, in all cases, the expert biomedical knowledge itself stands as authoritative and protective.

The Role of Prenatal Testing in Mother-Blame

By far the most common feature of mothers' narratives about their pregnancies is women's sense of responsibility for controlling fetal development through diet, broadly defined to include issues of drug use and alcohol consumption as well as nutritional intake. However, there are other arenas in which responsibility for pregnancy outcome is placed upon the mother as well. Most notable is that of prenatal screening technologies. While genetics has long been thought to represent life's natural and immutable givens, the widespread availability of prenatal testing has moved genetics into the domain of choice, and it has done so with particular consequences.

Despite the "promise" of gene therapy in the future, at present the only "cure" for a genetically based disability identified by prenatal screening is abortion of the fetus identified with the disability. Though disability rights advocates accurately argue that selective abortion after prenatal screening is a matter of preventing the birth of disabled people, the wider society has largely accepted the process under the morally less ambiguous rubric of preventing birth defects. The legislature of at least one state, Alabama, declared it to be state policy "to encourage the prevention of birth defects and mental retardation through education, genetic counseling and amniocentesis..." (Section 22-10A of the Alabama statutes, cited in Blumberg, 1998: 16). A woman who has access to information regarding her child's dis/ability status and fails to act on it may therefore be seen as responsible for the disability itself. This is borne out in a study in three European countries showing that prenatal screening is the single most important factor influencing both lay people's and health professionals' attribution of blame to mothers for the birth of a child with Down syndrome (Marteau and Drake, 1995). That the birth of a child with Down syndrome is a negative event for which "blame" is an appropriate response can and should be questioned; the point for my purposes here, however, is that access to informed "choice" through prenatal testing, far from liberating women, can paradoxically aid in perpetuating the notion of mother-blame, imprisoning some women within an atmosphere of guilt and shame.

The expectation of a "perfect" or "normal" baby if one faithfully complies with current expert advice is a specific manifestation of Americans' generalized belief in both linear progress and individual responsibility; it is in this sense the ultimate expression of faith in the possibility of control over nature. To fail to exercise control by implementing the available authoritative knowledge and technology has been culturally translated to mean something quite close to being responsible for the "imperfection" itself. Connie Brown, for instance, recalls that when a doctor came to talk to her in the hospital about her child's disability—the absence of a hand—he told her "'remember you didn't want that ultrasound…' That was probably the first thing he said—'Remember, you didn't want that ultrasound.'"

In another case I observed, a mother brought in her daughter for an evaluation at the Newborn Followup Program; she explained that for more than a year she had had concerns regarding the girl's development and physical appearance but that her child's pediatrician had repeatedly dismissed these concerns. The developmental specialist now examined the child and gave the mother devastating news: The child's symptoms were consistent with a storage disease, a fatal diagnosis. The girl would continue to deteriorate both physically and mentally; though there was an invasive experimental procedure being tested out of state that might inhibit the physical deterioration, in all likelihood death would occur within a few years. Painfully complicating the matter was the fact that the mother was now pregnant again; there was a high probability that the new baby would also have the disease. The burden of bearing such grave news weighed heavily on the staff; the case became the topic of many conversations among the residents and nurses. However, despite the tremendous sympathy the staff expressed for the mother, the issue of her personal obligation to exert control over nature remained. "The thing I don't understand," said a nurse during a conversation with other medical staff, "is that if she knew there was something wrong with her kid, why did she go ahead and get pregnant again?"

A powerful argument challenging feminists' use of fear of disability in support of reproductive choice has emerged from the disability rights movement (Blumberg, 1998; Hershey, 1994; see also Parens and Asch, 2000);[7] as will be discussed later in this book, its sentiments are often echoed in mothers' narratives *after* they have experienced mothering a disabled child for some length of time. However, the interviews suggest that the argument had only rarely been considered by women prior to the birth of their own child with a disability.

Most women report having had at least some type of prenatal testing during their pregnancies, the two most common tests being a blood test known as maternal alpha-fetoprotein (AFP) and ultrasound. Seven women in the study had also undergone amniocentesis, and only one had chorionic villae sampling. Screening results for a few women in the study indicated problems that led to further testing and to a decision on the part of the potential parent(s) about whether to continue the pregnancy. However, for the vast majority of women, the prenatal test results reassured them, falsely, that everything would be fine. Kim Boland, for example, is the mother of a child with Down syndrome and autism; pregnant at the age of 20, she claims that as for prenatal diagnostic tests, she had "everything but the amnio." When asked if she had ever thought about having a child with a disability, Kim responded, "No, because I thought as far as I knew, I had every test done possible; you know they did the test for spina bifida and all those." Kelly Strathmore described an emergency delivery in which she joked with the doctors, "I remembered yelling out 'I forgot to tell you, if you have a choice, save *me*,' and the doctor laughed." When I asked her if during that time she had been worried at all about a problem with the baby, she replied "No. I had amnio and everything… I had everything."

Lorraine Hamilton's son was born with agenesis of the corpus collosum; missing the part of the brain that connects the right and left hemispheres, he has severe mental retardation, visual impairment, and gross motor delays. Lorraine remembers wondering why this diagnosis did not show up on her AFP test; now she understands that the test is not designed to pick up this type of problem. Nevertheless, "with all the screenings and everything else you do if you're going for your pregnancy and then you do get a child with a problem, it's a real blow, a real shock," she claims. "You just assume everything's just fine; you just take care of yourself and you think it can't happen to me." Like eating right and avoiding drugs and alcohol, submitting to prenatal diagnostic tests seems to be understood by American women as part of prenatal care that, especially in the absence of positive results (indicating an abnormality), should ensure the birth of a normal, healthy baby.

The purposes for prenatal screening are generally presented to prospective American mothers in terms of (1) providing information that could be used to make a decision regarding continuation or termination of a particular pregnancy and (2) providing reassurance that a fetus is normal. The suggestion by medical practitioners that either function "needs" to be fulfilled validates the culturally constructed assumption that disability is a socially devalued birth outcome. Browner and Press argue convincingly that acceptance of prenatal testing is widespread because in an era of scrutiny of pregnant women's behavior, testing provides a means for women to reassure themselves and others that they are doing everything possible to eliminate the risk of maternally induced poor fetal outcomes; a pregnant woman who receives negative results can then, as they describe, quickly transform test results "into a non-event" (1995: 318). For a mother of a child newly diagnosed with disabilities who had only recently felt reassured by prenatal test results, the powerfully negative image of disability is all the fresher and the shock of her lack of control over pregnancy outcome all the greater. This suggests more than the simple observation that the impact of prenatal testing on those who have normal and those who have abnormal pregnancy outcomes is different. Prenatal testing culturally widens the moral distance between mothers of "normal" children and mothers of disabled children.

Increasingly widespread use of prenatal diagnostic screening technologies, like the popularization of expert biomedical knowledge about preferred prenatal and pre-conception diets, thus may contribute to the notion that "bad" outcomes are preventable *tragedies*. If so, it makes sense to seriously consider whether prenatal testing provides more data for women's informed choices and/or supports existing discriminatory attitudes toward disabled people. Like injury prevention campaigns—such as one using an ad for seatbelts that reads "If you think seat belts are confining, think about a wheelchair"—promotion of prenatal diagnostic screening technologies publicly implies that disabled people are an outcome to be avoided.[8] In the first case, what is represented is that which one should not become; in the other case, that which one should prevent from coming into existence. From the perspective of disability rights activists, both, even if inadvertently, encourage the social and political oppression of disabled people.

For our purposes here, what is noteworthy is that both injury prevention campaigns and the "normalization" of prenatal screening technologies (Browner and Press, 1995) promote the notion that disability is usually avoidable, albeit, in the case of genetic defects determined in prenatal tests, only through selective abortion. Even if a mother of a disabled infant who had prenatal testing and received reassuring results knows she did everything in her power during pregnancy to have a "normal" baby, the very availability of prenatal diagnostic testing may contribute to her perception (as well as the reality) that she is held accountable by others for the disability.

Speaking as it does for the rights of women, feminism might be expected to provide a counter-discourse to that of mother-blame. That it has not in part reflects what Janet Read refers to as a longstanding "uncomfortable relationship between feminism and mothers and motherhood" (2000: 75). However, there is more involved here than debate over the role of motherhood in reducing women's autonomy or on the wisdom of celebrating a woman's culture of caring. Cultural interpretations of what constitutes a life worth living intertwine with Euro-American feminist positions on reproductive choice. By combining a commitment to a woman's right to control her body with the current ready availability of information on the genetic status of a fetus, some feminists have argued specifically in favor of holding women individually accountable for the birth of disabled children. The most striking example, perhaps, is Laura Purdy's tracts on the immorality of knowingly giving birth to infants with high risk for disability or disease, found in her book *Reproducing Persons: Issues in Feminist Bioethics* (1996). At one point, Purdy argues on the basis of the demands of love. "The thought that I might bring to life a child with serious physical or mental problems when I could, by doing something different, bring forth one without them, is utterly incomprehensible to me. Isn't that what love means?" (1996: 58). Wary of arguments that might mean women giving up the "barely won" right to control their bodies and lives and of perpetuating the burden placed on women to be the primary caretakers of children, Purdy argues that to fail to exercise control as offered by genetic counseling is immoral. It is, after all, "one thing to have to cope with difficulties that could not have been avoided; it is quite another when they could have been" (1996: 65). This argument, based on what Purdy defines as feminist principles, is remarkably consistent with what mothers of disabled infants describe as the accusatory attitude they face in the larger society in which mothers carry out their daily lives (i.e., the insinuation that they didn't love their children enough to make the right choices to protect them, or in this case, to prevent their very birth).

I suggest that Purdy's argument is also ironically consistent with a patriarchal society that defines women primarily in terms of their reproductive roles and domestic responsibilities as rearers of individual children. Responding to disability rights advocate Martha Saxton's position that she would like to welcome any child born to her, Purdy counters that "despite the social costs of certain decisions about reproduction, the main focus here still needs to be on *what happens to children* (emphasis mine)..." (1996: 66; see also Steinbock and McClamrock, 1994 for a similar perspective).

This position assumes that an impairment in and of itself prevents a child from having a satisfying life; it suggests that even if society's response to the impairment rather than the impairment itself would cause the greatest difficulty for a child, a woman should not enter her hopes for and efforts toward societal change into her decision-making process. According to this view, the moral choice can be made only on the narrow basis of a woman's responsibility to prevent the birth of a specific child who it is presumed will have a less happy life than another child who might otherwise be born. Women's agency as political and social actors is dismissed in this argument.

American mothers of disabled children have joined disability rights activists in demanding *societal* responsibility to protect the civil rights of disabled people and to include all citizens in public life; however, the rhetoric of reproductive choice *individualize*s decisions and responsibilities (Landsman, 1998: 94). As biomedical information expands on how to protect the fetal environment in general and on the genetic status of any fetus in particular, we might expect that the vocabulary of informed choice will continue to lend itself to a discourse of individual mother-blame.

The rhetoric of choice and control simultaneously spoken in various domains of U.S. life—including biomedicine, feminism, and public health—enables people both to envision the possibility of "perfect" babies and to see "less-than-perfect" infants as the justifiable outcome of a woman's less-than-perfect choices (Landsman, 1998). The vast majority of women in this study consciously strived to exercise control over their pregnancies. The threefold combination of their access to medical care, the availability of prenatal testing technologies, and their general compliance with expert knowledge regarding diet led them to expect that they would have a "normal" child. For pregnant women the imagined disabled child is indeed the "other" (Press, et. al., 1998). However, while the "otherness" of the disabled child is clearly borne out by the narratives I collected from mothers of disabled children (and will be discussed in greater detail in later chapters), what is also revealed is the shock of the "otherness" of one's *own* new identity. Having done "everything right," the last thing most women imagined was that she would find herself the mother of a disabled child.

3

DIMINISHED MOTHERHOOD

I remember people stopping by, and I wanted so badly for somebody to say congratulations. Instead, I'm in this room by myself. People sent some flowers, but nobody knew what to say or to do, and it was the most horrible feeling, because… like it is a tragedy and it is horrible, but especially the first-time mom, you want some real experience. I don't know. Probably if they said "congratulations," I would have chopped their head off and said, what do you mean "congratulations?" This is not a good thing. This is a terrible thing to go through.

(Jane Sawyer, on the premature birth of her daughter)

The current American context is one in which most believe the available choices and technologies exist for creating a perfectly normal baby. For the public, new technologies such as intracytoplasmic sperm injection, gestational surrogacy, selective embryo reduction, egg donation, sperm sorting, pre-implantation genetic diagnosis, and a range of other prenatal testing technologies have both raised the ethically ambiguous specter of "designer" babies and greatly complicated the term *mother* in North American culture. If babies can ensue from technological and legal interventions independent of heterosexual intercourse, what should be the defining criteria of "real" motherhood? Should we prioritize the contribution of genetic material, the provision of the womb that carries the fetus and from which the baby is delivered, or nurturance of a child after it is born? Each of these components of motherhood may now be fulfilled by a different individual; new technologies and social arrangements allow for a broad array of maternal claims.

Yet each of the claims to the term *real mother* ultimately rests upon a culturally acknowledged and valued "real child." How is motherhood experienced and interpreted by those whose young children do not meet society's standards as such? This question moves us quickly into the realm of personhood. Personhood is here distinguished both from self, which refers to a reflexive locus of experience (see Harris, 1989: 601), and from human. "If personhood is seen as being not simply human, but human in a way that is valued and meaningful, then individuals can be persons to a greater or lesser extent" (Whyte and Ingstad, 1995: 11)." While disability scholars generally agree that "the marginal status of people with disabilities is a variable cultural pattern, not a natural occurrence present in all societies" (Scheer, 1994: 249), in North American society disability is known to diminish personhood (Longmore, 1997; Mitchell and Snyder, 1997; Murphy, 1987; Wendell, 1996; see also Goffman, 1963).[1] Thus we can ask the question: For American mothers of disabled infants, is motherhood diminished as well?

"It's Like You Don't Have a Baby:" Motherhood and the (Less-Than-Full) Personhood of Disabled Infants

The birth of a disabled child diminishes motherhood in the United States to the extent that within the culture there are gradations of personhood, with (dis)ability a criterion for determining a child's level of personhood; the socially constructed reduced personhood of a child is linked to women's experience of motherhood. In interviews, mothers expressed these notions either as representing their own belief at some point in time or as their perception of what other Americans believe; in this chapter, I examine the impact of these dominant discourses of disability and motherhood on the experience of individual mothers of children with or at risk for disabilities. As we shall later see, such beliefs are open to change through the transformative experience of mothering a disabled child.

Given the divisive social issues of abortion, euthanasia, and assisted suicide, much scholarship on personhood in Euro-American societies has been focused on analysis of the cultural criteria for determining the chronological beginning and endpoints of personhood. Biology serves as the dominant discourse informing Western ontology; the "biological facts" of conception, pregnancy, and fetal life serve as powerful, symbolic sources of meaning in the abortion debate, Franklin argues, precisely because they provide the key cultural resources for the construction of personhood (1991). Conklin and Morgan similarly argue that while there may be variation in the relative weight given to individualism versus sociality, there is

> notable consistency in North Americans' basic assumptions about how the criteria for determining personhood should be established. Personhood is assumed to be located in biology, in the capacity of the individual body to perform specific functions.
>
> (1996: 665)

The linkage of this biologically based definition of personhood to the abortion debate in the United States was made explicit during the 1984 debates between presidential candidates.

> President Reagan noted his belief that a fetus warranted constitutional protection as soon as it became a human being. He said that he must believe this occurred at the moment of conception *unless scientists could more clearly establish when human life began.*
>
> (Goldenring, 1985: 198)

In taking this position, Reagan not only located personhood in biology; he set the terms of the abortion debate as a matter of determining the starting point of personhood, and equated "person"—the category of entity to which state protection applies—with "human."

A person, Reagan assumed, comes into existence at the moment at which an entity may be defined as an individual human life. Anthropologists doing cross-cultural research, however, have found it useful to distinguish between the concepts of person and human. Human refers to a type of living entity. However, though "everywhere there is a human kind embracing the home society or at least its socially dominant members" (Harris, 1989: 601), there is cross-cultural variation in the types of individuals to whom the term is applied and in the biophysical processes asserted as its defining features. For example, fetuses are *not* universally considered human; nor are twins.[2] Among the Songye, those defined as "bad" or "faulty" children, including albino, dwarf, and hydrocephalic children, are considered supernaturals who have been in contact with sorcerers in the anti-world; they are not believed to be human beings, and they are expected to die (Devlieger,

1995: 96). On the Alto do Cruziero in rural northeast Brazil, sick infants are identified as "little critters" that have no feelings (Scheper-Hughes, 1992: 373–374). Among the Nuer, it is claimed, a disabled infant was interpreted as a hippopotamus that had mistakenly been born to human parents; the child would be returned to its proper home by being thrown into the river (Scheer and Groce, 1988: 28). Summarizing references in the literature on Southern Africa, Deliane Bruck notes that breech birth, cutting the upper teeth first, and being delivered of a mother who had not menstruated between births all precluded an infant's being allowed to become a human (cited in Whyte, 1995: 271).

In contrast to human, *person* refers to a being that is publicly considered an agent in the world (Harris, 1989). Personhood is contingent on social recognition (Morgan, 1996b: 25); it speaks to social value. Personhood and humanness may be defined separately or, as in the United States, as occurring (under "normal" circumstances) simultaneously. Within the latter contexts, language that is dehumanizing necessarily also reduces or denies personhood. Morgan suggests that in societies where the two are defined separately, a determination of humanity must precede the attribution of personhood (1990: 25); however, the ethnographic record provides numerous examples in which not all beings classified as persons are living humans and of many societies in which nonhuman entities are conceptualized as persons (Harris, 1989: 602; Moore, 1994: 32). Among the Navajo, for instance, nonhuman entities such as baskets, birds, houses, and snakes, have qualities of persons (Schwarz, 1997: 609). In the United States, where humanness *is* a prerequisite for personhood, there is nevertheless still not consensus on when in the process of human development personhood appears; thus the controversy over the morality not only of abortion but of research on and destruction of human embryos; embryos can be understood to be human entities, but are they persons? And despite the argument for fetal personhood espoused by some in American culture, miscarried fetuses, though understood as having been living human entities, are not generally treated as having been persons; there are, for instance, no culturally sanctioned rituals to mark pregnancy loss (Layne, 1997) as there are to mark the death of individuals who have already been established as persons.

The North American definition of personhood has been contrasted in the anthropological literature with conceptions of personhood that follow a more relational or sociocentric model and which are generally found in non-Western societies. Though there is important cross-cultural variation in relational conceptions of personhood, such models generally present the person not as an autonomous individual but as constituted by social relations. Among the Wari' Indians of Brazil, for example, personhood is acquired gradually (Conklin and Morgan, 1996); for the 'Are 'Are of the Solomon Islands, "the land that nourishes the child is also constituted of what constitutes the living person" (Strathern, 1992: 126); among the Navajo, the notion of personhood is informed by the principle of synecdoche such that the boundaries of the person are extended to include everything that can come into contact with an individual (Schwartz, 1997); and among the Punan Bah of Sarawak, personhood is acquired only after an ancestor spirit takes permanent residence in the child at approximately six months of age, before which the child is considered only "blood" and can be aborted with no moral problems (Nicolaisen, 1995: 43). Morgan cites numerous examples from the ethnographic record in which the socially significant event of naming a child, rather than the moment of its birth or conception, marks the beginning of personhood (1996: 29–30). In contrast, in the United States, personhood is generally (though as we shall see, not consistently) conferred on humans at the moment of birth; there is a conflation of biological birth and social birth.

Conklin and Morgan argue that because North Americans look to the autonomous individual body for fixed, structural markers of personhood, fetal personhood in the United States is an all-or-nothing proposition (1996: 660).[3] If the fetus is defined as a person, it can hold individual rights equal to that of the pregnant woman in whose body it resides; the concept of fetal personhood thereby allows for maternal-fetal conflict. Indeed, it can be argued that the rights of the fetus have now come to supercede the rights of pregnant women themselves. As the previous chapter has described, American mothers of disabled children have given birth in a context in which the fetus is widely viewed as a potential victim threatened by its mother during pregnancy and in which women are generally held accountable for any damage done to a fetus.

Fears about the political implications of such a concept of fetal personhood have left their mark on scholarship. Feminists have largely been silent on the concerns of women experiencing pregnancy loss, for instance, because to validate a woman's perception of a fetus as a baby whose loss of life is worth grieving is perceived by many as an acknowledgement of fetal personhood and thereby as a threat to women's control of their own bodies (Layne, 1997).[4] Feminists have largely left the issue of personhood to be framed by the abortion debate and thus to be phrased primarily in terms of: when does a fetus *become* a person?

Bioethicists and family members addressing end-of-life decisions, on the other hand, debate structural markers that would indicate when the *loss or absence* of personhood has occurred. Among bioethicists in the United States and much of Europe, brain functioning has been widely considered as the structural marker identifying both the beginning and end points of personhood (see Kushner, 1984; also Joralemon, 1995: 342–333, and Lock, 2002). Sentience (the capacity to experience pleasure and pain) and/or self-consciousness are used to define personhood in justifications for withholding aggressive treatment from defective newborns (Anspach, 1993: 28), in arguments in favor of allowing the killing of disabled infants (Singer, 1993), in debate over the disposition of human embryos (Gillon, 1991: 61; Poplawski and Gillett, 1991) and, as came to the fore in the highly publicized case of Terri Schiavo, in decisions to withdraw artificial hydration and nutrition from patients in "persistent vegetative states" (Zeman, 1997).

These cases of decision making at the margins of life are moments when professional and popular discourses on personhood interact to both contest and support each other. Politically, the focus on the margins has left feminists and disability rights scholars without the vocabulary with which to reach common ground; feminists are concerned with the implications for women of *attributing* full personhood to fetuses, while disability rights advocates are concerned with the consequences of *denying* full personhood to those with disabilities. Feminists have thus been open to disability rights activists' charges of complicity in the dominant "cure 'em or kill 'em mentality" toward disabled people.

Tension largely stems from pro-choice advocates' use of fear of disability in efforts to support abortion rights. Key medical professionals advocating for the legalization of abortion in the United States in the 1960s used the Sherry Finkbine case of a pregnancy possibly affected by thalidomide, believing "there was general support—both public and professional—for the idea that clear evidence of fetal abnormality was a legitimate indication for abortion" (Luker, 1984: 82). More recently, in response to legislative efforts to ban late abortions, Family Planning Advocates of New York State distributed flyers identifying as one of the two categories of "the most desperate and vulnerable women" who need access to legal abortion after 20 weeks those "women carrying severely deformed fetuses"; among the circumstances listed as reasons for abortions after the first trimester are "severe fetal abnormalities" including chromosomal disorders such as cystic fibrosis, severe Down syndrome, and sickle cell anemia (Family Planning Advocates of New York State, 1993). In a separate flyer rejecting demands for consent laws, the organization argues that by requiring physicians to discuss risks of late-term abortions and/or details of late-state fetal development, such laws would be particularly cruel for "the woman who discovers that her fetus is severely deformed" (Family Planning Advocates of New York State, 1996). With a focus on dramatic and painful decision making at the beginning and end points of life, the question of how personhood may be diminished as a common, *ongoing* feature of American life is left relatively unexamined, yet it is at the heart of the everyday experience of mothers of disabled infants and children.[5]

Noting the widespread circulation of photos taken from sonograms as "first baby pictures," Rapp argues cogently that there is an evolving politics of representation affecting many if not all pregnancies in the United States, in which the fetus has both a domesticated and a public presence" (1997: 32). The physical similarity of fetuses to those already unanimously defined as persons, a similarity that, as Rapp points out, is not inherently apparent in sonograms but which must be interpreted by technicians, has been recognized by the right-to-life movement as one of its strongest arguments against abortion and has been the centerpiece of its public representations. At the same time, the pro-choice movement has long used the *dis*similarity of potentially deformed children to persons in support of an abortion rights position. In this way, both sides in the abortion debate have naturalized disability as intrinsic to the individual rather than as socially constructed, and both have argued from the position that "biological facts" are the criteria for personhood. Questions regarding the role of prenatal imaging technologies in promoting a concept of fetal personhood or regarding the impact of technologies to detect and define cognitive functioning have taken on importance and urgency in scholarship on the cultural construction of personhood in large part because of their application to the divisive social issues of abortion and euthanasia.[6]

Pointing to the moral controversies presented to physicians by the "explosion of medical technologies," Morrow (2000: 1146) notes that justification for refusal to treat imperiled infants also derives from their questionable ontological status. In the bioethical literature, newborns, though human, have been noted to lack the characteristics of personhood, such as certain intrinsic cognitive capacities, and the ability to deliberate rationally (Morrow, 2000; Singer, 1993, 1995). By contrast, in The Netherlands for example, non-treatment of newborns with impairments may be based on physician and parent judgment of anticipated quality of life (see Vermeulen, 2004) rather than of personhood itself.

In American public debates on personhood, then, the focus has been on the points at which an autonomous, internally controlled corporeal unit can be defined as coming into or out of being. The assumption is that if we could reach consensus on the fixed structural markers of personhood located within the biology of this bounded unit and develop the technology to detect their presence or absence in fetuses and comatose patients, debate would disappear on some of our stickiest moral dilemmas. Conklin and Morgan argue that "locating personhood in fetal biology is consistent with a conception of personhood as a quality that accrues quickly and is fixed at a particular point in the gestational cycle" (1996: 665). Comparing North American concepts of personhood to those of the Wari' Indians of Brazil, they claim that because North Americans look for personhood within the biological body, a person can be created with minimal social interaction. And "when personhood is understood to be ascribed by nonsocial factors, it cannot be readily rescinded, attenuated, or truncated by social action. Western persons, once established, are not easily undone" (Conklin and Morgan, 1996: 665).

However, if we shift the focus of analysis away from the question of when in the gestational cycle personhood appears and toward the question of to whom personhood is attributed, we find that personhood is not necessarily an-all-or-nothing proposition in North American culture after all, nor is it permanently fixed at any specific time. Indeed, the first dilemma for many mothers of disabled infants is finding that the fetus to whom they may have attributed personhood in their womb is now an individual whose personhood is held in question by others, and indeed often by the mother herself. "When she was born and people heard there was something wrong, like the congratulations disappears. You don't get any of that. It's like you didn't have a baby," recalled Lily Beckett about the birth of her daughter with Down syndrome and a heart defect. Lily's story about being grateful for the doctor's delay in giving her the diagnosis reveals the way in which full personhood can indeed be rescinded by disability in U.S. culture.

> You know, a lot of people complained about Dr. Stevens and the part about not saying anything. But then I thought, I never would have had that part of it if he had said something. I'm actually grateful that he had done that because we were thrilled, you know. We have this baby girl and calling all of our friends. And we did have that part of it. It was the part afterwards that we had to call everybody back and say—well, we *did* have a baby, but things didn't go according to plan.

The fact that her child's disability wasn't known to her at first enabled Lily and others to establish her daughter as a baby and therefore for Lily to have, however briefly, a "part" of the experience of "real" motherhood. When the new information—the child's diagnosis of disability—was later transmitted publicly, the consequent negation of her child's full personhood diminished her experience of her own motherhood. Lily's perception of other people's perceptions of her child and of her motherhood is not at all unusual. Contrary to the traditional response of congratulations on the birth of a baby, the mother of a child with disabilities is often treated as if she has no baby to celebrate. Suzanne Dalton describes going back to work while her premature babies were in the NICU, "and people would whisper or wouldn't even talk at all, like I was never pregnant." Similarly, Angela Petrocelli, whose son has cerebral palsy, notes that when other people see him, "they think there's not a baby there." Jenna Mosher worries that her nondisabled child might feel like "an only child or worse, like, 'oh look, we were disappointed by this one, you better really put out because you're it.'"

Consistent with the arguments made by Franklin and by Conklin and Morgan, in all the above instances it is biology that serves as the source of the criteria for assigning or withdrawing personhood. However, that Americans utilize what they understand to be a nonsocial source for ascribing personhood (i.e., "biological facts") does not therefore disentangle biology from society in the United States. Bodies, in all their perceived "naturalness," are, after all, culturally constructed; as Lily's experience reveals, an individual human being before and after a diagnosis of Down syndrome does not have the same body. One might argue that it is simply the same body with its "true" biological constitution now revealed. However, the revelation of the extra chromosome, culturally marking disability, negates the initial definition of the body as a baby girl and thereby removes the attribution of full personhood to it, culturally transforming the body-person into something else. Thus it is "as if you didn't have a baby." The presumed "fundamentally unchangeable essence" that Morgan describes as characteristic of established persons in the West (1996: 55) has indeed been changed through knowledge of a child's disability. And yet the disabled body is medically cared for and given legal rights, its personhood not wholly denied, but rather diminished or, in some instances, provisional.

Disabled infant bodies challenge the all-or-nothing-ness quality those focused on the abortion debate have associated with North American personhood; they also challenge the conflation of either conception or biological birth with social personhood. Feminist scholars have rightfully noted with concern that biological birth and social personhood, historically conflated, have recently been uncoupled. New imaging technologies and avid consumption of infertility treatments have encouraged the attribution of personhood to fetuses well *prior* to birth; they have led to the development of the category of fetal, or even embryonic, persons (Becker, 2000; Casper, 1998; Hartouni, 1999; Morgan, 1996a: 59; Petchesky, 1987; Oaks, 2001; Rothman, 1986; Taylor, 1998), with concomitant implications for the abortion controversy and for women's health and rights. However, what has not been addressed is how entities defined by pregnant women as fetal "persons" in the womb may become "non-persons" or "less-than-full persons" after birth.

Rituals of Personhood

When a disability is known from birth, the cultural markers publicly acknowledging birth and motherhood are attenuated, delayed, or simply foregone altogether. When I asked about what she had planned for the day of her newborn's discharge from the hospital, Ashley Burkart, the mother of a 10-week-old boy with spina bifida, commented, "I thought my mom would be here, and we would have family here, and it would be a big show off thing. I had announcements actually in my drawer that I was going to do, but I never. I don't know. I just didn't." Jane Sawyer, whose premature baby suffered a serious bleed in her brain resulting in cerebral palsy, spoke with sorrow of abandoned celebrations and the loss of the kind of experience of motherhood she had planned, a loss that derives from the less-than-full personhood of her potentially disabled child.

> It's like nobody wanted to see pictures of her. You know what I mean? Nobody like oohed and aahed.... All the rituals. I missed out on showers. I missed out on everything.... You know, you don't send out announcements, because what's there to announce? That you had a one-pound-five-ounce baby, you know? It's all those rituals. They shouldn't mean anything, but they do.

Donna Leiden similarly recalls the decision she made about her son's baptism. The Sunday after her baby was born, the family had gone to mass and observed another child being baptized.

> I mean here is this perfect little baby getting marched down the aisle; it was like, oh, this sucks. You know. I was embarrassed by him (her son). He was deformed. But, I mean, I wasn't going to do that.... When I was pregnant with Keith I was thinking, oh, that's going to be Keith getting walked down that aisle by Father Graham, and no way. I wouldn't do that, because I would have lost it in front of all these people.

Rites of passage establish the personhood of a baby, but they also validate the motherhood of the woman who gave it birth. Here are babies whose births are neither announced nor celebrated and whose personhood remains ambiguous at best. Layne has described strategies whereby in the absence of a baby, would-have-been mothers of stillborn infants and those who have experienced pregnancy loss construct their would-have-been babies as real for themselves and for a public that denies their existence (Layne, 1999, 2003). Mothers of disabled infants face not the absent baby but a diminished one, a son or daughter whose full personhood is not culturally recognized; their own motherhood is not denied but attenuated.

Lennart Nilsson's famous photographs of fetuses, first appearing in *LIFE* magazine in 1965, have been utilized in anti-abortion campaigns precisely because they stress the physical resemblance of the developing fetus to a healthy full-term baby, which in the United States is consensually defined as a person. To the extent that these pictures have succeeded in encouraging public acceptance of the concept of fetal personhood, they have done so based on what appear to be the "biological facts" that in the United States serve as the criteria for personhood. At the same time, the dramatic reduction in the gestational age of viability that has occurred as the result of advances in neonatology has resulted in saving the lives of babies who might earlier have been defined as miscarried fetuses. Yet contrary to the imagery of "babies" in the womb presented by the right-to-life movement, upon viewing their infants *outside* the womb for the first time, mothers of very premature infants, even those who had earlier attributed personhood to their fetuses, do not necessarily see their infants in the NICU as "real babies."

Rather, the language used by many mothers portrays not-quite-a-person or even nonhuman imagery, delaying or attenuating personhood in a society in which humanness and personhood are conflated. "The first thing they said is 'It's a little boy.' You kind of want to be happy about this, but it's a fetus, it's not a baby," remarked Suzanne Dalton about her son born at under 24 weeks' gestation. Recalling her daughter's NICU experience, Michelle White said "I could hold her little dropper. It was like feeding a guinea pig almost." Mary Jane Pickard's one-pound baby drew so much attention from visitors to the NICU that she complained to her husband, "I feel like he is a freak from the circus or something." Another mother related how when she went to the grocery store she could not buy or even look at a package of chicken because of the images it brought forth; the packaged chicken weighed more than her own son, then in the NICU.

The field of developmental pediatrics acknowledges the distinction between premature and full-term babies; in determining the developmental age of a baby born prematurely, medical staff do not go by the infant's date of birth but rather assign an age adjusted to the due date. A baby born at 25 weeks gestation that has lived in the NICU for

13 weeks, for instance, will still not have attained a "corrected age" of 1 day old. Full personhood, here as everywhere culturally constructed, is for these babies ambiguous and/or provisional.[7]

Though aborted fetuses are portrayed by members of the right-to-life movement as murdered *persons*, miscarried fetuses, which are often interpreted by medical personnel as having been "defective," are not prominently portrayed as persons in the movement's rhetoric. Even for those who accept the notion of fetal personhood, then, the personhood of a fetus that would develop into a disabled child is attenuated in comparison with one who would otherwise develop into a "normal" child. Though the precise moment for defining someone as a person—conception or birth—may serve as a locus of debate in the abortion controversy, the birth of disabled babies suggests that for North Americans, personhood may not necessarily be assigned absolutely at one point or another but rather earned and/or reduced in increments. In this sense, North American conceptions of personhood allow not only for persons and nonpersons, as public debates over fetal personhood and brain death would imply, but for *gradations* of personhood.

Mothers encountering a child different than their expectations may vacillate between visions of the disabled child as a real baby and as something "other." On seeing her daughter for the first time, Jane Sawyer remembers, "I didn't see her as her, I didn't have the attachment to her." It wasn't until later, Jane says, that "I guess I saw her as a baby... ." Jean Hill brought her four-month-old (corrected age) to Newborn Followup after a lengthy hospital stay. She described the process of sitting in the NICU day after day waiting for answers only to receive different information from different doctors "and by the time you get done, it's like do I have a kid left?" After Keisha Sellers[8] learned that her baby's brain was damaged and that he might never walk, she cried as she told the silent group in the examining room that "he was never meant to be." During her pregnancy, Keisha had received treatment at a hospital, where she was told the fetus was dead, and a D&C was subsequently performed; a couple of weeks later, she was in the hospital again with pain, "they telling me it's gas, and it never got better. It never got better. And the baby was dead, and then I knew something was going to be wrong with that baby... ." In an agonizing expression of the ambiguous status of her child's personhood, she sobbed, "I have a death certificate and a birth certificate for the same baby! Should have got rid of the baby, didn't want to get rid of it."

A neonatologist came to talk to Suzanne Dalton after it was determined that her premature son had had a serious brain hemorrhage. Recognizing the tentative personhood the grim prognosis implied, Suzanne described the doctor as "wonderful" because "he laid out all the facts and then at the end... he just made Matthew a *baby* again." That Matthew might *not* really be a baby (owing to the facts of brain damage initially laid out by the doctor) is the subtext of her comment. The particular neonatologist described here appears in numerous narratives in which he plays the same role—the doctor who appreciates the infant as a full person, the one who recognizes, and helped parents to recognize, not only specific personality characteristics of their child but the child's agency as well. What Suzanne claimed stood out for her was that he told her, "Matthew is a special little guy, he's really fighting." In such a way, the doctor makes sense of the child; Matthew's act of living has now become suspended in "webs of social significance" (Geertz, 1973: 5). By placing him within a valued story, the doctor has invested the child with culture.

Achieving recognition from medical staff and/or family members as a fighter against the adversity of potential disability is a theme repeated by most mothers in their NICU stories and in statements during the NICU support group meetings. An infant's efforts to progress away from a diagnosis of disability and toward a trajectory of normal development is a criterion for attribution of personhood to a child at risk, a point that will be discussed in greater detail in the next chapter.

Doctors, Denial, and the Authorization of Personhood

Women whose children were born with an identified disability, or risk of disability, described a loss of the "real experience" of first-time motherhood; this was the case for mothers of infants born very prematurely or with Down syndrome, for example. Detection of conditions such as autism, cerebral palsy, and muscular dystrophy is less certain (Hedderly, Baird, and McConachie, 2003: 21); rarely are these disorders determined in the hospital at birth. Mothers receiving a diagnosis of their child's disability in the course of a later developmental exam often view the *physician* as diminishing the personhood of the child. Talking about her child's examination, Diane McDonald explains,

> The evaluation, I think, was a totally foreign process to me, and an eye-opener, because here they were objectively categorizing my child in a way that I never saw him that way. And it hurt. I mean, I cried. I cried when they told me that my two-and-a-half-year old had the cognitive ability of a nine-month old.

The medical language here provides a quantitative measure of the child's deficit. A mother can know precisely how much less of a child she has. The functions and implications of quantification of deficit will be discussed in the next chapter.

Qualitative medical markers of disability also diminish personhood. As a "cackle of medical students" surrounded Jenna Mosher's seven-week-old boy, they held a textbook open to a page describing a related syndrome, "and they're saying, look at his ears, look at this—you know I felt like—he's not a circus freak!" Becky Romano, whose toddler was diagnosed with a chromosomal abnormality, similarly reports the impact of the developmental pediatrician's evaluation, and her own struggle to recapture, for herself, her own definition of her child and her role of mother:

> There were days I would just—being part-time too, and being home a lot, I would just sit and cry. I would look at Billy and just cry.... Like even with this latest thing with Dr. Jones about the attention deficit. I was so devastated when I came out of there I said, that's it. We're going to Disney World next year.

Physicians at the Newborn Followup Program generally feel compelled to give a definitive, unambiguous diagnosis; they are often uncomfortable when, for lack of clear medical indicators, they find themselves unable to do so. They are generally aware of research (such as that by Quine and Pahl, 1986; Quine and Rutter, 1994; O'Sullivan, Mahoney, and Robinson, 1992; and Sloper and Turner, 1993) suggesting that parents are dissatisfied if they feel they are not given sufficient information or if they were not informed of a disability as early as possible in their child's life. Doctors and nurses make conscious efforts to explain as much as they believe a parent can understand, in a manner appropriate to what they judge a parent's level of education to be. And they often quite reasonably assume that in requesting information mothers are also asking the doctors to predict the future level of disability of their children; indeed, it is very often the case that parents overtly request such predictions: "When will she walk?" "Will his learning catch up with other kids?" "Will she grow out of it?" or, as I heard a mother ask in a case of a diagnosis of autism, "Will he ever love me?" The developmental specialists and residents doing their rotation in developmental pediatrics are therefore often troubled that the predictions and labels they provide in response to such questions nevertheless so often lead to bad feelings.

Physician labeling of a child with a particular disability challenges the mother's ability to define her own child. Regardless of the clarity with which doctors may explain diagnoses in medical and/or lay terms, in the short period of time they have with parents during an evaluation they are unable to disassociate certain terms from the cultural devaluation of a person so labeled (Landsman, 2000). If she is to maintain her belief in her child's full personhood, an American mother therefore may first attempt to disassociate her child from the diagnosis that culturally diminishes him or her. This attempt is what physicians and psychologists refer to as the stage of "denial." Rejection or reinterpretation of the physician's label and prognosis is common; I suggest that it is found across all classes and educational levels in large part because discrimination against persons with disabilities does so as well (Landsman, 2000: 177).

In narratives collected in the initial round of interviews, I found mothers most frequently reject the application of a label to their child if that label is one about which there are firmly entrenched negative stereotypes. A mother is more likely to assent to a diagnosis of periventricular leukomalacia or pervasive developmental disorder, which conjure up no specific images in American culture, than to one of cerebral palsy, mental retardation, or autism, about which a mother is likely to already have some awareness and preconceived opinion. For example, mothers of children diagnosed with autism often refer to the 1988 film *Rain Man* and contrast their child to the movie's autistic savant main character played by actor Dustin Hoffman. After doing some reading on the subject, Peggy Hoffmeister felt that a label of autism didn't really fit her son; contrasting the term *autism* with pervasive developmental disorder (PDD), her son's official diagnosis at the time of the interview, Peggy herself noted differing public reactions: "PDD is a nice term to use; nobody knows what it means, and say he has pervasive developmental disorder—nobody stops to think what the words mean and say, 'Oh!'"

Upon first hearing a diagnosis of cerebral palsy, mothers often incorrectly assume they are being informed both that their child will be unable ever to walk and that the child will inevitably have mental retardation; in American culture, mental retardation may hold the lowest position in the "pecking order of disabilities" (Ferguson, 1996: 20). At the time of the first interview, Angela Petrocelli's son had recently been diagnosed only with the term *spastic diplegia*, a term that medical staff, but few mothers, understand as a *form* of cerebral palsy indicating spasticity (stiffness) in the lower extremities; at a visit to the doctor a year later, the term *cerebral palsy* (CP) was used with the mother for the first time. Angela describes the diagnosis:

> **Angela**: He still has spastic diplegia as a more specific form and now he's definitely a child with CP.
>
> **Gail**: Was that hard to hear or to see in writing?
>
> **Angela**: Yeah, I'd rather hear spastic diplegia—sounds worse, I don't know. But I think people associate—even me myself before, to see or hear CP kind of makes me think the child is also retarded when I know absolutely that's not the case. So I think I still see that image of maybe a very, very, severe child—and maybe the child does have mental retardation—but I think just because they're called CP all these kids get lumped into—actually, do you find that?

Terms that generally reside exclusively within the domain of biomedicine—spastic diplegia, hemiparesis, periventricular leuko-malasia, hypotonia, pervasive developmental disorder—are deemed more acceptable than those with broader cultural saliency, like cerebral palsy or mental retardation. In part, this may be because the first set of terms appear to refer to illnesses or conditions that are temporary and curable (and thus rightfully in the domain of medicine), whereas the latter indicate permanent disability and thus culturally justify the attribution of less than full personhood. Sonya Somich, for example, was angered that just because her premature daughter requires the use of oxygen, the infant is defined by others as handicapped; commenting on the provision of a handicapped parking permit for her to use when "lugging around" the oxygen tank, she explains "I wasn't even thinking along those lines, because to me, Katrina is not handicapped…. It just aggravates me that people are so narrow-minded sometimes into thinking that if the baby needs medical attention or whatever, then there is something wrong with the child." Sonya thus stresses the distinction between the neutral diagnosis of a (temporary) problem requiring medical attention and the socially pejorative diagnosis of a long-term disability. When doctors label a child with a disability, they are in many instances asking women to apply to one body two seemingly incompatible concepts: their loved child and a diagnosis culturally associated with less than full personhood.

Mothers often question or resist such value-laden diagnoses. Resistance comes in many forms, including claims that the doctor only "played" with the child during the evaluation; that parents were given contradictory information from specialists elsewhere, such as at the larger children's hospitals in Boston or Buffalo; that with time and appropriate therapies (such as massage for spasticity or applied behavioral analysis for autism), the child will overcome his or her symptoms; or that the child is perfectly able but either too shy, tired, or unwilling to perform tasks for the doctor within the brief time frame and particular context of the evaluation. Questioning the doctor's prognosis of cerebral palsy, Angela Petrocelli points out that her son

> doesn't perform well in front of people that he doesn't see regularly enough. So he doesn't—to me, he doesn't do what I know he can do and then we get this report based on 20 minutes of this kid turning into my shoulder, keeping his head down, so—I find a lot of doctors—I don't know if they agree with therapists, but they don't have such an optimistic outlook.

Doctors often respond to mothers' denials by reiterating or providing additional medical facts in order to convince parents of the validity of the diagnosis. In the case of Becky Romano above, the physician later told me his intent in stressing the physical markers of disability had been to provide the mother with information about how he knew the diagnosis was correct.[9] Rather than arrogantly expecting blind acceptance of his authority, his goal had been to share his knowledge and reveal to the mother his reasoning process; in this way, he felt, the mother would come to see the same evidence as he did in her child, and reach the same conclusions. However, a mother may experience this type of session not as information sharing but rather as the doctor's authorizing the withdrawal of her child's full personhood: "I was looking at my son like he was some ugly dog for like six months after that first visit with Dr. Jones," Becky recalled in her second interview.

During and after a child's evaluation, physicians and nurses often engage in analysis of whether the mother "gets it." "Getting it" refers to a mother's understanding that what she is hearing is bad news, generally that the diagnosis is serious and that it is permanent. Not "getting it" is of concern to the medical staff, in part because it may result in the mother failing to seek the medical and therapeutic interventions from which they believe the child would benefit but also because they fear the mother may leave the office with hopes that are too high and that may be painfully dashed at later time. Thus, "Do you think she gets it?" is often the starting point of conversation when developmental pediatricians, nurses, and residents congregate in the meeting room after an evaluation to discuss a case, especially if signals from the mother seemed equivocal. The clearest indicator to the medical staff that a woman gets it is if she cries. As mothers generally try not to do this in front of the doctors and usually apologize when they do so, mothers and doctors are often at cross-purposes at this most difficult moment.

In the following excerpt, a doctor has just evaluated a three-and-a-half-year-old boy who had been previously diagnosed with PDD. Receiving little visible or verbal response from the mother to indicate that she "gets it," the doctor in turn gives progressively more disheartening information.

> **Doctor:** What I would have loved to have seen is some very definitive changes in each of those areas: using language as a tool, making sustained efforts to connect with people, being productive in his play...those things are happening, but they're happening still to very small degree.... Am I kind of on target here?
> **(No audible response from parents)**
> **Doctor:** So one of the issues that I come up with myself is, compared to where he was eight months ago has he made those major changes

that say "gee, this is headed very much in the right direction?" And the answer to that from my point of view is "no." He hasn't made those big changes to say, "gee, we're really feeling positive." I don't mean to be not optimistic and say they couldn't happen

Mom: Uh-huh

Doctor: It's clear he's got a great amount of potential, but that big league board hasn't been there

Mom: Right

Doctor: Um, and as the time goes on… if you don't see that progress it makes it harder for us to in the future, just statistically

Mom: Mmm

Doctor: So if you have somebody that's two, two-and-a-half that's having these difficulties you may see big improvement within a year. At three-and-a-half the chances of that big improvement coming are less.

Mom: Uh huh

Doctor: At five, there's much less. So, I think your idea of saying that you want more intensity, you want to look at programs very targeted to this issue, I think that's a good plan and I'd push you to do that if you weren't doing it…. If you were to ask if this is still pervasive developmental disorder, there's no question that this is the problem. And where is it on the continuum of difficulties? If you try to think of it as a line from very minor difficulties in socialization to being very severe… he's not on the *most* severe end, but he's not in the middle either, he's sort of what we'd call moderately severe.

Mom: Mmm

Doctor: And I didn't want to use the term autism in the past because he was so young. At this point I would use that term.

Mom: Uh huh

Doctor: It's consistent with that way of thinking… it's a more serious situation.

Mom: Uh huh

Doctor: … So I guess the message I'm leaving today or what I feel is he's made some improvements

Dad: Right

Doctor: but not the spectacular ones that everybody hopes for, that the issues here are *not* minor. They're pretty serious.

Mom: Uh huh

Doctor: And looking at a program that's highly intensive…

(description of potential school programs)

Mom: Now, he's not out of the age where, it's still an important age, right? It's not too late for him to turn around and like go to regular kindergarten?

Doctor: Is there a chance that he'll be talking well in kindergarten and managing on his own so you can say he's going to learn from that experience? Yes, there is a chance. But to be honest with you, it's pretty slim.

Mom: Mmm huh

Doctor: When the issues are not making rapid progress you have to say that the chances of him getting out of the woods in the next couple of years are pretty slim. It does happen, but it's very unusual.

Mom: Uh huh

Doctor: And the worry that everybody has is that this is going to turn out to be that long-term condition that's going to be exceptionally disabling to him. So on the face value you have to say, the odds are not in your favor, but they're not zero.

Mom: Uh-huh

Doctor: But if you look at it in more depth, in some school districts they would expect him—

Mom: But it's still not, I mean, out of the question, that he would ever go to regular school? He's still young enough where he could get a little better?

In this case, the doctor and nurses were troubled by the woman's lack of expressed sorrow when being given such serious news and about her focus on the possibility of her child becoming relatively normal by the time he reached school-age; following the exam, discussion immediately ensued about whether the mother "got it."[10] When instead of crying or otherwise indicating that they see their child in a new light, (i.e., as permanently disabled), mothers *"deny,"* resist, or seem to ignore a diagnosis, doctors presume that what is being denied by the mother is the medical diagnosis itself; therefore, they may bolster the diagnosis with repetition, extension, or elaboration of the "biological facts" that serve as the medical criteria for the diagnosis. I suggest, however, that what is being denied are not always the "biological facts" themselves but rather the child's diminished personhood for which in the broader culture, the biological facts are made to serve as evidence.

On Norms, Personhood, and Perfection

If the permanence of a child's disability is a threat to his or her personhood and to his or her social valuation and acceptance, the ambivalence of a mother's own interpretations regarding her child's personhood and value is in turn a source of guilt. "And then, like months and months of this, it's like get rid of this kid, and I wish he never existed, and then you go through the guilt, you know, I love this child, I hate this child, I love this child, I hate this child, " Jennifer Borden recalled. "At first, you go through that brief little time where you feel like I don't want this child if he's going to be handicapped, which is so selfish-sounding," admitted Becky Romano. Similarly, Laurel Messerschmidt found that shortly after receiving a diagnosis of cerebral palsy for her daughter "one of the things that kind of surprised me is that there was like sort of a point where I wanted to push Ellen away." Laurel's language, like that of many of the doctors, reflects the ambiguous status of the child's personhood:

> I just sort of thought of the stuff we learned in school about when an animal perceives one of the pups is not going to make it, sort of push him away, and it was sort of like an unconscious thought that rose to the surface to a certain extent. And after a short time, it's sort of the—she's not perfect, so I'm not sure I want her—type of thing.

Countering the fears of social critics that routine prenatal diagnosis will lead women to seek to have only "perfect babies," Press, et al. (1998) claim that analysis of statements made by pregnant women in their study suggest that the majority do not seek "perfect babies" but rather "perfectly normal babies." I agree that for most pregnant women who consciously adhere to the prescribed prenatal diet, the goal is a normal baby. The data from this study of mothers of disabled children, however, suggest that "perfect" and "normal" have been conflated in the United States. Prenatal screening, selective abortion, and dissemination of information on the impact of maternal behavior on the fetus support a climate in which pregnant women assume that "perfect" children are within reach of all mothers who have access to prenatal care and who comply with biomedical advice. To put it another way, the assumption is that perfect babies are (or should be) the norm.

Though in the next chapter I discuss the notion of the norm in relation to narratives of linear progress, it is worth examining here the historical development of the concept of the norm. Lennard J. Davis refers to a quantification of the human body that began in the nineteenth century. The idea of a norm, Davis reminds us, "is less a condition of human nature than it is a feature of a certain kind of society" (1995: 24). Based on lexicographical information, Davis dates the emergence into consciousness in English of the idea of the norm to the period of approximately 1840–1860.

Preceding the concept of the norm in relation to the body was the concept of the "ideal," a word dating to the seventeenth century. Davis asks us to envision a world "in which the hegemony of normalcy doesn't exist" (1995: 24). What we would find, he claims, is the *ideal* body, as exemplified in nude Venuses. The ideal, divine body is simply unattainable by humans. The very notion of an ideal body implies that "the human body as visualized in art or imagination must be composed from the ideal parts of living models. These models individually can never embody the ideal since an ideal, by definition, can never be found in this world" (1995: 25). Ideal bodies are associated with gods and goddesses; they are found not in the real world but rather only in mythology, poetry, and art. As Davis explains, in a culture with an ideal form of the body, *all* individual members of the population are below the ideal; there can be no demand that people have bodies that conform to the ideal.

Davis traces the emergence of the concept of the norm in European culture, and in particular the notion of the norm as imperative, to the development of the field of statistics (1995: 23–49). The French statistician Quetelet, Davis tells us, took the "law of error" used by astronomers to locate a star by plotting all the sightings and then averaging the errors and applied it to the distribution of human features such as height and weight. Quetelet then formulated the concept of the average man, representing the average of all human attributes in a given country. Davis argues that Quetelet's notion of the average man, conceptualized in both physical and moral terms, provided scientific justification for the middle class and specifically addressed the body such that the notion "of physical beauty as an exceptional ideal became transformed into beauty as the average" (Davis, 1995: 28). Galton's later development of the normal distribution curve and his revision of it into ranked quartiles, further lent itself to eugenic purposes; MacKenzie argues that it was in fact the needs of eugenics that in large part determined the content of Galton's statistical theory (1981: 52). In a society in which the concept of the norm is an imperative and is applied to the body, those falling outside the normal bell curve are deviants. In essence, Galton created a new kind of ideal.

> This statistical ideal is unlike the classical ideal which contains no imperative to be the ideal. The new ideal of ranked order is powered by the imperative of the norm, and then is supplemented by the notion of progress, human perfectibility, and the elimination of deviance, to create a dominating, hegemonic vision of what the human body should be.
>
> (Davis, 1995: 35)

The development of the hegemony of the norm was illustrated in the United States in the "better-baby" contests held at county and state fairs between 1910 and 1930. According to Alexandra Minna Stern, in the United States "being deemed 'the best' required a score as near to perfect as possible on a set of physical, psychological, and physiological scales, most of which were statistically measured according to bell curves" (Stern, 2002: 69). At better-baby contests in the Midwest, judges utilized a scorecard approved by the American Medical Association. Points were deducted for a broad range of what were considered defects, and "slow reactions to the mental tests or perceived lack of muscular co-ordination lowered a child's score, as did deviations from the national standards for height and weight (based on age), and weight-to-height ratio" (2002: 76). Being "better," Stern argues, thus "meant being 'normal,' which, in turn, meant embodying to the closest decimal point the standards of growth being codified in the emergent field of pediatric medicine" (2002: 69). With their eugenic goals and assessment of children through indicators that generated statistical abstractions, the contests helped "to bring about a reconceptualization of the perfectibility of infants"; the desire of parents of the 1890s for their children to manifest physical beauty,

Stern claims, had by the 1930s been supplanted by a focus on norms and deviation (2002: 77).

As Davis and Stern each demonstrate, the concept of the normal is a historically situated cultural construction. For disabled people themselves, the implications of a shift from the notion of the perfect body as an unattainable ideal to the imperative of the attainable norm include being on the receiving end of a negative moral evaluation. However, what are its implications for the mothers who bring such people into the world? With prenatal screening and information on how to avoid birth defects through prenatal diet now routine parts of a woman's experience of pregnancy, the tools to enable the elimination of deviance appear to be readily available. In this context, "perfect" and "normal" are taken to be one and the same. In this sense, Browner and Press's claim that pregnant women don't seek "perfect" babies but rather "perfectly normal" babies suggests a distinction that does not exist, for perfection is taken to be a goal that normal prospective mothers are obligated to seek and attain.

Mothers' narratives thus often express surprise that after doing everything right during their pregnancies, their child is diagnosed with a disability (i.e., is not "perfect"). Judith Larson describes her reaction upon receiving a pediatrician's advice to contact a specialist. "I mean, we knew she slept a lot and she wasn't very good at eating, drinking her bottles, but it never really occurred to us that she wasn't perfect, and that was kind of shocking." During developmental pediatric examinations, doctors themselves conflate the terms *perfect* and *normal*. The following excerpt is typical of cases in which the testing procedures indicate no disabilities or developmental delays. It is taken from a doctor's comments to a mother at the conclusion of his evaluation of her one-year-old daughter, who had had complications at birth: "But when we look at her development today, how she plays with toys, and how she talks, and uses her hands, and how she's walking, she's perfect.... She has normal development. Everything we look at is normal, good, and we don't expect any problems from this girl."

"Perfect" here refers to the child's fit within the normal curve of physical, cognitive, and social development as measured in standardized tests; it indicates the absence of imperfections that would mark the child as abnormal and qualify her for intervention services. Which particular aspects of development, appearance, or behavior are tested for and for which a norm may be determined, may vary over time or from one evaluation site to another. However, for a doctor to say that a child is "perfect" or that he or she is "normal" in his or her development is considered one and the same thing.

Forty-one percent of women in the study make spontaneous reference in their narratives to "perfect" babies. The reference to perfect babies may be in describing an expectation they once had or a wish they still have. Sometimes it is used as a commentary on the discrimination their children might face in a society driven by expectations of perfection and conformity. The term often appears in reference to other mothers' children as they move through the milestones that mark development and full personhood in both the practice of pediatrics and popular culture in the United States, leaving their own child behind.

> I mean, I have a friend who has three perfect children... and I guess I only resent it when I'll say something like—something to the effect of "Well, you know, Daniel's still not eating solid food," and she'll just immediately say, "Oh, but look, at least he's eating baby foods and things." And I feel like saying "Well, what the hell do you know, your kids can make their own peanut butter and jelly sandwiches at the age of four."
>
> (Jenna Mosher)

Whether referring to their own perceptions of other people's children or other people's perceptions of *their* children, mothers of all classes, ages, and educational levels represented in the study refer to "perfect" children; even when criticizing the term and/or redefining it, they recognize it as a term that is used to distinguish those children who fit the norm from those who don't. Mothers, aided by mainstream public discourse and the medical community that measures child development in terms of deviation from the norm, thus participate in an interpretation of disability articulated by Erving Goffman in his famous study, *Stigma* (Goffman, 1963). Geyla Frank contrasts this interpretation to the anthropological viewpoint expressed by Margaret Mead, whose work suggests that American culture can be represented by its diversity. "While Goffman viewed disability as a matter of deviance from the able-bodied American norm, Mead saw it as merely one variation within a broad range of possibilities" (Frank, 2000: 61). As will be discussed in later chapters, mothers themselves may move between these approaches. However, regardless of their personal interpretations of disability as either deviance or variation, numerous mothers in the study report that others—be they strangers, friends, or extended family members—often openly question the value of their disabled children and in turn extend that devaluation to question the wisdom of investing time and energy in their nurturance. These women understand their own motherhood to be publicly devalued.

> I called him [a college friend] after Brent came home and told him, and he was surprised at first, and then he kind of, he made a very... like with a remark of, well, he'll be developmentally delayed, or he will have developmental problems, or something, just assuming.... And I was kind of thrown by that. I thought, wow, because he has two perfectly healthy children, and I kind of—that really kind of bothered me, and I haven't heard from him since, and I feel like, you know, because I didn't have the ideal baby, he is treating me differently.
>
> (Mary Jane Pickard)

> I think that they somehow think, oh, "I'm sorry for you," you know... and we even had one woman say to us, she said, "Well, now you need to decide if you're going to sink your whole life into Ryan, or if you're going to have more kids and create a normal family environment." And I thought to myself, what is she saying by that... are you saying that we are not normal? You know, "Your family is something less" or whatever.
>
> (Tina Graham)

Diminished Personhood and Diminished Motherhood

If perfect babies are an attainable norm, then the mothers who attain, nurture, and commit to less-than-perfect babies are themselves *ab*normal, their families "something less." Those for whom the disabled child is their only child may question the validity of their experience of giving birth and their identity as mothers. "I always wanted to do that grunting and pushing and yelling nasty things at my husband, and then have that beautiful baby come out, and I'll never have that," stated one young Navy wife, the mother of a premature baby who had been diagnosed as blind. Suzanne Dalton similarly feels excluded from the community of normal American new mothers:

> And when all the mothers sit around and like to talk about deliveries which some of them like to do... I can't sit around and say I was in labor for so many hours and my husband did this thing and I yelled at him. I don't have good stories to tell. I have bad stories and no one wants to hear the bad stories. And sometimes I want to tell someone about it. I want to say here's what my experience was but no one wants to hear that. It's a real downer because when mothers get together to talk about their deliveries it's how they came out strong and survived.

Angela Petrocelli found that her extended family thought she should be excluded from future motherhood altogether, for fear that this could happen again. "I guess what bothers me the most is that I should become sterile because of this. This is a reason for sterilization, and you're not to have anymore kids or do this to anymore kids, or do this to this family again."

Toward the end of an interview, first-time mother Jane Sawyer began to ask *me* questions about how I dealt with having a disabled daughter. "Are you proud?" she then asked me. Thinking I understood her question, I began to respond "yes" and to describe how very proud I was of my daughter. Jane interrupted me. "No, I mean are you proud of *yourself*, are you proud of yourself as a *mother*?" During the interview with Jane, I had been genuinely troubled by the pain she had exposed in her story. As she changed the terms of the interview, asking me questions, I had felt my role shifting from that of objective interviewer toward that of support person. However, perhaps because my own motherhood felt to me already firmly established through my other two conventionally successful school-age children, what I had missed in her question was the linkage she made between her daughter's diminished personhood and her own diminished motherhood. It was a linkage I would hear again and again in the narratives of other women in the study. "I feel sometimes as a failure as a human being because I didn't have a perfect child," reflects Alice Brooks, whose daughter Susan has Down syndrome. "I do love her dearly," she continues, "but you wonder, you know, what did I do wrong to have a child like this?"

As we have seen, biomedicine and popular culture have provided a historically specific vocabulary with which to answer this question for a mother herself and for the public that would scrutinize her behaviors during pregnancy. Some mothers—crack addicts, alcohol abusers, and poor, teenage or otherwise "bad" mothers—are themselves to blame. Those mothers who appear to have done "everything right"—who followed the accepted practices of obtaining regular prenatal care and diagnostic tests and who dutifully complied with the recommended diet, including the elimination of alcohol, cigarettes, and drugs—yet nevertheless have a child with a disability, therefore pose a particular challenge in American society. It is to such women it is often told, "God gives special children to special parents."[11]

Special Kids for Special Parents?

Mothers consistently report the statement "God gives special kids to special parents" as something told to them by others. Some women had read in the newspaper or been sent by well-meaning friends or relatives a reprint of a 1980 Erma Bombeck column. "Do you ever wonder how mothers of handicapped children are chosen?" Bombeck (1993: C-2) asks in the widely circulated column, which was reprinted in the major local newspaper in 1993; the column also hung on the wall at the Ronald McDonald House, which provides housing for out-of-town parents of hospitalized children. The column provides a description of God instructing an inquisitive angel to give a particular woman a handicapped child on the basis of the woman's specific qualities; these qualities include the woman's knowledge of laughter, a feeling of self and independence that empowers her to take a child who has his own world and make it live in hers, the right amount of selfishness to enable her to separate herself from the child occasionally, and the ability to rise above ignorance, cruelty, and prejudice. In Bombeck's scenario, such a special mother will have God at her side every minute of the day, for she is doing His work.

Those few mothers in the study who found the notion comforting generally did so in the early days following a child's diagnosis of disability. Such mothers acknowledged it as a reassuring statement of faith on the part of friends or family that they were capable of coping well with the struggles ahead. It served as another version of the saying that God never gives you more than you can handle. Many found it comforting regardless of their spiritual beliefs.

> That's sort of comforting.... Not because I really believe that there is a God or anything but just because it's the fact that they care enough.... So, maybe on a bad day it would be nice to believe that there is somebody up there saying this woman is capable, she's the one that needs to be raising this child. That's a nice thought.
>
> (Dawn Woodward)

> I was talking to my cousin and she says "You know, Mary, only certain people are blessed with certain kinds of kids and certain people can deal with it and certain people can't, but my own belief is He chose you because He knew you could do it." And that made me kind of happy to hear from just a relative of mine saying that.
>
> (Mary Summers)

Yet after a year of mothering a child with a disability, few of the mothers interviewed accepted the validity of the saying (Landsman, 1999: 143). One seeming exception was Patricia Marks, who had only recently reinterpreted the traumatic birth of her premature son (who has cerebral palsy) as "training" for which she was chosen by God for the purpose of preparing her for the adoption of premature twin girls 11 years later. By agreeing to take children who were, in Patricia's words, "not white, not babies, and not perfect," she and her husband rose to the top of the Department of Social Services' list of prospective adoptive parents for two white premature infants whose prognosis involved multiple disabilities.

> When we were coming back from the hospital and we were coming back with two babies, and two oxygen tanks, two SIDS monitors, and a nurse for, I think it was either 12 or 16 hours a day... "Oh, my God," Joe said to me, "Are you going to be able to do this?" I said, "It has already been decided that we can do this," and I know we've been chosen, and that has helped me through some of the scares we've had, was knowing that—because I was this obviously hand-picked person that I would not be faced with anything that I could not deal with. I have been more confident as a result of that. There has never been any doubt in either one of us that this is a match made in heaven. You also feel more confident in

your parenting, and we also both felt that they were our reward for doing a good job the first time we got picked...

Patricia continued her story by reflecting back on her reaction to her 11-year-old son Sam's premature birth and subsequent disabilities.

As a mom, I spent 11 years wondering what I did wrong. It was my body. Who else could you say?... One of these cold winter days when I was dealing with major cabin fever here, it hit me that I didn't do anything wrong. It was training, and I could finally mark that off the list. I used to feel for years, that when my time was up and I hopefully went up there, my first question was going to be, so what did I do wrong? So what made that happen? And now I knew I could mark that off the list of things that had been stored back there and that you worried about. My dad said the day they came to see them (the twin girls), that on the way up he remembered talking to me when Sam was just a few days old. I was still in the hospital, and I was crying. "Why couldn't I have a baby like everybody else does?"... He said, it took you 11 years, he said, but you have your answer now. He says, "because of two little girls coming along the line that needed you."

Patricia's story overlays her being chosen as a special mother for special children with being chosen, after long, agonizing years of waiting, to be the adoptive mother of the two girls nobody else seemed to want; her "special child–special mother" story and her "adoption success" story merge into one. Yet even so, her story portrays her current status as "special" not as a quality intrinsic to her, but rather as the result of "training" obtained through the experience of mothering her first child. Her specialness was earned.

Most women in the study came to reject the notion that they were chosen by God because they were special, many with surprising vehemence and anger. This rejection cut across all classes, religions, ages, and educational levels represented in the study. Just a few of the many interview excerpts in which the issue is raised by mothers follow:

But that's a crock of bull, okay? They say, well, you know you have to— God—because you have patience or whatever. You have no choice. This is it. You know either you give them up, send them away to a home or you deal with it. It's not in between. I choose to deal with it.

(Alice Brooks)

You do get sick of people saying to you, because I've had quite a few people come up and say, "Oh, you know, God gives special children to special people." Shut up! It's just like some of the dumber things people say. It's not really that bad, maybe because I never had another one before him. I've just adjusted. He's really not that bad. He's really kind of cute. He's got lots of personality. He's not, you know, this *thing*.

(Jennifer Borden)

People say "Oh, my God, I would never be able to do it. I can't believe you're doing it." But I don't think it's that bad. I don't know if it's because I'm doing it or whatever, but for some reason, I don't think it's like, "How could you have dealt with that? I would go crazy." But you wouldn't. If you had to do it, you had to do it and you wouldn't go crazy, because you can't.

(Katie Allen)

Yeah, I—I've heard that.... Someone cut that out for me and gave it to me.... I'd rather be the person it didn't happen—I'd rather have it happen to the other person.

(Angela Petrocelli)

I mean, I realize they are trying to be flattering, and I'm usually a little embarrassed by that. It's very kind of them saying that, but I don't think that I—well, I think we have a lot of love.... We do have a lot to offer to him, but I think we are even more blessed to have him than he is to have us.

(Lorraine Hamilton)

I've heard that a lot... and I just say, I think you just handle what is given to you. You know, it's either that or crumble, and some can do it, some can't because obviously, there are people who can't handle it, and they either lose it or get rid of their child. I mean, it's just—luckily, we're able to handle it. I don't think that we are special parents, any specialer than any other parent because we were given one. We're lucky parents, really. I mean, we ran into a couple, an older couple in the mall one time with her, and they didn't say anything but "she will love you more than any child ever could," and I mean, you can see that they're probably right...

(Lily Beckett)

Now I'm not an atheist or anything, but that doesn't do much for me. I know I'm strong. I've been through a lot already.... In fact, I kind of resent it although I know people are trying to be kind and trying to help explain why these things happen. Again, my feeling is there is no explanation. It's totally random. It's nature. It's just life.

(Jenna Mosher)

At her first interview, Lisa Hart had noted that as she and her husband are gentle and loving people, it was possible that they were "meant to have a special baby." She had been told shortly after the traumatic birth of a child at risk for disabilities, that

> God never gives babies to parents who don't have extra love to take care of them, sick babies to parents that can't take care of them, and I think, yeah, it does take a special person to have a baby with problems and be there for them and love them and help them out in a way. I'm sure you're one of those good people just by the way you talk about your daughter.

At this first interview, Lisa had not only accepted the adage for herself but attributed this "special parent" quality to others, including me. Yet when interviewed 14 months later, with her child still fed by gastric tube and now diagnosed with cerebral palsy and potentially with mental retardation, she had clearly reinterpreted the statement. Recalling a time when someone had made the statement to her, she claims to have replied, "If they're such a blessing how come everybody doesn't pray to have one?"

In rebuffing the statement "God gives special kids to special parents," mothers are reacting in part to the saying's romantic glossing over of the emotional and practical hardships involved in parenting a disabled child. More significantly, however, they reject the manner in which the statement diminishes the personhood and value of their child ("He's not really that bad.... He's not, you know, this *thing*"). They object as well to the implication that prior to the child's birth they must have been fundamentally different from normal women in order to have been given an abnormal child (countering with "It's nature. It's just life"). That they are *now* different from other parents is apparent to most mothers. Ironically, however, the difference in part lies in their newfound ability to recognize how very much *like* everyone else they once were.

> You know that whole idea of... this only happens to special people—an interesting thing—I find it annoying actually when people say that. I think it certainly *makes* you different.... You know, "You're special parents." We're not special parents, we're average normal people who had this crazy thing happen to us. And we're doing the best we can, and maybe in the end we might turn out to be special parents, but we're just normal people struggling with, you know, making the best out of the situation we've got.
>
> (Suzanne Dalton)

Like many of the women in the study, this mother reflects that prior to having a disabled child, she also assumed that only special, different people could handle it.

> I remember saying the thing, I know I'm not special. I know I couldn't deal with that, if that happened to me—I mean, because I used to teach swimming to handicapped children... and I thought, you know, it really is a wonderful special parent who—and it just is so—it's almost like this is what it is, because when I said that it removed me completely from the experience of it. Which I *was* completely removed. It could never happen to *me*. It only happens to wonderful special people.... I mean, at the time I said to Steve, I know I'm not special, I know I can't do this. And that's what bothered me. It's almost condescending to feel as though... only special people can handle this sort of thing. No, it's like average normal people who have to deal with it... I mean, you just do what—you become a parent, I mean.

Though mothers of disabled children generally reject it, the formula "God only gives special children to special parents" continues to have broad public appeal. That it does so speaks to its support for the dominant discourse of reproduction in North American life. The adage removes reproductive outcome from the domain of biological facts for one unique category of people ("special" parents) while leaving intact trust in its functioning for "normal people." The concept of being "special" supports the belief that the "normal" state of affairs is indeed that nature is within our control and that progress itself is natural (Landsman, 1999: 141–142).

Research, however, indicates that despite genetic screening and the decreasing age of viability in prematurity, childhood disability rates have not been reduced. For example, while prenatal diagnosis has prevented an increase in Down syndrome live-birth prevalence in New York State, it has not *reduced* the live birth of children with Down syndrome significantly, in part because the percentage and number of women in the population above the age of 30, those with a higher risk for Down syndrome in the fetus, has increased, as has the birth rate among such women (Olsen, Cross, Gensburg, and Hughes, 1996). Olsen et al. predict that "if recent demographic trends in New York's female population continue and if use of prenatal diagnosis remains at the 1992 level of 48 percent, then New York's DS live birth prevalence will very likely remain constant or even increase" (1996: 998).

Prevalence of major neurodevelopmental disabilities among extremely immature infants (born before 26 weeks' gestation) similarly does not show any reduction over time in spite of dramatic advances in neonatology (Lorenz, Woodliever, Jetton, and Paneth, 1998). In reviewing the literature since 1970, Lorenz, et al. find that the more aggressive treatment of neonates and higher survival rates have actually led to a "steadily increasing prevalence of children with disabilities" (1998: 425); this finding is consistent with that of a study by Hack, Taylor, Klein, and Eiben, et al. (1994), published in the *New England Journal of Medicine*, in which school-age outcomes of premature births were assessed. The rate of preterm and low-birth-weight rates have also been increasing. In New York, the rate of infants born preterm increased more than 10% between 1994 and 2004; the rate of infants born with low birth weight in New York between 1994 and 2004 increased almost 8%, closely matching statistics for the United States (Perinatal Data Snapshots: www.marchofdimes.com.peristats, April 2007).

Bhusan, Paneth, and Kieley (1993) estimate that the childhood prevalence of cerebral palsy rose about 20% between 1960 and 1986 in the United States and that the 1980s witnessed a rise in the birth cohort population of cerebral palsy in the industrialized world. In turn, the National Institute on Disability and Rehabilitation Research reports that disability rates for children have also "risen considerably" since 1990 (Kaye, Laplante, Carlson, and Wenger, 1996: 2). "In earlier generations, when viability was limited by pulmonary maturity," Thomas McElrath explains, "the neonate either overcame the deficit or perished. The middle ground of long-term morbidity was more limited in scope.... Today... severe intraventricular hemorrhage or neonatal cerebral white matter disease... creates a much broader gray-zone between death and truly unaffected development" (2002: 44). Compared with the mid-1980s, for instance, the incidence of cerebral palsy in 23 to 25 week neonates appears unchanged, while mental delay among extremely low birthweight infants is even more common than cerebral palsy (McElrath, 2002: 56). In a study done at a major perinatal center, survival and impairment rates were compared in two periods, corresponding to the introduction of surfactant therapy in 1990; in the second period, both survival rates and neonatal morbidity rates increased (Wilson-Costello, Friedman, Minich, Fanaroff, and Hack, 2005: 997). Watts and Saigal also note that improved survival rates and constant impairment rates have resulted in an increase in the absolute numbers of infants with impairment (2006: 2221). Low severity dysfunctions such as learning disabilities, borderline mental retardation, ADHD, and behavioral problems appear to be increasing and are estimated to occur in as many as 50–70% of very-low-birth-weight babies (Aylward, 2002: 234). In short, in the United States the development of neonatal intensive care units, the advent of exogenous pulmonary surfactant, and increasingly aggressive intervention have contributed to increased neonatal survival rates at earlier gestational ages and thereby to the persistence and/or increase of childhood disabilities.

Despite these trends, well documented in the medical research literature, the adage that God chooses special parents for special children enables its speaker to retain faith that increased knowledge *does* result in increased control over pregnancy outcomes. With this formulation, the rhetoric shifts from what the mother herself *did* during pregnancy, which "should" have resulted in perfection, to what she *is* (special); the "fact" of her uniqueness is validated and made apparent by what she received (a special child) (Landsman, 1999: 142). The statement in this way not only maintains intact faith in the possibility of quality control but supports both the cultural mandate to have perfect/normal babies and the diminution both of the personhood of disabled children and of the motherhood of those who give birth to them.

In contrast to the saying, interviews reveal mothers struggling to describe the ambiguity of recognizing a child's profound difference from other children *and*, simultaneously, its full personhood; mothers lay claim equally to their own "specialness" born of the experience of raising a disabled child and to the conviction that mothers of disabled children are just ordinary people in extraordinary circumstances. While appreciating the "special" qualities being attributed to them, most mothers of disabled children contend that these traits were not inborn, waiting to be discovered, but rather were acquired. To what was acquired and how, we will turn in later chapters.

Cultural and Historical Context of Diminished Motherhood

That diminished personhood of a child should necessarily have as its consequence the diminished motherhood of the woman who bore it is not a given. If such a linkage exists, as it appears to in the experiences of mothers in this study, it is to be explained rather than merely assumed. While there are some cross-cultural studies of societal attitudes toward disabled children, there is less information on the experiences of their parents. Scholarship on American mothers is found primarily in the literature on stages of grief and strategies for coping, with recent work on the latter addressing resiliency. The professional literature, as Hillyer laments, has been rife with mother-blame and weak on mothers' own accounts (1993: 96). How mothers of disabled infants have viewed their own motherhood in different times and places is not readily accessible. Explanations for the contemporary relationship between diminished personhood of the child and diminished motherhood are necessarily speculative. However, we can begin to explore the issue by looking at the time period and cultural context within which mothers in the study are living.

Pregnant women are currently portrayed in biomedicine, public health, and popular culture as the potential enemies of their developing fetuses. The medical finding that the drug thalidomide was linked to birth defects encouraged this shift in thinking. So also did the development of medical imaging technologies that encouraged viewing the fetus as having needs and, by extension, rights, separate and apart from those of the mother. No longer a safe haven for the developing baby, the womb is currently understood as permeable, vulnerable to dangers delivered by selfish, careless women, the "bad" mothers who bring crack babies into the world or who fail to comply with the advice of medical experts. In contrast, late nineteenth-century medical doctrines portrayed the "female animal" as "the creature organized around the uterus, the scene of fruitful production, of nurturing" (Haraway, 1986: 114), and indeed woman suffragists of the time drew specifically on this essentialist notion of women as inherent nurturers in their "government as housekeeper" analogy; they argued that society needed the special skills and experiences of motherhood (Landsman, 1992: 255). This argument was buttressed by evangelical Protestantism that both sought to circumscribe women's roles within the domestic domain and "elevated and endorsed women's moral character" (Cott, 1987: 17). The cultural scene was such that Elizabeth Cady Stanton saw it expedient for the woman suffrage movement to argue that the "greatest civilizing power all along the pathway of natural development has been found in the wisdom and tender sentiments growing out of motherhood" (1891: 7). A strong cultural association between motherhood and morality simultaneously constrained women's public activities and raised their moral status.

In the current public imagery, however, it is not women who have symbolic moral power but their children, in whose behalf the state and/ or biomedicine must often intervene. Rothman suggests that the shift in imagery from mother as protector to mother as potential enemy of her child represents not a change in maternal behavior itself but a reaction to the feminist movement. "If women can look out for our own interests, then, some fear, perhaps we cannot be trusted to look out for the interests of our children" (1989: 188). Documenting this lack of trust through the changing treatment of unwed mothers since World War II, Martha McMahon draws the conclusion that the moral worth of mothers may have gradually been replaced by the social worth of children (1995: 190). Whereas once motherhood was believed to hold redemptive power and white unwed mothers were encouraged to keep their babies, professionally run maternity homes now encourage adoption "in the best interests of the child." Citing research by Solinger and Nathanson, McMahon suggests as well that the lack of social services to black unwed mothers represents a lack of faith that such mothers are even capable of redemption. With idealized white womanhood having been removed from its moral pedestal (black womanhood never having had such a pedestal in dominant culture), she argues, motherhood now retains only a personal value, and a "social worth derived from association with valued children" (1995: 190).

Where does this leave the mothers of disabled infants and toddlers, mothers whose children hold little value in society and indeed are often portrayed as burdens upon society's scarce resources? If the social worth of motherhood is measured by its association with children of greater or lesser value, mothers of children who do not even attain the status of personhood fall well short of the mark. However, the linkage between a disabled child's diminished personhood and a woman's diminished motherhood is not exclusively a quantitative relationship; it is marked with blame and responsibility.

Accompanying the change in the American family from its role as a unit of production to one of consumption has been a shift from children as workers to children as commodities (Rothman, 1994: 140). Failing to meet standards of commodity uniformity and functional predictability, disabled children are "re-classified as irregulars, seconds, damaged goods" (Phillips, 1990: 850). "Too bad you got a lemon," Tina Graham feels she is being told in reference to her mentally retarded son. The commodification of babies that characterizes industrialized capitalist societies is consistent with a metaphor of pregnant women not only as producers but as consumers. Women facing an array of apparent (but often illusory) choices—regarding conceptive technologies, personal conduct during pregnancy, prenatal diagnosis, and neonatal intensive care—are called upon to become informed, savvy shoppers. Reproduction has, as Strathern reminds us, been "enterprised up." Children, no longer the embodiment of kin relations, are the embodiments of their parents choices (Strathern, 1992: 31–32). "Perfect" babies can now be understood as the norm; less-than-perfect babies as the consequence of individual women's poor choices (Landsman, 1998). Through careful consumption of medical care, tests, and advice, a woman should, after all, be able to obtain a healthy, perfect child (i.e., one without noticeable product defects).

Many of the narratives collected include mothers' abiding awareness that birth defects are considered grounds for rejection. Alice Brooks's comment that "either you give them up, send them away to a home or you deal with it" is not unusual. An expectation of parental rejection was occasionally brought to the attention of mothers in the study by well-meaning medical staff, friends, or relatives. After a blood test confirmed that Lily Beckett's daughter had Down syndrome, the doctor asked her how she planned to feed the baby. When she replied that she planned on breastfeeding, the doctor asked her, "Do you think you can still do that?" She reflected, "and that to me was a strange question, but I can understand it now, that they probably have a lot of people who just completely reject the baby after that."

Having grown up in a society in which disabled children were segregated from everyday life, mothers of disabled infants are well aware that in previous eras abandonment of disabled children to institutions was common and that some parents still make that choice today. However, for a variety of economic and social reasons, public sentiment has been turning against that option.[12] The federal legislation that encouraged states to establish early-intervention programs that provide services to children younger than three years old, the Individuals with Disabilities Education Act, mandated that such services are to be provided, to the maximum extent appropriate to the child's needs, in natural environments. "Natural environments" are those locations "that are normal or natural for the child's age peers who have no disability" (Early Intervention Coordinating Council, 1999: 15), that is, settings in which infants and toddlers *without* disabilities normally participate. For infants in particular, the natural environment has been widely and increasingly interpreted to be the home. Most statewide systems of early intervention provide home-based services to infants and toddlers with disabilities, but for reasons including staff attitudes, inappropriate curricula, and insufficient resources for disabled children, public natural environments inclusive of young disabled children are less prevalent (Bruder and Staff, 1998: 26). In the New York State Early Intervention Program's 1998–1999 program year, home was the primary location of early intervention services for 88% of infants and for 85% of one-year-olds. Only 7% of infants were served primarily at a service provider's facility (Early Intervention Coordinating Council, 1999: 15). Thus, women who themselves grew up with few if any role models, little exposure to disabled people, and no expectations that they would ever be in the position of mothering such individuals paradoxically find that they are now bearing primary responsibility for caring for their disabled young children.

With motherhood itself valued only in relation to the value of the child and with "perfection," the absence of product defects, conceived as a norm attainable by all women who have access to prenatal care and who are in compliance with medical expertise, women raising disabled children are, like their children, outside the norm. Being different in American society, they are not construed as being morally equal. Either they are worse than other mothers—"bad" mothers who avoid prenatal care and who risk harm to their fetuses—or they are better—special mothers chosen by God. They are to be condemned for their selfishness or admired for their sacrifice; either way, most are to be pitied for their plight. With their children categorically less than full persons, their own motherhood by association is itself diminished.

Yet culture is neither static nor uncontested. Women who nurture their disabled children challenge the cultural construction of diminished motherhood. The means by which they do so are explored in the next two chapters.

4

Mothers, Doctors, and Developmental Delays

On Denial, Personhood, and the Emplotment of Children's Lives

It's the teaching hospital, so you got nineteen residents, thirty-nine interns, you know, the whole bit, every single person coming in and every single person making sure I knew how disabled Kate was going to be and I, I finally one day, it's like, I have had it. I sat—this poor intern, he was just the last person who walked through the door that day, and I looked at him and I said, "I heard what you said. I am not a stupid person. On one hand you tell me we don't know; on the other hand you tell me no, no, no, and this is what is going to happen to her." I said, "I cannot get up in the morning if you take away my hope. I cannot." And I said, "because I'm not a stupid person, as the time goes by and I see she doesn't do these things, I'll accept it in my time, not your time, my time, little by little. But to think right now that she's never going to get any better, I can't go home and function."

(Anonymous mother of a disabled child speaking at a workshop for parents)

Disability and the Attribution of Personhood

Mothers in this study are nurturing children who would be disposed of in many cultures (Hrdy, 1999: 460). Committing oneself to such a child, the sociobiologist Sarah Hrdy argues, is counter to self-interest and, where it happens, it represents "true heroism," the kind of behavior that

91

"makes it awkward for even the most hard-core materialists to completely discount the existence of free will" (1999: 460). This formulation begs the question of why we find such "true heroism" (a problematic term) some places and not others.

Ethnographic data suggest that the denial of full personhood, and even of life itself, to infants born with disabilities is neither universal nor uncommon. Among the Punan Bah of Central Borneo, physically and mentally impaired children live as members of extended families, share in age- and gender-appropriate household work, and are acknowledged both as humans and as persons (Nicolaisen, 1995). In the early twentieth century, some 2% to 10% of the population of Cuna Indians of the San Blas Islands of Panama had inherited a dominant gene for albinism; sensitive to the light, affected males adapted the traditional male role of fisherman by becoming night fishermen, and "albinism was not considered a disability; instead, it was identified as simply one of the many characteristics of an individual" (Scheer, 1994: 245). Similarly, Beth Harry describes a Haitian family in which expectations of interdependence make it natural for a disabled son to do odd jobs around the house rather than seek employment elsewhere; in such a situation, "family members considered this a normal part of a family contract in which members play different roles and are not devalued for their inability to be economically productive" (2002: 135). However, among the Arunta of Central Australia, Morgan reports that a premature infant was interpreted as being the young of some other animal, such as a kangaroo, that mistakenly entered the body of the woman (Morgan, 1996b: 25). And it has been reported that among the Tarahumara Indians of the Sierra Madre mountains in Mexico, parents commonly abandon infants with birth defects in the hospital or let them die shortly after they are discharged (Mull and Mull, 1987).

Scheper-Hughes suggests that particularly in those societies in which there is a high rate of infant mortality, sickly or physically different neonates "may be sacrificed in order to protect scarce resources (including maternal love and attentive nurturing) for older, healthier siblings or the lives of those yet to be born" (Scheper-Hughes, 1990: 302). However, the denial of personhood and nurturance to disabled children is not exclusive to such societies. Drawing on the database of the group Disability Awareness in Action, a report prepared for the UN General Assembly Special Session on Children in 2001 documents ongoing violations of the human rights, including the right to life, of disabled children in *all* areas of the world. The report makes the claim that disabled children

> are commonly allowed to die, denied resuscitation or have treatment withheld. Parents of disabled children are put under unbearable pressure by cultural and religious beliefs that their child is the embodiment of sin and disgrace... NGO's working in the field consistently document, not just examples of children whose lives have not been protected, but evidence that such judgements are informed by policies which consider severely disabled children as of insufficient value to justify pro-active intervention to protect life.
>
> (Landsdown, 2001)

Meira Weiss reports that at the time of her initial study in Israel "50.8 percent of all children born in Israeli hospitals who manifested a major physical or medical defect were abandoned in hospital" (1998: 149). She argues that deformed children are defined by parents of all economic statuses and ethnic and religious backgrounds in Israel as "non-persons" and are described by parents using metaphors of monsters and animals. Such children, if taken into the home, experience territorial isolation. In the cases she describes, the disabled child and his or her belongings are physically and symbolically separated from the everyday life of the home. Weiss (1997) claims that by giving disabled Israeli children a specially demarcated area that is considered "non-home," parents leave intact both their concept of home and their denial of the personhood of a deformed child. She concludes that because this "common pattern of behavior was observed across sociodemographic boundaries, it attests to its deep-rooted psychological causes" (1997: 268–269) and reveals what she suggests may be a universal and "natural aversion to physical and, especially, facial deformity" (1998: 161).

Aversion to and discrimination against disabled people runs deep in American culture as well.[1] And yet my own findings are dramatically different from those reported by Weiss and do not support an explanation based on universal psychological causes. In the homes I visited, far from being territorially isolated, the disabled child was integrated into the family's living spaces. Mothers related both the pleasures and complications of having disabled children eat with their families at the kitchen table or travel in the family car. Disabled infants were held in laps or placed on blankets in the living room, their toys spread over the floor within easy reach; youngsters crawled, sat close by in positioning seats, cried, played, watched TV, and interrupted repeatedly as my interviews with their mothers proceeded.

Even if sleeping or not present in the home during the interview, evidence of the disabled children was abundant. In the trailer home of a child with cerebral palsy, a gastric tube used for feeding hangs over the kitchen sink; in another, the child's medicines are arranged on the counter in open view. Framed photographs of disabled infants and children are displayed on shelves and mantlepieces. Pediatric walkers and "special needs" strollers are parked in the hallways or entryways of homes; in one home, the furniture has been rearranged to accommodate the child's frequent seizures; in another, the piano bench is used for at-home sessions of applied behavioral analysis with an autistic child. Most mothers in the study describe themselves as surprised and devastated hearing of their child's disability and originally believed themselves unjustly miscast in the role of mother of a disabled child; but while many may have apparently rejected ("denied") the child's diagnosis, unlike in the case of Israeli parents, by the time of release from the hospital or within a short period after diagnosis, relatively few actively reject the personhood of their child. Instead, as we saw in the last chapter, it is often the doctor who is seen as diminishing the personhood of the child over and against the mother.

If discrimination against disabled people is widespread in both cultures, what might account for the difference between Israeli and American mothers' early responses to their disabled children? Is it the case that contemporary American mothers are simply, in Hrdy's terms, more "heroic" than women in Israel or other cultures? For the American women in my study, there is a readily available discourse that competes with the concept of disability as permanent impairment. This discourse enables mothers to simultaneously hold negative views of disability and acknowledge the full personhood of their disabled child. It takes form in the heroic disability success story we all know, the football player paralyzed in an accident who nevertheless defies doctors' predictions and walks again, the child hero who against all odds beats cancer and becomes an Olympic athlete, and so on. It is the story line that accounts for the broad public appeal of Christopher Reeve, an actor paralyzed in a horseback riding accident in 1995, who proclaimed that given enough research dollars spent on spinal cord injuries, he would walk again or stand and toast his doctors and friends on the occasion of his birthday (Reeve died in 2004, never having achieved this goal). It is the American story of upward mobility and linear progress, of the underdog who overcomes all odds through self-determination and force of will, and it is the plot within which many American women first experience mothering a young child with, or at risk for, disabilities.

Layne (1996) discusses the inappropriateness of culturally pervasive narratives of progress for parents trying to make sense of their children's health status in the neonatal intensive care unit (NICU). Like parents of the NICU "problem cases" to which Layne refers, mothers of disabled children also face the failure of their children to follow the ideal and normal trajectory, in this case, to attain particular developmental milestones at the expected times. Interview data suggest that many such parents shift their focus from an *absolute* timetable (used in the medical profession to determine disability or "delay") to the marking of a child's relative progress along a linear developmental scale. The very fact of forward movement in some domain itself stands as evidence for such parents of the inability of physicians to set developmental endpoints for children; it leaves open the possibility that disability is but a temporary condition which, with therapy, science, a child's intense motivation, and a mother's hard work, can be surpassed.

Doctors' Knowledge–Mothers' Knowledge

Mothers' narratives are replete with "the doctor was wrong" stories; many of these stories take the form of the child overcoming the gloomy predictions made by neonatologists, neurologists, or developmental specialists. Such stories become lessons of hope from which to draw strength when facing more bad news or, as in the following case, with which to teach other mothers of children newly diagnosed with disability.

And I told Suzanne, I said "No, you can tell them the same thing I tell them." I said "I will accept that they probably won't go to Harvard and they probably won't go to the Olympics," I said, "but those are the only two things I'm willing to write off my list." I said, "As far as I'm concerned, everything else is still possible." And they (children) keep proving me right.

(Patricia Marks)

It was common for mothers in the study to challenge the doctors' assessments of their children. Sometimes, as we shall see, this takes the form of a complaint against a particular doctor's style or level of knowledge, but more often it expresses a recognition that doctors simply *can't* know some things and shouldn't pretend to be able to predict a child's limits or abilities. As Terry Johnson, a married, college-educated white woman whose child was diagnosed first with Hirschsprung Disease and later with Cri du Chat syndrome, explains,

One of the things that I think I learned from the whole experience with the medical part of it is that you know, the doctor's word is not God, God's word. Whereas I think I wanted to do everything the pediatrician was telling me to do, like for those first few months, when deep down I kinda felt that really there was something more than what he was telling me. And I vowed, ever since she was diagnosed, that that's it. I mean just because a professional is saying this is what the case is, that doesn't necessarily mean that I have to go with that. So I think even if the developmentalist said to us that she's going to end up in an, you know, whatever, it wouldn't, I don't think anybody could tell at this point. And we would always strive to push her into making the most of herself and making progress and stuff like that…

Explaining why she doesn't want to hear a prognosis from a doctor about her son, who was born prematurely, Suzanne Dalton similarly states "what I realize is that, and I just feel really hopeful about him in that he's getting a lot of services and there's just so much that we don't know about the brain, you know, that I just don't really believe that anyone could tell me definitely anyway." Katie Allen is a 19-year-old white high-school dropout and single mother of a premature baby with brain damage. She *does* want to hear doctors' predictions; however, she makes a distinction between what doctors can actually know (very little) and what they think.

> They don't know. They say they can probably guess, but they don't want to say nothing. Sometimes people want to know what they think. They don't always just want to know what they know, they want to know what they think, too. People like opinions from more people that have seen other babies like that.

Brenda Wilson, a college-educated full-time homemaker, reflects,

> I was trying to find a doctor out there that could give me all the answers, but I just discovered that there isn't; no doctor out there could give me information.... I can't look at her neurologist and say, can you tell me when she's going to have another seizure?... They don't know. I don't know either.

Referring to physicians, Patricia Marks, a white, married adoptive mother of premature twin girls complains,

> I know that they don't know. And not only do they not know, but *nobody* knows. And at 19 months old, there is so much that you can't tell and that you don't know, that we get to complaint number two, don't speculate. If you don't know, *say* you don't know.

Sharon Miller, an African-American single mother raising a son with DeMorsier syndrome, makes a similar argument:

> I don't believe that they can make any type of expectations on it. I don't—I don't think they can. One, because... they're not talking to Robert's teachers. They're not talking to his speech, his OT [occupational therapist], his PT [physical therapist]. So, I don't think they can make any predictions on—outside of the physical, on what he can do, as far as his behavior, I don't think they can make that, and if they did tell, I wouldn't believe it, because they don't—they're not there.... I don't think I would believe anything that a doctor says, I don't. I almost—I argued with Dr. Williams about the mental retardation. I was like, is Robert mentally retarded in the sense that there's been brain damage, or is he mentally retarded because he doesn't know how to apply his knowledge, because

his schema is because he's blind and deaf, because of his disability?... I'm not trying to challenge his authority or anything.

Laura Robertson, whose daughter has a seizure disorder and developmental delays, compares a mother's nurturance-based knowledge with a physician's limited range of experience with any one particular child, and complains

> But then again, you're the parent. They don't always take your word for what it is... I said, you know, like she reaches for her little guys on the play gym. They're like, well, *we* don't see her reaching. So I went and took a picture of her doing it. She would do it. We videoed her having a seizure because nobody believed us that she was having seizures. Videoed it, and then brought it to the doctor and brought it to the neurologist... I think doctors need to realize that you know your baby, and you know, yeah, I'm a first-time mom, but when I say my baby's sick, she's sick. And when I say that she can do something, I'm not trying to say that they're wrong, I'm just trying to get what's best for her.

Lisa Hart described a similar process. She knew "just by listening to her" that her daughter aspirated while crying and did not aspirate when she was calm. Doctors, however, disagreed with her assessment. "And the doctors were like, 'no.' I'm like, well, 'yes.'" In the end of the story Lisa tells, an endoscopic test was performed, indicating that in fact the child did aspirate only when crying. Cheryl Benedetto is a young single mother whose infant son, born with a diaphragmatic hernia, had a cranial bleed resulting in severe impairments, including mental retardation and spasticity. Talking about her experience with doctors in the hospital, Cheryl stated, "like [Dr.] Keller, I had to tell him phenobarb needed to be—it's like you're so into his life, it's almost like the parent becomes the nurse, the doctor.... Because you know him. Who knows the baby better than you do?" Brenda Wilson, whose daughter had a stroke, also took an active role in her daughter's medical treatment, deciding for herself when the child could be weaned off of oxygen. When at a visit to the pulmonary specialist she was told to begin the process of weaning, she responded, "'Well, we already have.' They're like 'WHAT?' I said, 'I tried to get an appointment with you earlier. You wouldn't see me.'

Anyway, she was fine. She didn't have to be on oxygen as long as they said, because we knew our child."

Mothers repeatedly describe coming to recognize and value their own expertise. They attribute this expertise to two factors. First, as the quotes above indicate, these women argue that no one can know a child as well as its mother. During an interview, Sara Anderson reminded me that the day of the evaluation which I had observed, her daughter, diagnosed with microcephaly due to strep B infection, did not follow a red toy and when she dropped her head, she didn't show the reflexes to come back up. "She didn't do that with *them*. She does it with *me*." As Lisa Hart, whose daughter has cerebral palsy, describes her statement to doctors, "I said, 'I totally respect you guys as doctors, and I listen to what you tell me', I said, 'but I'm her parent. I'm with her 24 hours a day. I knew how she'd act.'" In this sense, mothers are laying claim to their own special form of knowledge, challenging biomedicine's position as what Brigitte Jordan (1993 [1978], 1997) calls "authoritative knowledge."[2]

But mothers of disabled infants and toddlers also suggest that mothers, because of their commitment to their child rather than to a stated prognosis or to their own professional ego, have the passion and freedom to gather the *same* biomedical information as physicians do, and in some instances, to come to know more than a particular medical practitioner not only about their child but about their child's disability and treatment options. "I don't think that there's pretty much anything, outside of medication, that he can have me hands down on as far as my son's condition," Sharon Miller claimed in reference to her son's physician. "Everything else, I can probably find a note or a book or something that I read or recall or have to find out, pick my brain for; outside of medication, I don't think there's nothing he can really tell me." For another mother, uncomfortable with a diagnosis of autism at her child's evaluation, the "first stop was the library on the way home"; on the basis of what she learned there, she scheduled an appointment for a second opinion at a hospital in another city. Pam Karcher, a single mother working part-time as a waitress, diagnosed her son's pervasive developmental disorder through information gathered on the internet; only later did she go to the developmental pediatrician for the access the doctor could provide to early intervention services she had already determined her child needed. Ann Meadows tells a similar story of diagnosing her child: "If I want to know something, I always head to the library, and I—within the two months I waited for my appointment with Dr. Jones, I had already figured out what was wrong with him. I knew before he ever said it. I could have told him." Nor was Lisa Hart surprised by the time she eventually received her child's ultimate diagnosis.

> Well, you know it was kind of odd because I had gotten a book on CP (cerebral palsy)… I had gone in the bookstore many times and looked at books and never wanted to really commit to anything like that, and finally, I bought that like probably just about the age when she was one and stuff, and if I had read it six months earlier, I would have diagnosed her with CP and not been waiting around like the doctors. I mean, she just had so many of the things… She was just—you know—everything in the book was her.… So it was just—you know, it wasn't a surprise to us because, you know, we definitely knew. You know, actually hearing it, you don't want your kid labeled with anything, you know, but it really wasn't a surprise to us at all.

Though Michelle White has only a high-school degree, she explains that she and her husband had "learned a lot, a *lot*, and were knowing what to look for in all different things." Observing her four-pound daughter, Michelle believed she was due for another blood transfusion. According to Michelle's story, doctors disagreed with her, but five days later the girl's temperature was so low it did not register on the thermometer, and she was rushed to the emergency room and placed under a heat lamp. At the hospital, the baby's body temperature was brought up to 91 degrees. "She was so anemic from not getting that blood transfusion that I had asked them for, " Michelle points out. This story line, in which a mother's knowledge is first dismissed by physicians, concludes by validating a mother's ability to access and correctly apply biomedical knowledge; it appears in different versions in interviews with women of all classes and educational levels. College-educated Brenda Wilson, for instance, "butted heads" often with a particular doctor during her daughter's hospital stay. Her daughter's condition worsened, she believes, because the physician made medical decisions that she herself had challenged:

> He took her off Lasix, which is a diuretic, and he took her off oxygen, and in the reports I read, it said do not take this child off Lasix or oxygen…

"We're taking care of her, Mrs. Wilson," this is what they would say to me. One doctor said to me, "you're not a nurse." I said, "I am *now*."

Denise Rivers tells a story in which she took her four-month-old daughter to a pediatrician, "well-known, supposedly the best," who simply told her she was "a nervous mom" with a healthy baby. Continuing to be concerned about the child's development at twelve and later at sixteen months, she returned to the pediatrician. After Denise verbally threatened the pediatrician, a brain scan was finally ordered. The scan showed the child had hydrocephalous, a life-threatening condition in which there is fluid buildup in the brain; emergency surgery was required to put in a shunt, and as a result of the hydrocephalous the child has mental retardation and motor impairments. Similarly, Jean Barbarino, a single working class mother, tells of her concerns about her infant son's development being ignored by physicians for a year:

> And I already knew what was wrong with my child (cerebral palsy) before he had told me. And I looked right in his face and I told him at the end of the appointment, "you know, I already knew this. I just need to hear it from you because you're a medical doctor and you can sign the papers saying that was what was wrong with him." He didn't like that very much.

Nancy Papagallo is a high-school graduate and single mother living on welfare. She prides herself on having obtained biomedical information about her child's condition, and uses it to criticize her infant son's physicians. She explained to me that she "went out and got a book on hearts, children's hearts, and it tells in there that they should have noticed the problem before instead of after when he was born. They should have known way before then." The following excerpt took place later in the interview, when a physical therapist had come to work with the baby.

> **Nancy**: Guess what I did? The day before yesterday, when it was nice out, I took a walk to the library. I found a book on child's hearts!
> **Therapist**: Oh, did you? Good. Did the reference person help you?
> **Nancy**: Yes, I and I'm reading it real fast.
> **Therapist** (to me): Nancy wants to try and educate herself on his condition, so that was a step we thought would be good.

Nancy: And like the words in black in there I'm writing down and I'm like looking at the back at the the book where the diary is to find out what they mean…. And that's—I came across it in that book, okay? And what made me really upset about the part that I read is that I wish the doctors looked more clear when I was pregnant… where I said that they could have known before birth, during the time that he was in my stomach, they could have found the problem, and I'm really going to get down to it, starting now. Why didn't they find out there was something wrong with him, and two to three hours later after I had him. Come on!

In their narrative analysis of a Latina woman's decision regarding amniocentesis, Browner, Preloran, and Cox remind us that across groups in United States, an incidence of illness triggers information seeking; "what varies by ethnicity (and by social class)," they argue, "is not that locally acquired lay epidemiological information influences women's decisions about health care for one group but not for others. The variance lies in the sources of that information" (1999). Potential sources of lay epidemiological information for mothers in addition to printed material and Web sites include each woman's personal network of friends, family, neighbors, co-workers, religious advisers, and the like. That most women in this study primarily report seeking information not from these sources but rather from published or internet sources, and later, from other parents and from the therapists treating their child may be owing to the lack of ethnic diversity in the study population. Another likely factor, however, is the isolation of mothers of disabled infants and young children. Most women in this study grew up in an era in which they had little contact with disabled people; they cannot readily find lay experts in the immediate networks within which they lived prior to the birth of their disabled child. Women who in other domains of medical decision making might ordinarily consult with their mothers, siblings, or friends, often describe such people as well-meaning but incapable of understanding in this particular situation; thus they turn instead to the biomedical knowledge available from an array of public sources. Sharon Miller, who had challenged her doctor about his prognosis of mental retardation for her son with DeMorsier syndrome, points out

I just pulled that out of books and off of the Internet, and I think that's where doctors are gonna start getting in trouble, because people are,

I mean, you can go through the Mayo Clinic [Web site], put in your disease, and pull it off. Pull off data pages and reference pages or search engines for that stuff, and they're challenged by it, and they shouldn't be… At least take the information not as a threat; but Dr. Williams is getting much better.

This mother, like others, sees herself as capable of teaching doctors about her child's disability. In drawing on resources on the Internet and in bookstores, newsstands, and public libraries, mothers are not challenging the position of biomedical knowledge itself as authoritative knowledge. Rather they are denying exclusivity in whatever area such knowledge can reside. Indeed, they cite their own facility with biomedicine as authoritative knowledge in justifying their claim to equal power relations with the specific physicians treating and evaluating their children. It is in this sense that Sharon Miller sees hope for her son's doctor; by virtue of his recently appearing to be less threatened by mothers' biomedical knowledge, Dr. Williams is judged to be "getting much better."

But whereas women challenge physicians' knowledge on the basis of mothers' own facility with biomedical sources and of their intimate knowledge of their own child, they may also experience doctors' predictions about their children as inauthentic because such predictions do not fit within the plot of the story through which mothers structure their actions and experience. It is to this plot that I now turn.

Developmental Delay

Mothers who resist the power of individual medical practitioners to define and set limits for their disabled children find institutional support for their linear narratives of hope in the form of the state's early intervention (EI) program. This program provides various services—including physical therapy, speech therapy, occupational therapy, nursing, and special education—to those children newborn to age three meeting specific criteria. It is the position of this system that "early intervention can reduce the number of children with disabilities or reduce the severity of their disabling condition" (Early Intervention Coordinating Council, 1999: 6); the possibility of mitigating or even eliminating disability is thus to some extent implied for participants in the program.

The key term for eligibility for early intervention services, as stated in the federal legislation, is "developmental delay," a term the majority of those interviewed used in describing their children. The lead agency for the early intervention program in New York State is the Department of Health. This agency defines developmental delay as meaning "that a child has not attained developmental milestones expected for the child's age adjusted for prematurity in one or more of the following areas of development: cognitive, physical (including vision and hearing), communication, social-emotional, or adaptive development" (New York State Department of Health, 1998: 4). A developmental delay, for purposes of obtaining early intervention services, must be "a delay measured by qualified professionals using informed clinical opinion, appropriate diagnostic procedures, and/or instruments, and documented as a 12 month delay in one functional area, or a 33% delay in one functional area or a 25% delay in each of two areas" (NYSDOH). Alternatively, if standardized instruments are individually administered in an evaluation, a delay can be documented as a score of at least 2.0 standard deviation below the mean in one functional area or a score of at least 1.5 standard deviation below the mean in each of two functional areas.

The specific assessment tool used at the site at which this research was carried out is the Revised Gesell Developmental Schedules. The schedules measure the attainment of specific developmental milestones at four-week intervals beginning at an adjusted age of four weeks and continuing through 56 weeks; milestones are then measured in three-month intervals from 15 months through 24 months of age, and in six-month intervals thereafter until the child reaches three years of age. According to this scale, for instance, an infant of 24 weeks should approach and grasp a rattle with two hands, while four weeks later the child should approach and grasp a small cube or bell with only one hand; in gross motor development at 24 weeks, the child should be able to sit well leaning on his or her hands, while at 28 weeks he or she should sit erect for about one minute. The developmental pediatrician marks whether a child has attained each developmental milestone and whether the milestone has been reported as attained by the parent or has been directly observed by the pediatrician during the evaluation itself.

The historical basis of developmental assessment of very young children is a *maturation* model, in which arbitrary cut-off points are used to define motor development or language development as delayed (McConachie, 1995: 112). A well-developed set of developmental norms is the legacy of research carried out by Gesell and McGraw in the 1940s (Kamm, Thein, and Jensen, 1990: 764). Observing regularities in the patterns and sequence of movements attained by infants, they concluded that the regularities "reflected regularities in brain maturation, a genetically driven process common to all infants;" this "maturational explanation was accepted as gospel and is still believed widely today" (Thelen, 1995: 79). A large literature now suggests that children proceed through "motor stages in an orderly fashion; attainment of these functions is clear-cut and dramatic" (First and Palfrey, 1994: 480). Rolling front to back precedes rolling back to front, for instance; both are followed by, in sequential order, sitting independently, creeping on tummy, and crawling on hands and knees.

A maturation model suggests that these transformations of early life follow a preset program; but as Konner explains, this neglects "the environment's shaping role, which, in the nervous system at least, includes learning. So development.... is more than maturation, requiring constant negotiation with the environment" (2002: 279). And though motor development may consist of relatively orderly stages, there may be less consistency in how children proceed through other domains of development, calling into question the appropriateness of a maturation model in these areas. In particular, McConachie faults the model for its treatment of intelligence as quantifiable and fixed and for its presumption that development should be linear and predictable through childhood. "However, the reality is very different; research with young children who have impairments indicates that the course of early development is discontinuous" (McConachie, 1995: 112). Measurement is inherently inexact, McConachie argues, because the tests are designed "as if sensory and physical impairments can be separated out from more cognitively loaded skills" (McConachie, 1995: 113). She argues instead that impairment in one area can have consequences in other areas, as in the case of a child who cannot reach out to touch something dangerous, is consequently not exposed to responses such as "No, that's hot!" and thus has reduced *opportunities*, rather than reduced *ability*, to learn language.

Children in the United States are nevertheless routinely measured against a standard linear scale of development. As children at the Newborn Followup Program are tested in the various domains, they are rated along this linear scale, such that a baby whose chronological age is nine months may be determined to have the cognitive development of a four-month-old and the gross motor development of a six-month-old. The evaluator calculates the percentage of delay in each domain by comparing the child's developmental age in that domain against the standard scale. Thus regardless of any rhetoric about "differences" among children, the necessarily quantitative measures present disabled children as different only in terms of their lower placement on a linear model of development; the linear model itself remains in place, with disabled children defined as behind or delayed.

While analysis of cross-cultural views of child development are beyond the scope of this book, it is important to point out here that there is indeed variation in how development is understood to proceed. The Beng of the Ivory Coast, for instance, assume that the newborn, a reincarnation of a previous full life, emerges not from a restricted uterine environment from which it *begins* its process of development but from a rich existence in a place called *wrugbe;* what English speakers would term the afterlife for the Beng is more appropriately considered beforelife (Gottlieb, 1998: 123). Beng babies may be tempted to return to wrugbe, and parents are thus cautioned to make life comfortable and attractive for the child; a diviner's instructions to parents to buy jewelry for a crying baby, for instance, "may serve to remind parents that the infant, while seemingly helpless and unable to communicate, was recently living a full life elsewhere and thus needs to be respected as a fellow person rather than being viewed as a suffering, wordless creature" (126). Beng infants, owing to their previous existence in wrugbe, are considered to be multilingual, capable of understanding not only Beng but *all* languages. "In sum, Beng infants are doing the opposite of learning new languages subsequent to a prelinguistic phase, as a popular Western folk model posits. Instead, they are *losing* old languages..." (128). The point of this digression is that the Western model of an orderly, cumulative acquisition of developmentally appropriate skills from a starting point near zero is, like the Beng model, also culturally specific; the model in turn has effects both on child rearing practices and on the experiences of mothers whose children fail to conform to the expected trajectory of development.

A child newborn to three years old in New York State is currently eligible for early intervention services if the child has a diagnosed disability (such as cerebral palsy, spina bifida, or Down syndrome) or if the child is determined to have sufficient developmental delay as outlined above. Developmental pediatricians are among those designated to determine eligibility for the early intervention program but have mixed feelings regarding the term *developmental delay*. When asked to define the term, one doctor at the Newborn Followup Program responded, "It means your child is mentally retarded but I don't have the courage to tell you." Abrams and Goodman (1998) similarly consider the term developmental delay a euphemism used for purposes of softening and masking the truth. They point out that the term *mental retardation*, which now seems harsh, was itself once a euphemism designed to suggest slowed-down mental processes rather than imperfect or insufficient ones. With time and familiarity, they suggest, the "masking" power of the term *mental retardation* eroded, leading it to be subsumed by the "even more euphemistic term, 'developmental delay' or 'developmental disability'" (88).

Mental retardation in particular is by many definitions incurable. "If we miss a chance at prevention, the consequences are usually devastating and irreversible, and we get no second chance. We can treat, we can ameliorate, and we can rehabilitate, but we cannot cure a person of mental retardation," Alexander points out in a review of the research (1998: 50).[3] The term *developmental delay*, by comparison, presupposes that permanency of the delay has not been established. In the words of a pediatric neurology text, "All mentally retarded individuals exhibit developmental delay. However, not all children with developmental delay remain behind" (Coker, 1989: 1). A developmental pediatrician at the Newborn Followup Program explained the term *retardation* to parents during an evaluation: "It would indicate that there would be some significant future difficulty down the road with these areas of learning. And that you hit the wall sooner than another kid." Note that the metaphor "hitting the wall" removes the child from the progression along the line of developmental milestones, a progression that the term *developmental delay*, conversely, suggests is merely followed at a slower pace.

When asked to explain the term's meaning in the non-cognitive domains to which it is also applied, the same physician at the Newborn Followup Program commented that it is equivalent to saying "You're short." That is, it tells you that you are currently short relative to other people but not whether you will eventually catch up to the norm or remain short all your life. For some physicians, this lack of specificity is problematic. For mothers, however, especially those who have just heard their child diagnosed with delay, the ambiguity inherent in the term may be its very appeal. Both the generic term *disabled* and its more specific manifestations (cerebral palsy, Down syndrome, autism, mental retardation, etc.) carry the implication of permanency. By contrast, developmental delay suggests simply a different *rate* on a linear progression toward normalcy. A train may be delayed, but it will reach the station; so a child with a developmental delay may be slow to walk or to speak but, mothers may believe, will eventually meet up with his or her peers.

Negotiating Emplotment

Individuals use narratives to repair the disruption caused when culturally specific expectations about the course of life are not met (Becker, 1997: 4; see also Ginsburg, 1989). Gay Becker theorizes that people edit their stories in such a way as to make the current condition of disruption consistent with past experience or with dominant cultural ideology, that is, to make meaning and sense out of the changes they are facing. However "repair of disruption" need not be achieved exclusively by establishing consistency with past experience. As we shall see in later chapters, mothers' narratives may instead be stories of profound transformation, of revelation—even celebration—of a break from a former self and a critique of cultural values that had shaped their earlier views of motherhood and personhood. Nevertheless, stories *first* told by mothers encountering a difficult diagnosis, as those discussed in this chapter, do often work to create consistency between current personal experience and the mainstream cultural expectations about the course of life with which most mothers had grown up.

The American narratives Becker analyzes are those told by people whose own lives have been directly disrupted—by illness, stroke, job loss, or infertility, and the like. These narratives tend to share a particular plot or pattern, she argues, because of a common American focus on a linear, orderly unfolding of life, and the emphasis on the individual in relation to society (Becker, 1997: 5). With infertility, for instance, the attainment of biological parenthood as a culturally expected stage of life is unreachable; the "normal" course of life has been disrupted. What constitutes the disruption in the life course of mothers of children identified with disabilities seems at first too obvious to ask. And yet its apparent obviousness rests on culturally and historically specific beliefs about motherhood, personhood, and disability. Why should the birth of a child with an impairment inevitably make unreachable a woman's attainment of the culturally expected stage of motherhood? If the status of mother of a child with an impairment represents a disruption that initially calls for repair, it is because "real" motherhood in American culture is contingent upon the birth, not of a child but of a "normal" child.

As discussed in earlier chapters, "real" motherhood is threatened or diminished in large part because the potential for full personhood of a child born to such a woman is in question.[4] More specifically, the child's current or projected failure to attain developmental milestones makes its full personhood ambiguous. Thus, as mothers of newly diagnosed disabled children tell stories to recreate order in their own lives (i.e., as they reconstruct their "real" motherhood), the stories they tell are about their *children*, whose lives they attempt to emplot in culturally specific ways. Recall Weiss's analysis of Israeli representation of disabled children. Using metaphors of monsters and animals, Israeli mothers' narratives deny the personhood of a disabled child, enabling abandonment and/or territorial isolation; by employing the concept of developmental delay, however, American mothers' narratives instead *assert* personhood, or at the very least, the potential for its future attainment, and thereby encourage ongoing nurturance.

To have meaning for its teller or hearer, scholars of narrative point out, a story must have a plot. Plot is an organizing feature of narrative, forging "meaningful totalities out of scattered events" (Ricoeur, 1981: 278). The different parts that comprise a narrative—its protagonists and events— "are selected and shaped in terms of a putative story or plot that then 'contains' them" (Bruner, 1991: 8). These parts are themselves constituted in interaction with the whole; each event or character has relevance only as it contributes to the story. Through plot, then, events are made to unfold in a temporal sequence, but the meaning of a story ultimately can only be determined by its ending (Good, et al., 1994: 855).

How will the story turn out? What meaning will the present have from the perspective of the ending? These questions structure the process of emplotment when people are still living within unfinished stories. Our "chief tool in making sense of narrative, the master trope of its strange logic," is this very "anticipation of retrospection" (Brooks, quoted in Good, et al., 1994: 855). While not the case for all women in the study, most mothers of young children newly diagnosed with or at risk for disability order or emplot the scattered events of their children's lives in anticipation of a specific and culturally acceptable ending—that of overcoming (or at the very least, reducing) disability. Each separate incident—a physician's grim prediction, a friend's well-meaning but hurtful comment that a woman is wasting her life in devotion to her disabled child, an article found on the Internet, an exchange on a listserv, or a half-hour session with a physical therapist—becomes an obstacle to overcome or an opportunity to seize along an epic journey toward this hoped-for conclusion (Landsman, 2003).

One mother takes photographs of particularly painful moments in the NICU for the purpose of being able to later proudly show her prematurely born child the difficulties he courageously overcame; during an early intervention session, another vows she will return in five years with her daughter's first report card to shove in the face of the medical resident who had once pronounced her child mentally retarded; yet another places a basketball in her preemie son's crib, anticipating that even though five of his tiny, fragile toes had broken off, he will be "the first five-toed basketball player in history." The emplotment process is not just a post hoc editing of the events of experience to create a sense of consistency with the past; the narrative is performative, such that the ongoing events of life are experienced by actors in the form of the story whose desired ending mothers claim to know and which they work to bring to fruition.

Women in this study entered into their personal experience of childhood disability with culturally constructed definitions of personhood and motherhood. In the context of such definitions, narratives of developmental delay, implying the potential for developmental progress, enable hope. As Cheryl Mattingly argues, "Life is not experienced as one thing after another because actors work to create a story-like quality to their actions. Being an actor at all means trying to make certain things happen, to bring about desirable endings, to search possibilities that lead in hopeful directions" (1998: 47). Developmental examinations, at which time diagnoses are often determined and prognoses discussed, provide particularly relevant moments for parents and doctors to search and/or challenge these possibilities; they can and often do become sites at which competing plot lines for the child are put forward and sometimes negotiated (Landsman, 2003: 1952). This negotiation process will be analyzed through a particular situation described below. In the following extensive excerpt, Brenda Wilson discusses with the developmental pediatrician the diagnosis for her daughter, Lisa. Lisa had become seriously ill with a respiratory infection at five months of age and was transferred to a hospital across the state in Buffalo, where she had been placed on a machine to undergo extra-corporeal membrane oxygenation (ECMO). Lisa suffered a stroke, a major but common complication of the ECMO procedure. Eleven months later at a developmental exam, the meaning of the consequences of that stroke—the potential endings to Lisa's story—are negotiated between doctor and mother (BW).

Doctor: Okay. Do you have some particular things that you'd like to talk about or questions you want—

BW: Well, first of all, you know, I think it's important to stress that we've accepted Lisa for how she is and we're determined to make her the best little girl that she can be. Of course, my concern as a parent is what the future holds for her, but I mean that's even with my four-year old too. What I've seen in the past eight months has been incredible, so I'd like to say Lisa is going to develop at a slower rate than other children. If she'll ever catch up, I don't know. But with the services we are getting, I've seen an improvement, of course, and I'd like to continue, of course with that. But I like to see different doctors and get their ideas, you know. That's why we went to Boston to, you know, we went in there and they said "we've seen this, we've seen this." This is common to their, you know, out there.

Doctor: To their practice.

BW: Yeah...

Doctor: So, from the physical standpoint, I feel really positive about how she's doing. Really, very positive. The other thing that I would comment on today, is that, well, first having seen her from hospitalization, onward, I have a perspective that's been very helpful to me. And I would fully agree with you, when I consider where she was, even after the hospitalization the first time you came here, where there was really very little awareness of her outside environment, vision that was questionable, she's obviously made some very important strides forward, extremely important strides forward... So, let me put it in a bigger picture. The first thing that happens is, or what had not been happening, is you get visual information, and for her it was almost like on a blank screen, it wasn't registering. Now the visual information is coming in and it's registering, not 100%, but it is registering. The next stage has to be to take the register of that information and apply it to your previous experience, to your memory. But it means something about something that happened before or that could happen is going to give me a tool that I hadn't had before. That's the next jump that has to happen for her. Okay, now she made the jump to vision, now she has to put the vision together with learning thought processes. Okay, that's another big jump. That's a *huge* jump. So if you look at her current status she has made, you can't give a number to the progression because it went from almost zero to something more concrete in terms of where she was with her learning. So its been maybe a thousand times better, but that thousand times better has to come up by another thousand to really make the impact in terms of learning that has to occur. So she's at another critical stage, and by critical stage I mean the next year or two. Okay. And the critical stage has to do with what I call integration of information. So now she has some open channels, now she has to put those channels together and make sense out of them. If that happens, if she gets into that issue and begins to understand how things relate to one another, visually, touch, hearing, she's going to continue strong progress in learning. If they stay separate channels—and that is a distinct risk—mental retardation is clearly going to be present.

BW: I don't agree with that, though.

Doctor: I said "if."

BW: Okay, but I think to bring mental retardation into it at this point, is kind of premature, don't you? I mean, from just speaking to neurologists in Boston and everything…

Doctor: I'm a different way of thinking because I'm giving the best case and worst case here, all right?

BW: Okay.

Doctor: That's how I look at my job, kind of put this in that perspective. Okay. You say what is mental retardation? Mental retardation is that difficulty with taking information, making sense of it and applying it your life. Okay. And what I was just saying about taking that vision information, making sense out if it, and applying it to learning, if she doesn't make that jump, you're going to be in a situation where learning is not going to occur the way you want it to.

BW: A delay.

Doctor: Not delayed. I'm talking about if that jump doesn't occur, it will be delayed but there will be a permanent effect and that's mental retardation.

BW: All right, so effectively she would plateau and go no farther?

Doctor: She would plateau in areas that are critical to what we're going to call functional capabilities, okay?

BW: Okay—

Doctor: How do you take care of yourself, how do you communicate, how do you manage in your environment? Now that's the core issue of mental retardation. You don't have the understanding to make it through life, even with the physical disabilities. If you ask the question is she retarded today, the answer is that she's in the process of development and some clinicians would say she has strong signs of mental retardation…. Okay. She hasn't had experience with vision for a couple years almost. Now she's got to take that and somehow use it. If it occurs, she's going to be in really good shape. But if it doesn't occur, you're going to recognize learning is progressing but nowhere near the rate it needs to. What happens generally at two to three years of age are tremendous accomplishments, at two and three years of age. So while she might make progress, the other two and three year olds made a huge jump forward. So you're going to see a gap.

BW: We already see a gap.

Doctor: But what I'm saying is that a gap could actually increase even though she's making progress, the other kids could be way ahead. I'm pointing out worry markers along the way here. That's what I have to do, that's my job.

BW: I know that, I know that, I know that. But from what I understand, I mean, I have a question—if someone, an adult, has a stroke, are they labeled mentally retarded?

Doctor: No, mental retardation has to be in the developmental period. So it has to be during childhood.... Now that's the worst case. Let's get away from that worst-case issue. Okay. Again, if she was still at the point of saying vision hadn't improved, we'd all be saying, "Gee, what's her future?" The question I think that is a legitimate one is, as she's getting closer to two, as her health is stable, is she at the physical standpoint of say, more intensive service in terms of being in a classroom situation for four hours a day? Would that be to her developmental benefit?... I mean you have the whole array of services so I don't offhand have another one to add to that, and I think the idea of stabilizing her ankles in such a way that she has more support down below is going to help with her stance. [Turning to physical therapist] Are there some issues from your standpoint that you wanted to talk about?

Physician/parent communication is often represented in terms of the physician "giving" and the parent "receiving" bad news; this interaction, however, exemplifies how diagnoses and prognoses may instead be negotiated among actors. The mother opens the conversation by positioning the physician as only one of the sources from whom she may legitimately seek and accept information; pointing out that there are specialists in Boston with greater experience in these matters, she indicates that she is prepared to discredit the doctor's evaluation, though not biomedicine itself, if need be. Most significantly, she actively frames the entire evaluation and discussion in terms of her daughter's "incredible" improvement since the last visit. The doctor initiates his commentary by acknowledging the girl's progress, thereby validating the mother's observations and establishing common ground. However, the ensuing negotiation is in large part over the role that progress plays within a larger story. Within which plot should Lisa's "progress" be embodied?

The girl's present developmental status in itself can be meaningful to neither participant in this exchange; it makes sense only when viewed from a position of "anticipation of retrospection." Using the narrative strategy of foreshadowing, the different actors therefore cast events in terms of a future trajectory (Ochs and Capps, 2001: 5) each presumes to know. For the mother, Lisa's progress in regaining vision is incorporated as an event in a temporal sequence leading toward the hoped-for ending; the child is temporarily delayed in reaching developmental milestones relative to her peers, yet is proceeding along a linear trajectory appropriate to, and characteristic of, recovery after a stroke. Lisa's current medical status attains meaning because in the plot of the story her mother tells, the developmental distance the girl has traversed in the past, is made to portend the future. However, for the doctor the progress made is inadequate to qualify as "delay"; he interprets its significance to the story not through a comparison of the girl's current status with where she has come from but rather with where she needs to go, a transition he describes as "a huge jump." In this story, Lisa's current condition is a "worry marker" embedded within the plot of permanent disability. Delay versus disability: Mother and physician have emplotted Lisa's life differently, and the otherwise "scattered events"—such as the return of her vision, and a newfound awareness of her outside environment—are organized into different totalities accordingly (Landsman, 2003: 1954).

At the time of her developmental examination, Lisa herself is still in the midst of the stories being told about her; with her future yet to be realized, a conclusion cannot be known. Having introduced their competing plot lines, mother and doctor can therefore negotiate the prognosis. The physician proposes the likely possibility of mental retardation. The mother rejects this label as premature; she cites authoritative sources ("neurologists from Boston") and counters with the discourse of developmental delay. In response, the physician backs off slightly, reminding her that this is only one possible story ("I said 'if'") and represents a worst-case scenario: if a significant developmental jump does not occur, not only will Lisa be delayed "but there will be a permanent effect and that's mental retardation." Like Brenda, he too cites authoritative support for his emplotment of events ("some clinicians would say she has strong signs of mental retardation"); labeling the projected increasing gap between Lisa and her normal peers, he dismisses the significance the mother has assigned to Lisa's progress. Once again, Brenda interprets the predicted future gap in terms of the existing gap;

that is, in terms of developmental delay rather than permanent mental retardation. Incorporating her daughter's experiences within a known and valued American story of struggle, hard work, and progress, Lisa creates consistency between her personal experience and mainstream cultural expectations about the normal course of life.

At the end of this excerpt, the physician attempts to resolve the discrepancy between the two stories by directing the conversation away from projected endings and toward concrete actions upon which all can agree. He puts forth questions about more immediate strategies—would more intensive services be helpful? Should her ankles be braced? With the latter question, the doctor abandons the mental retardation-delay debate altogether and turns from the mother to the physical therapist.

After conversation with the physical therapist, the doctor turns again to Brenda, asking if she has other issues she would like to talk about; she replies curtly, "no." The physician again retreats from his stance on mental retardation, for the moment accommodating his story to hers. "I want to emphasize the extremely strong progress she's made, from where she started to where she is now. And more encouraging, the visual changes that have occurred recently...." This time the mother responds more expansively, educating him on the value of hope.

> **BW**: Right, right, yeah. That kept us going because when they labeled her legally blind, they had felt it was a cortical impairment and they gave us that hope that cortical impairment, you can regain your sight and that's what kept us hoping. As to why that happened, we don't know why, at this point we don't know if it had something to do with the spasms. She's been having spasms all along.
>
> **Doctor**: It may have something to do with that.
>
> **Physical therapist**: Are there any suggestions that you have?
>
> **Doctor**: I think you covered it extremely well. Like I said, I know I have been impressed with Mrs. Wilson from the beginning in terms of her desire and capabilities in understanding her daughter's needs to follow through. I would say you have a model program, from the administrative side of things it sounds fine. I'm sure you have a group of therapists that are excellent. And [turning to Brenda] your strong attitude about "we're going to find the best for her" is really what works.

In the interaction above, the doctor publicly acknowledges the mother's competence and commitment; her persistent efforts to get the best for her daughter have been effective. In response, Brenda offers her reflections on the disparity between how she and the doctor have emplotted the events surrounding the girl's stroke:

> **BW**: I guess that's why I'm so like, I didn't mean to jump on you about the mental retardation, but how I get through this is, I have a child with a stroke and that's you know, until someone can actually say to me, your daughter's mentally retarded, I can't even hear that word right yet. I know in the back of my mind it's there, but I just take it one day at a time and I try not to focus on that, 'cause I know if you do focus on that, then she's not going to get where she is today.

From the mother's perspective, a plot in which the likely conclusion of the story is permanent disability leads to resignation rather than to constructive action. Were Brenda to have believed the physician's ending, she suggests, she would not have worked to bring about the dramatic progress that has been achieved. Her lived experience of mothering and her choice of actions take form within the story of progress she tells. Developmental delay is not just a euphemism or a mechanism of denial for purposes of her own psychological comfort but is conceptualized as taking action on behalf of her child. To the extent that she can engage others in the story, she mobilizes their experience, expertise, and energy toward the hoped-for goal as well.

The very permanence of disability, the reaching of a plateau or what is sometimes called "hitting the wall," dislodges a child from the course of linear development which in American culture marks the full personhood of "normal" children. The story one tells about a child is therefore performative; it can create or withdraw the potential for full personhood. However, narratives at this site are performative in yet another way; within the context of state early intervention programs, the plot negotiated by mother and evaluator sets in motion the treatment plan for a child and family. Early intervention is both a financial investment for counties and a privacy-invading investment of time and energy for parents. For a story to result in early intervention services, there must, from the point of view of the early intervention system, be a significant enough "delay" or gap between the child's performance and that of its "normal" peers to warrant expenditure of public funds. However, as Brenda's statement above implies, for a mother to commit to early intervention, the story must also entail sufficient hope that the gap can be reduced or eliminated through a mother's hard work and a child's program of therapy.

In the case above, Lisa's well-being is a goal to which both doctor and mother are committed, albeit in different ways. Unable to reconcile their competing plot lines, they instead negotiate a story whose ending is tentative and open-ended. Brenda's final statements to the doctor assert her daughter's value. She offers her daughter as a reference for others going through the trying experience of ECMO. "So I hope it doesn't happen to anybody," she tells the physician, "but if it does, I'd like to use Lisa as a reference, because she's incredible, an incredible kid."

"Hopes are Like Elastic": On Narratives of Uncertainty

Lisa is here described as "incredible" because she persevered and overcame tremendous obstacles. She survived a devastating illness and its high-risk treatment; she regained her sight after a damaging stroke; and within the next year, to the delight of her family and physical therapist, Lisa learned to walk unassisted, a much-anticipated accomplishment celebrated with a party and numerous photographs. Like the developmental milestones reached by other children for whom doctors had made dismal predictions, these events lend themselves to emplotment within a story of progress. Hope "is inextricably linked to notions of progress, which are embedded in U.S. values of activity, achievement, and a focus on the future" (Becker, 2000: 179).

Stories in which a child does not conform to the normative rate of reaching developmental milestones in specific domains but nevertheless progresses toward them are common in narratives of mothers across all ages, educational levels, and marital status. By leaving a prognosis undetermined, the stories allow hope for a future without disability (Landsman, 2003: 1956). This fact, and not just women's intimidation by medical professionals, may discourage some women from pursuing definitive medical prognoses. When Amy Garrison was told that her premature baby suffered periventricular leukomalacia, she chose not to ask what could happen as a consequence because she'd "rather just take things one step at a time; I don't want to think he's going to be different." Maria Peters, who dropped out of college in order to care for her baby who is blind and has cerebral palsy, bitterly recounts a doctor's frightening prognosis at the time of birth. "He was like pessimistic about the whole situation, and I was like, 'Thanks a lot.' I felt, I was really mad." Maria believes that if the doctor had to give a dismal prognosis it should have been told to her husband rather than to her, for "Jeff wouldn't have run back and say that to me. He's like 'you know, this stuff might not happen. He [the baby] might not be able to get through this, but we're going to pray and hope,' instead of what he (the doctor) said to me." Becky Romano acknowledged that when the doctor writes an evaluation for her child "they got to make it sound bad so that, you know, you can get the services," but, she complains "this guy [the doctor] doesn't give him a break. I mean, can't he just say this kid's come a great distance? He can't do it. Can't do it." Mothers here resist the medical use of absolute scales, favoring relative progress as a predictor of their child's future.

Talking about one of her premature twins who is labeled by physicians as at risk for disability, 33-year-old Suzanne Dalton states

> I'm not dumb. I know there's probably going to be some effect, but I'm also not going to treat him like he's disabled yet, because they're doing better than they would have expected him to do so far... I continue to believe that the right attention and all the loving attention and all the special services that we can take advantage of that he will be fine.

By utilizing a concept of developmental delay, mothers can, for a time at least, continue to hold received negative stereotypes of disabled people simultaneously with belief in the full personhood of their own disabled child; their child's full personhood will eventually be achieved through "loving attention" and "special services." The fact of her son's progress, especially beyond doctors' stated expectations, permits Suzanne to not treat her son "like he's disabled yet," just as Lisa's progress is pointed to by her mother to justify a story of delay rather than mental retardation. What "being disabled" means in American culture can remain intact in general, but irrelevant for a particular child.

While such mothers are often assumed to be "in denial" in the sense of being unable to accept reality, it is the case that early screening for disability (physical or cognitive), though of great value generally, is not always predictive for any individual child. Nelson and Ellenberg cite a number of studies documenting that "motor abnormalities detected in early childhood may subsequently lessen in degree, change in kind, or disappear altogether" (1982: 539); their own study indicated that of 229 children diagnosed with cerebral palsy at one year of age, 118 were free of motor impairments when they were retested at the age of seven. Such children are referred to by Nelson and Ellenberg as children who "outgrew" cerebral palsy, though for some such children problems in other domains (i.e., lower IQ) later became apparent (see also Ross, Lipper, and Auld, 1985). Though some findings on ultrasound can be good predictors of cerebral palsy while an infant is in the NICU, it cannot tell the magnitude of diffuse damage, and ultrasoundography for extremely preterm infants "leaves much to be desired. Some children considered to be at high risk for developmental dysfunction do much better than expected, and some considered to be likely to do well do not" (Damman and Leviton, 2006: 728). As the latter point out, determining a prognosis for a premature infant poses problems because many recognized clinical predictors are not useful in practice and because a child's future is influenced by numerous factors, many of which occur after an infant leaves the hospital (2006: 727).

In a study examining the sensitivity and specificity of two motor assessment tools, Harris (1987) found a high rate of "false positives" for cerebral palsy for the Movement Assessment of Infants (MAI) tool when administered to low-birth-weight babies who returned from the NICU for follow-up; Bierman-van Eendenburg, et al. (1981) also found a high rate of false positives using the Prechtl neonatal neurological examination. They account for these findings by the fact that

> dysfunction of the nervous system at birth is not necessarily permanent....
> Recovery will depend on the type, localisation and extent of the insult.
> Moreover, the nervous system is a very sensitive organ system which may
> react to temporary stresses in a reversible way...
>
> (1981: 300)

"Although infants with neurologic handicap at follow-up are mainly those who had earlier abnormalities," Dubowitz, et al. similarly state, "many infants with abnormal neurological signs in the newborn period do turn out to be normal" (Dubowitz, et al., 1984). A "wide range of neurologic abnormalities may be transient in some children during the first year of life," particularly in the case of premature infants who may have had "multiple insults during the neonatal period but do not sustain permanent brain injury" (Morgan and Aldag, 1996: 692). As Harris points out simply, "Often a diagnosis of CP at one year and even two years of age is unreliable" (1987: 12).

Early identification of cognitive impairment may be equally difficult. A study conducted in Australia indicated that while an "assessment done at two years of age was valuable in the identification of most of the severely disabled children," it was also the case that "developmental delay at two years of age did not always portend intellectual impairment at eight years of age" (Victorian Infant Collaborative Study Group, 1991: 761).

In other examples, a study of a commonly used screening test, the Denver II, indicated a high over-referral rate; in a sample of 104 children of three months to 72 months of age, "almost half the children without developmental problems also received suspect scores" (Glascoe, et al., 1992: 1224). The predictive value of a subnormal score on the commonly used Bayley Scales of Infant Development II Mental Development Index for later, school age cognitive function has also been shown to be poor (Hack, et al., 2005). And in a review of current assessment practices, McConachie points out that "generally assessments before the age of two years have little predictive validity for later intelligence assessments" (1995: 112). For extremely premature children, a variety of studies have illustrated the impreciseness of early cognitive development scores in predicting later outcomes (Watts and Saigal, 2006: 223). Environment has a moderating influence on learning disorders (Aylward, 2002: 238), and improvements in scores are particularly associated with two-parent households and higher maternal education (Watts and Saigal, 223).

None of the mothers I interviewed had read these studies; their own anecdotes in which doctors' expectations of death or predictions of a particular impairment did not come to pass are emplotted within the larger story wherein they serve as evidence that the child may yet again surpass gloomy predictions and escape the label of disability. For American mothers of children at risk for disability, "progress" in some domain of development serves as a marker of provisional normalcy in a story of developmental delay rather than of disability.

Suzanne's earlier quote, however, raises a number of related and paradoxical issues for physicians, not the least of which is: Do parents really want to be given a definitive prognosis? How much do they want to be told? In evaluations I observed, parents did commonly ask the physician to predict a child's future level of impairment in some area of development. Yet in private interviews, mothers expressed a much different perspective. Single mom Cheryl Benedetto, for instance, claims "I wouldn't want anybody to tell me 'this is what's going to happen to him' because I don't want to hear the bad news now, and then to be depressed about it his whole life and worry about it. I wouldn't want anyone to tell me 'this is what's going to happen to him.'" Speaking about her son, teenage mother Katie Allen figures, "If we do exercises with him everyday why wouldn't he be better? I don't understand why he couldn't change." She acknowledges that "the doctor knows more than me about babies with problems so I can't really say he don't have a problem, because I'm not sure, but... I'm not going to think that he does until something shows me that he does." Katie described it as "unfair" for the doctor to be negative in his predictions. I recall, as my own infant daughter, suffering from hypoxia, lay in a coma day after day in the NICU with an uncertain prognosis, hearing many people say to me in sympathetic tones, "The not knowing must be the hardest part." I numbly and politely nodded my assent, but in truth it wasn't how I felt at all; instead, I imagined myself responding angrily "So, would I rather know for *sure* that she'll die? Would it be easier to be told that she'll *definitely* stay in a coma?" Indeed, I thought, the really hardest thing would not to be told "we don't know," but rather "we do know, and it's awful."

These examples seem to fly in the face of "common sense" that uncertainty is in itself anxiety-producing. Recent research in Germany also suggests a psychological benefit of diagnostic certainty for mothers of disabled children. Lenhard, Breitenbach, Ebert, Schindelhauer-Deutscher, and Henn (2005) compared mothers of children with Down syndrome (a precise genetic diagnosis) with mothers of nondisabled children and with mothers of children with mental retardation of unknown etiology. Down syndrome was taken to represent a disability in which there is certainty of both etiology and prognosis. Data were collected through questionnaires. Mothers were compared for level of anxiety, feelings of guilt, and emotional burden. The researchers found that mothers of children with Down syndrome scored comparably to mothers of nondisabled children but that there were "broad psychoemotional disadvantages for mothers of children with a mental retardation of unknown etiology" (Lenhard, et al., 170). They conclude from this finding that diagnostic uncertainty is a strong independent determinant of emotional burden for parents. Qualitative data collected from mothers in my study suggest an alternate conclusion: The emotional burden may derive not from an uncertain prognosis but from the uncertain *etiology*. The latter, as we have seen, lends itself well to mother-blame and feelings of guilt. Uncertain prognosis, on the other hand, may lend itself to anxiety but also to hope.

In American medical practice, disclosure is considered the norm, and "frankness is valued" (Good, et al., 1994: 858). At the Newborn Followup Program, residents doing their monthly rotation in developmental pediatrics often talked about their painful responsibility to make parents "face reality." Yet when I asked residents what that meant, they repeatedly responded in terms that defined "reality" not as the uncertainty that more accurately characterized their predictive knowledge about an infant in the NICU but in terms of the "worst-case scenario" for which, they believed, a parent must be prepared. Parents bringing their children to the Newborn Followup Program *do* often ask the doctors for their prognoses; doctors attempt to comply as fully as they believe a parent can understand or handle. However, when Denise Rivers was given the opportunity to have her daughter, Paula, who has hydrocephaly, undergo a diagnostic MRI, she refused. The following is an excerpt from a second interview.

> **Denise**: MRIs tell you how much [damage] was done and we haven't
> —we're not ready for that, you know, not yet, you know. We don't want
> to know.
> **Gail**: When you say you're not ready to know, and you don't—
> **Denise**: I mean, can they—they told me that they would get—they could
> get like an MRI, and say this much damage was done. This is where it's
> at.
> **Gail**: You don't really want to know that?
> **Denise**: I don't want to know.

Gail: Why?

Denise: I don't know.

Gail: I'm really interested in that because some people say oh, I just can't stand to not know, and other people say "I really want to keep things open"—

Denise: They give her wide—we take her everyday for—just for her, you know, she's Paula. For us, it's not different. For us, it's not— I don't want to know. Same thing I would never have done it to any of my other kids. I don't want to know, you know. You appreciate life more, I guess, if you like—you just do. It's different.

Gail: Yeah.

Denise: And I don't want to put any boundaries on her either. I mean, we never thought we'd hear her talk, and she's motoring on now, so.

Denise here reiterates the desire described by many mothers to treat their disabled children the same as they would those without disabilities. As Ann Meadows points out "*nobody* knows their future." Terry Johnson, whose second child has Cri du Chat syndrome, was angered that a genetic counselor would attempt to predict a future for her middle child:

> She said, "Well, you're right, Mrs. Johnson, you don't—we don't know where Colleen is going to be and, you know, she's going to go at her own pace, but don't expect her to go to college." And it's like, gee, that was very nice! That's what we really needed to hear right now. I don't know if my *other* kid is going to college. I'm going to worry about Colleen going to college?

Mothers express concern that a label will follow a child to school and limit his or her options owing to society's prejudice. However, what is most interesting here about the narratives is the concern that mothers express about how they *themselves* would set unfair limits on their child's potential if they were to believe a prognosis of disability. Suzanne Dalton makes just this point about her twins, one of whom has been diagnosed with cerebral palsy:

> **Suzanne**: I don't know if I would want to live with the idea that someone told me, no, he'll *never* walk, and he'll be in wheelchair. Everyone adjusts to that, but I think I would rather adjust to it on my time rather than have

them say, this is what we *know*…. So, I really don't—overall, I would say,
"No, I don't want anyone to tell me definitively this is what Matthew's
life is going to be like." Because that way I still have—if they tell me, you
know, it's going to be great, that would be wonderful, but at least if I don't
know that, I can help—I can be part of it with him and be proud of him
and, you know, all that. And if it is worse than what I want, then I'll lose
hope for him and I don't want to lose hope for him because I still believe
that anything is possible, so, you know…. Do you know what I mean,
like you scale down, or change your hopes, so everything—hopes just are
like elastic, you know…. Next year maybe something will be different,
and I'll just have different hopes or different dreams for him, you know.
But, if someone told me definitively, I feel like I would lose all that, you
know. And I don't want to lose that. And I don't want to lose my positive
outlook for him, you know, because I just think that that does a lot for a
baby to have parents who would just expect he's going to be the best that
he can be, you know, rather than someone saying, "Well, this is what he's
going to end up like." You know, I wouldn't even want anyone to tell me
what Louise is going to end up like.

Gail: Yeah.

Suzanne: You know, I don't want to know.

What these mothers suggest, as did Brenda Wilson earlier, is
that if one believes that their child has specific limits, one will stop
encouraging the child to achieve; in turn, the child will step off the
(delayed) track of developmental progression. Thus, mothers suggest,
in some instances the best one can do for one's child is to *not* seek a
prognosis, or to not let oneself believe a doctor's prognosis if it is bad.
Maureen Quinlan, for instance, weighs the consequences of belief in
the doctor's prognosis versus her religious convictions: "I can believe
what I know has happened already in my life, which is that God heals,
or I can choose to believe what they're (physicians) all telling me, you
know, and I can just accept this thing." Asked if she wants people to
tell her more about her daughter's prognosis, Terry Johnson responds.
"No. Honestly, no. Because if I know then it's—I feel like I might not
push as much." Patricia Marks is explicit about how this process works.
She warns doctors not to speculate that a child will have serious and
permanent disabilities, because "if you're wrong and a parent takes you

seriously, then you got a parent who's not going to work with the kid because (they think) they're never going to be able to do it anyway. And I think they're doing more damage to the child in the long run." Becky Romano similarly points out,

> Had I been a parent who really believes in doctors and really thought that was it for Billy, I don't know if I would have gotten him the therapy and the services that he needed.... If I did find out from the beginning "this is how it's going to be," maybe it would have been detrimental because I wouldn't have pushed so much for Billy.

Though "the hardest thing for me to deal with is the what-ifs or the not knowing," Becky decided that "as long as the doctors can't say 100%, there's always hope." Lisa Hart also makes the association of uncertainty with hope, claiming that "It's kind of hard not knowing, but I guess it's kind of good not knowing. Like I have a girlfriend who two weeks before she was born had a baby with Down's syndrome. She is like, 'I wish I at least got the hope that you guys have.'"[5] Even those mothers whose children are classified by other mothers of disabled children as having set, determinable prognoses and/or are saddened by the fact that their children have not progressed steadily along the appropriate trajectory hold to a notion of development over time with no set end-point and continue to seek therapies. Pam Karcher, for instance, gets "little waves of doubt now and then." However, she keeps in mind what someone said to her in a conversation on the internet, that

> it's you know, two steps forward and one step back. I'm like, that's a good way to think of it.... You know, he's talking wonderful. His speech is blossoming. He's starting to communicate. It's a joy to see it everyday. But then he'll do little things like that—like the autistic traits will come back and it's like a little bit of a letdown, but then you've got to like not let that let you down. You say, well, look where he's been. Look where he is now.

As for her expectations for the future, Pam thinks her son is "going to be a perfectly normal oddball just like the rest of the family." At her first interview, Peggy Hoffmeister, mother of a child whose original diagnosis is pervasive developmental disorder, claimed that her son's "just got this little glitch, and it's something that can possibly even be

overcome because we got it so early. Catching it at age two is quite early."
Upon learning that his diagnosis was changed to the more serious one
of "full blown" autism, Peggy commented in her second interview:

> ... and even working at it very conscientiously and thoughtfully over
> the last year, he's still not—he's not talking.... So, well, we're still
> waiting, though, for things to click him on—they say it often takes a
> while, but many of the children will sort of like flip over and all of a
> sudden, language will start to make sense to them and be able to express
> themselves.... I'm just mostly—I'm just kind of sad that it's taking so
> long, but it can take this long. He's still only three and a half, so a lot of
> things can happen...

Normalizing Motherhood: On Denial and Doing What's Best for the Child

On the surface of it, many mothers appear to be simply putting up
with the unavoidable uncertainty inherent in their child's particular
condition. However, those who choose not to put themselves in a
position to hear difficult prognoses and/or those who actively ignore
or reject such prognoses—in other words, those who are commonly
labeled as "in denial"—often do so in the name of *doing what is best for
their children*. Though denial has long been understood by psychologists
and social workers as a strategy mothers use to cope with a stressful
situation,[6] mothers themselves (using different terms) claim this as a
strategy to ensure commitment to, and action on behalf of, their child.
In a culture in which disability diminishes personhood, to deny the
permanence of the disability is also to assert the child's potential for
achieving full personhood. This move justifies the value of the child
not only for society as a whole but for the mother herself. In this way,
"denial" can help ensure a commitment to nurturance, and beyond that,
to advocacy in the child's behalf, including obtaining early intervention
services and refusing to let the child be "written off" by others. The
long-term value of mothers' resistance to doctors' dismal prognoses
may extend into adulthood; in her capacity as manager of an internship
program for disabled college students, Laureen Summers, who herself
is disabled, notes that "the most successful students are the ones whose

families have fought for them, despite the warnings from doctors, counselors, and teachers. These parents knew that their children were smart and could persevere" (Summers, 2004: 120).

It is possible to interpret the interesting findings of Markens, Browner, and Press (1999) regarding women's decisions to refuse prenatal screening in this light as well. They were interested in learning why some women turn down the opportunity to obtain information about the disability status of their fetus. They find that "refusal did not signify rejection of and/or resistance to the offerings of science and technology"; nor were differences between refusers and accepters of prenatal screening linked to different views on abortion (1999: 359). Rather, both refusers and accepters in their study used the biomedical concept of risks to make their decisions. The risk explicitly referred to by refusers of maternal alpha-fetoprotein screening were those of miscarriage posed by the testing procedures. I suggest, however, that it is possible that an additional risk being considered by test refusers who held an anti-abortion stance was that of losing one's resolve; that is, concern that despite theoretically and morally opposing selective abortion, in the face of a definitive prenatal diagnosis of disability, one might end up opting for abortion anyway. Discrimination against disability is so great, and social supports for raising disabled children so few, that in order to stand by an anti-abortion stance, it may be that one almost has to not know or not give oneself the information that would lead to the existence of a choice. (One mother in my study, for instance, reported that upon receiving amniocentesis results indicating Down syndrome, her obstetrician automatically scheduled an abortion for her, and that throughout the pregnancy she had to actively justify her decision to bear the child to friends and relatives as well as to medical personnel).

Bolstered by new reproductive technologies that encourage a conceptual separation of mother and fetus, personhood may be a given at or even before birth for many American parents; nevertheless, a child is also understood as a work in progress whose very development can be affected by both parental and societal actions. In American society, as in Israel and elsewhere, discrimination against disabled people is rampant. Indeed, in interviews, many mothers refer to their own previous prejudices. Therefore, in the process of facing a child's new label of disability, an American mother may simultaneously feel that a permanent impairment diminishes a child's personhood, *and* that the impairment itself can be eliminated or reduced through therapy and a mother's hard work, such that the child's true (nondisabled) self can be revealed. Like pregnant women who refuse prenatal testing, mothers who choose not to request or accept the prognoses of permanent disability are protecting their existing baby from maternal rejection and from the risks that rejection poses to the developing child.

Disability rights activists argue for the coexistence of disability and full personhood, a stance in which "disability is seen as diversity of the human condition and not an undesirable trait to be cured or fixed" (Gilson and DePoy, 2000: 207). As we shall see, many mothers themselves come to adopt the latter position or at the very least to hold it in tension with the desire to have their child progress along society's approved developmental sequence. However, for women just embarking on mothering a disabled child, emplotment of events within a story of developmental delay, including the act of defying bad prognoses and their implied limits, serves to normalize motherhood. As Suzanne Dalton has reflected regarding a definitive diagnosis, "if I don't know that, I can help—I can be part of it with him and be proud of him." To help and to be proud of one's child are inherent features of contemporary American motherhood. The paradox of being both a special mother and a normal mother, never completely resolved, is thereby addressed.

A plot line in which a woman assists a child on the morally approved path of overcoming disability shifts a mother of a disabled child from the alternative characters she plays in the reigning American stories (i.e., from either the "bad" mother who must have done something wrong to harm her fetus/baby or the "special" mother who was chosen by God to bear the burden of raising a special child) to the role simply of a normal mother doing the best for her child. Brenda Wilson sums up how her efforts on behalf of her daughter are in reality no different than the actions taken by mothers across the generations of her family:

> I don't know if you've heard that song, "Because I Love You," that new song that's out... from that movie, *Up Close and Personal*. It says, you were my voice when I couldn't speak. You were my eyes, when I couldn't see, and it goes on, and my mother called me crying, and she goes, "Did you hear that song? It reminds me of you and Lisa." I said, "Yeah, I did mom, but

it reminds me of you and me." And it goes on and on. It's just the circle of life, really. My mother almost died, and my grandmother was at her bedside almost every day, and my mother was with me, and I was with my daughter, and that kept me going, my mother, you know, and you must fight for your kid until the end. No matter what.... You're never going to regret fighting for your child. You're never going to look back and regret it.

Narratives of Hope: On Competing Concepts of the Brain

In describing their child in terms of developmental delay, mothers can hold off the cultural attribution of less than full personhood to their child and retain their own commitment to nurture their disabled infant. Elements that appear repeatedly in the "overcoming disability" story told by mothers are (1) progress achieved through early intervention, (2) findings from the field of neuroscience (especially the concept of neuroplasticity), (3) a child's intense motivation, and (4) a mother's hard work and refusal to give up on her child. Physicians also use some of these same elements, particularly a child's level of motivation, in framing the stories they tell to parents. "In the learning achievement area, I was very impressed with her; she seems to really try hard, doesn't she?" a physician prefaces his remarks about the progress of a girl diagnosed with spastic diplegia. In the following two excerpts—the first from an evaluation of a child suspected of mental retardation, the other from a follow-up evaluation of a child diagnosed with cerebral palsy—the examining physician comments explicitly on the presumed causal relationship between a child's motivation and the projected eventual outcome.

> The second piece of what I see today is what we were saying a little bit about at the beginning, is personality or style of approach. What I see with him is that either for reasons that are only known to him or because that is just the way he is, he also is gun shy; he does not like to pursue activities that will more likely lead toward stress or failure. And that issue can play a role in terms of how well he does. So if you are learning the skills and are enthusiastic about it, you are going to do much better.

> The important thing today I'm going to say is she has made tremendous progress. She has gone much more quickly getting out of her walker than

I would have guessed. And that tells me that she has a very strong will. She wanted to do it. She did it, right? That's what I experienced today. And that quality of saying, "I have a goal, I want to do this right and I'm gonna get it done" is a wonderful quality. You take two people who have any kind of problem and you say one is going to be so motivated to do something about it and the other one isn't. Who's going to go farther?

Except when a child is labeled "unmotivated," physicians' associations of motivation with outcome generally resonate well with mothers' own narratives of hope. However, when emplotting events in anticipation of a less hopeful ending, physicians most often utilize an interpretation of the brain that competes with the image portrayed in the overcoming disability stories told by the mothers. The description of brain damage physicians put forward in explaining a child's permanent disability to a parent is largely based on a structural or localization model of the central nervous system. In this model, when there is damage to the central nervous system causing a loss of irreplaceable cells, there is a resultant loss of function. "In the traditional world of medicine," Bernard Brucker explains,

> everybody is so embedded in this structure-function relationship that the way they even determine structural losses is by investigating function. And where people start to get some functional return spontaneously... they say obviously this person cannot gain any further function because we know they have damage to the structure and you cannot get more function once significant parts of the central nervous system are disturbed.
>
> (Brucker, 1998)

This model assumes that complex functions are discretely localized in specific areas of the brain and does not address that it might be possible to reorganize how the brain uses motor neuron cells; the structural model thus does not take into account the concept of neuroplasticity appearing in the more recent literature of neuroscience, an important feature of which is the capacity of the brain for adaptation to change, for "structural reorganization following injury" (Brucker, 1998). In explaining a diagnosis of cerebral palsy, for instance, it is not uncommon for a doctor talking to the parent of a premature baby to bring out a diagram of the brain, indicating the locations in the brain that control specific functions. The doctor might discuss with the parent(s) the location of damage determined through an MRI or ultrasound and then in turn describe the functional deficit and/or specific type of cerebral palsy, such as spastic diplegia or hemiparesis, that is assumed to inevitably follow from damage in that area. Conversely, the doctor might discuss how deficits such as motor delay or spasticity (manifesting as stiffness) noted through observation of a child's behavior are indications of the part of the brain that must therefore have been damaged. Structural damage is described as determining loss of function, and loss of function is taken as proof of irreversible structural damage.

In the following excerpt, a doctor explains to a couple the prognosis for their 10-month-old boy, differentiating between delay and permanent damage:

> He's delayed, but he also has damage to the brain. That damage to the brain, it won't get worse, but it might not get a lot better... I know he doesn't like to use that right hand. It's hard for him to use that right hand because the part of the brain that works that right hand is dead. It's dead, injured, not completely but it's been very seriously injured, okay? Same thing with his legs. He wants to use those legs, he wants to stand up, but it's really hard for him because those parts of the brain that work those legs, they are damaged, and I look at him today and I see these things that he is doing. They tell me that this problem isn't going to go away in a year. This problem will be here a long, long time. That there's a chance it will never go away.... I want to say this is a real serious problem so the odds are not real good here.

A Pakistani mother uses her sister as an interpreter to ask, regarding her infant daughter, "She's behind? She's late-blooming? She has delay?" The doctor responds,

> Um, well, definitely she's delayed. There's no question about that. The question that's most difficult is: Is this something that's going to be a problem for now, and when she's older is going to get much better and go away? Or is this the first sign of a problem that's going to be now, later, later, later? Okay?... Maybe this is the first sign this is going to be permanent.... The problem she has with body control is not because her

muscles are stiff or because of the nerves, it's because the control from her brain is wrong, just like with the vision; it's been damaged or it just didn't develop properly. That part of the brain that has to do with body control is working very poorly, that part of the brain that has to do with vision is working very poorly, that part of the brain that has to do with learning is probably also working very poorly.

Similarly, progress of a child with a speech delay is monitored to determine whether there is an injury to the brain, as in this excerpt from an evaluation: "If it's minimal progress in the next six months, then you have to think about a more serious kind of speech problem where the brain, rather than just slow at figuring out how to talk, it may be severely impaired in that area." In the foregoing examples, the child's behavior or function is used to extrapolate the existence and specific location of structural damage. In the following two excerpts, conversely, different physicians explain to parents that documented structural damage determines future impairment of function:

Sometimes, if it is not that bad, it is not like dead tissue, it can recover over a long time.... But it is not completely damaged. So, in that case, maybe that is the case with her and that is why she was doing pretty good and that is why she appears very good in other areas... and if you really want to find out, maybe an MRI will show that, because an MRI will show you a really small lesion that we cannot see on the ultrasound, the MRI will show that.

Let me just explain a few things to you. This is a picture of the inside of the brain and this is the bottom of the brain. And this is where the arteries come in... What they saw in the nursery was that on the left side of the brain, there was an injury to this artery. And the important question is, what does that mean? Well, this artery feeds this area of the brain.... Sometimes these areas are actually damaged, they actually die because they're supposed to be fed, so without oxygen and enough food for long enough that the brain can't survive and it dies in this area. So they couldn't say for sure from the first scan because he was too young... This area right here is involved in your body control, your movement. This area back here is involved in more with your tone and your speech and this area here has a little bit to do with how you pay attention and the way you think. So when you see this artery involved, it involves so many things—thinking, body control and talking—that we get concerned because so many things are controlled by this one artery.... So this part of the brain, the left side of the brain controls the right side of the body. It gets switched around so we would be looking for a problem on the right side of the body.

There is a strong common sense appeal to the localization model: "If damage to the nervous system always causes a permanent loss of behavioral function, isn't it logical to suppose that the behavioral loss is caused by the destruction of the specific nerve cells that 'control' the function?" (Stein, Brailowsky, and Will, 1995: 22). However, some scholars argue that the techniques used in experiments verifying the model do not explore other options. What, for instance, would it mean if one could relearn conditioned responses with special training, even though the nerve cells were no longer present? (Stein, et al., 22). Experiments in neurobiology "show that experience changes the wiring in our brain because it changes the activity in our neurons (Zull, 2002: 116). Animal research has "resulted in current conceptualization of the brain as a flexible system with frequently shifting connections" and has "also fostered our growing awareness of how experience itself both induces and guides plasticity" such that the clinical process can be thought of as one in which the therapist "deliberately directs experience-guided plasticity" (Holland, 2004: 255). Summarizing what had been learned about children's brains in recent years, Shore (1997) states that "the brain is not a static entity" nor are an individual's capacities fixed at birth. Rather, "The brain itself can be altered – or helped to compensate for problems – with timely, intensive intervention" (Shore, 1997: x).

In their book entitled *Brain Repair*, Stein, et al. (1995) argue for looking at those cases that have previously been considered to be exceptions. These are precisely the "doctors were wrong" stories told by parents, stories in which gloomy predictions did not come to pass, or profound difficulties were overcome with will and effort. Such stories assert the child's personhood, justify maternal commitment of time and resources, and normalize the experience of motherhood; "overcoming the odds" in these stories represents joint and ongoing agency on the part of mothers and the disabled children they nurture.

Amy Garrison talked about the hope given by her son's physical therapist, who she said told her that

> unlike an adult, a baby's brain is just starting to grow, and the parts that are damaged, there are parts of the brain that we don't even use and maybe that part of the brain can take over the spot that is not working right and, do you know what I'm trying to say? Which gives me lots of hope.

Mothers, in seeking information with which to construct their own narratives of hope, gather information not only from early intervention service providers (physical therapists, special educators, speech and language pathologists, etc.) but from popularly available reports from the field of neuroscience that are not always incorporated into the information parents receive through the clinicians evaluating their children. While mothers may challenge or reinterpret a particular individual medical practitioner's prognosis about a child, mothers of children with central nervous system damage (often those who survived premature birth) appear to hold in high esteem the field of neuroscience. The latter is used by mothers to validate the notion of linear progression and to question the ability of individual doctors to set limits on their child's development.

Summaries of scientific research in the field of brain development are easily accessed through popular media. A *New York Times* article entitled "Studies Show Talking with Infants Shapes Basis of Ability to Think" points to the works of researchers such as Dr. Esther Thelen of Indiana University, who explains "Experience in the first year of life lays the basis for networks of neurons that enable us to be smart, creative and adaptable in all the years that follow (Blakeslee, 1997: 153). "Using the tools of modern cognitive science," another *New York Times* article reports, scientists are asking such questions as "How does experience shape the brain's circuits? How changeable are those circuits later in life?" (Blakeslee, 1995: 158). With such titles as "Fertile Minds" (Nash, 1997), "Cultivating the Mind" (Lach, 1997), "The Surprising News" (Polaneczky, 1998), "Retraining Your Brain" (Greenwald, 1999) and "How to Build a Baby's Brain" (Begley, 1997), popular magazines such as *Time, Redbook,* and *Newsweek* describe the brain in terms of computer circuitry, (re)wiring, and flexibility and highlight the role of experience in brain development:

When a baby is born, primitive structures in the brain—those controlling respiration, reflexes and heartbeat—are already wired. But in higher regions of the cortex, neural circuits are rudimentary at best; the vast majority of the 1,000 trillion connections (synapses) that the newborn's billions of neurons will eventually make are therefore determined by early experience.

Connections that are reinforced by a baby's exposure to language, images, sounds, facial expressions and even lessons in cause and effect... become permanent. Tentative connections that are not reinforced by early experience are eliminated.

(Lach, 1997: 38)

A baby's brain is a work in progress, trillions of neurons waiting to be wired into a mind.... Some of the neurons have already been hard-wired.... But trillions more are like the Pentium chips in a computer before the factory preloads the software. They are pure and of almost infinite potential, unprogrammed circuits that might one day compose rap songs and do calculus, erupt in fury and melt in ecstasy. If the neurons are used, they become integrated into the circuitry of the brain by connecting to other neurons; if they are not used, they may die. It is the experiences of childhood, determining which neurons are used, that wire the circuits of the brain as surely as a programmer at a keyboard reconfigures the circuits in a computer. Which keys are typed—which experiences a child has— determines whether a child grows up to be intelligent or dull, fearful or self-assured, articulate or tongue-tied. Early experiences are so powerful, says pediatric neurobiologist Harry Chugani of Wayne State University that "they can completely change the way a person turns out."

(Begley, 1996)

Of all the discoveries that have poured out of neuroscience labs in recent years, the finding that the electrical activity of brain cells changes the physical structure of the brain is perhaps the most breathtaking... while the brain contains virtually all the nerve cells it will ever have, the pattern of wiring between them has yet to stabilize. Up to this point, says Shatz, "what the brain has done is lay out circuits that are its best guess about what's required for vision, for language, for whatever." And now it is up to neural activity—no longer spontaneous, but driven by a flood of sensory experiences—to take this rough blueprint and progressively refine it.

(Nash, 1997: 50)

Nothing you do or don't do will change how your child's heart chambers develop, or how many eggs her ovaries hold, or how her kidneys function. But proper stimulation, meaning a rich and diverse environment, will make her brain grow denser, her thought processes quicker, her perception keener—and ultimately make her more competent and happier person... (T)hink of your child's genetic brain matter as the hardware he's born with. His experiences—via stimulation—are the software that dictates how much of that hardware ever gets used.

(Polaneczky, 1998: 103–104)

Such findings have significant policy implications, suggesting the value of quality daycare and of early childhood education programs for all children. The implications for young children with brain damage or other impairments related to the brain are presented as even more dramatic, suggesting that damage can actually be corrected. "The remarkable plasticity of the brain has put scientists in hot pursuit of novel ways to treat a host of ailments," *Time* magazine reports; while scientists used to believe that "the brain you were born with was the brain you got... today researchers are showing that the brain can constantly revise its 'maps' of neural circuits that serve as operating panels for the body and mind" (Greenwald, 1999: 52–53). The magazine *Parenting* quotes a specialist in developmental and behavioral pediatrics in its article on developmental delay: "There's a lot of evidence that a good deal of catching up can be done in the preschool years.... There's a wonderful plasticity to the way that young children develop" (Garrison, quoted in Sachs, 1997). *Newsweek* reports that "three out of 100 newborns suffer birth defects. But more and more of them can now hope to lead normal lives" (Riccitiello and Adler, 1997: 46). "It is possible," the *Newsweek* article states, "for a Down syndrome child to hold a job and live at least a version of the sort of life that every parent dreams of from the moment he or she hears the fateful news that a child has 'a problem.' A normal life" (Riccitiello and Adler, 50).

At the White House Conference on Early Childhood Development and Learning, David Hamburg, the president of the Carnegie Corporation of New York reportedly lamented that "there is a wide gap between scientific knowledge and the public's"; concern was raised that "despite the media attention given to research on how early-childhood experiences determine the brain's wiring, many parents have not heard the message" (Begley and Wingert, 1997: 72). However, mothers of disabled children in this study do appear to have heard the message and often use it both to structure the stories they tell about their child and to justify the plot to others.

Circulation of expert knowledge is affected by the hearer/re-teller's personal engagement with the issues. Parents hoping that their child will overcome his or her disabilities find research on the plasticity of the brain, and in particular on the way in which experience can "rewire" the brain, inherently optimistic. In her first interview, Suzanne Dalton described "doing a ton of reading" after being told her premature infants were at risk for cerebral palsy, "and the thing I came out of it with is in babies you just don't know. Their brains are very elastic in that other parts of the brain can pick up part of what has been damaged." Cheryl Benedetto, whose child also suffered a stroke while on ECMO, speculates about the prospects for her son in similar terms: "I guess children use different parts of their brain, and they're saying we only use ten percent of our brain.... Maybe he taps into those other parts... I mean, he's come a long way from where they (doctors) said he was going to."

"I'm a Synapse-Builder": On Mothers' Hopes and Burdens

Such research supports a story of developmental delay with potential linear progress, setting agendas for both child and mother. "There's a short circuit getting it from here to there," remarked Pam Karcher, about the brain of her son with pervasive development disorder; "I'm like, 'We have to help him build another circuit.'" In the following narrative, Patricia Marks refers to reading a recent magazine article on early brain development; she too incorporates the information there into the ongoing story of her twin daughters with cerebral palsy, a story that includes doctors' predictions and in which she as a mother is presented as a central character moving the plot toward its hoped-for conclusion:

> Dr. Kureshi says she has cortical visual impairment. And cortical visual impairment means that the brain center in her brain is not going to ever process what she's been seeing.... And I asked Dr. Lester when we went

there in October about this.... He's says "No... It's too early to say. I don't
make that diagnosis until they're much further down the road," which
prompted me to say, "Thank you for not speculating about my child."
And, did you read that *Time* magazine article in February about how
a baby's—how a child's brain develops?... And to me the whole thing
made perfect sense. Why am I not working now, right? Because I'm a
synapse-builder. That's what this whole period of their lives, this whole
reason, this is—and then you know what? That's why I know Suzannne
Dalton's kids are going to be okay, I can tell from talking to her that those
kids live with synapse-builders and they will keep going like I did.

While conflicting with the more static structural or localization
model of brain damage commonly used by physicians to explain a
child's permanent disability to a mother, the metaphor of mothers as
"synapse-builders" engaged in rewiring the brain of a disabled child is
both consistent with some recent research in neuroscience and easily
incorporated within the story of temporary developmental delay. "The
brain's ability to change and to recover lost functions is especially remarkable in the first decade of life," Shore states in *Rethinking the Brain*, a
report based on the proceedings of a national conference on early brain
development (1997: 36). "The bottom line is that the brain's plasticity
presents us with immense opportunities and weighty responsibilities"
(37), both of which are keenly felt by women in the study.

In short, publicized recent neuroscientific findings suggest that a
child's experience can affect brain circuitry and functional outcome.
As mothers are largely considered responsible for providing the
appropriate experiences for their children, there is a moral component
to developmental progress not only for the child but also for the
mother. For the child, this moral component is what it has long been
in U.S. culture; the child's efforts to progress fit neatly within the plot
of the courageous "overcoming disability" story. Each event, each
developmental milestone achieved, anticipates the story's ending of
the impermanence of severe disability and the establishment of full
personhood; that a child "chooses" to work toward this end is in itself a
sign of the child's moral worth.

Mothers recognize the performative qualities of the different stories
that might be told of their child; if one experiences life according to

one story—permanent brain damage—the child is in danger of being "written off," of living without the investment of time and effort by medical personnel and perhaps even by mothers themselves. If, however, one experiences the events in a disabled child's life according to a story of developmental delay and of potential reorganization of the brain, parental investment is both justified and essential.

The child's developmental progress is a validation of a mother's efforts in the hard work of nurturance, including that of securing for her child, as early as possible, expert interventions. The child's progress is a woman's simultaneous claim to normal motherhood and to special motherhood in which she gives above and beyond the norm. The story is more than a selective representation of events that justifies her commitment; a mother's actions—her refusal to give up on her child's ability to progress, her determination to get various early intervention therapies, her efforts to teach and provide stimulation to a child—are integral to the plot and are experienced as moving forward the child's story toward the (hoped-for) conclusion. Mothers here are actors in the story, but they also act having adopted "the point of view of a narrator, reading... actions backward from an ending" they somehow know (Mattingly, 1998: 44) or hope for.

When, as is often the case, the child's story is narrated by a doctor "reading back" from an ending different from that of the mother, the collision of the two stories within the confines of the doctor's office is jarring. Mothers' reactions reveal the moral implications they draw from the different endings for both child and mother. Lisa Hart compares doctors in these terms: "One thing you don't get from a lot of doctors, you know, is 'you're doing a good job. She's really coming along'... they're really good at our pediatrician's office about saying, 'you know, we see a lot of good changes.... She's really coming along, you know. Good job for *her* and good job for *you*.'" Alice Brooks similarly explains that what she "really wanted" from the developmental specialist at a follow-up visit was "that pat on the back, that reassurance that, yeah, we're doing a good job, she's going the way she should." If, instead of such reassurance, the doctor's story doesn't recognize, or even present as possible, developmental progress toward overcoming permanent disability, parental efforts toward attaining full personhood for the child may appear unrewarded or futile, and "real" motherhood for the woman an unattainable goal.

In the following excerpt, a mother of two boys diagnosed with pervasive developmental disorder (PDD), a disorder on the autistic spectrum, speaks:

> With PDD, you know, it can go either way, they can have a good outcome or a bad one, and if you don't get the intervention, which is what you have to fight all the systems with, it will directly affect how your child comes out.... Like I said, with the horizon being that if you go this direction it's going to be sunny, if you go this direction it's going to be cloudy, and you want to make sure you're walking in the right direction at all times. That's where it's so hard with PDD or mild autism... as opposed to severe autism where they really give them a prognosis of well, they're going to have to have adult supervision when they get adults. But they haven't given that to my boys.... . So you're up to bat all the time, all the time. And when you think you've hit the ball, they call a foul.

Mothers believe that the story one tells and can get others to hear matters. It may affect the mobilization of resources, the support of extended family members, the commitment of a mother herself, and the allocation of interventions which, in a story of temporary developmental delay, would help move a child along the trajectory toward overcoming disability, and in doing so, affirm the child's full personhood.[7] However, as Maureen Quinlin tells us earlier, the story has its costs, too: If disability can indeed be overcome with effort, then a mother is "always up to bat." Mothers thus express in their narratives both the boundless hope and ever-present, exhausting burdens inherent in a child's open-ended prognosis.

What does this examination of the developmental delay/overcoming disability story tell us about the relationship of narrative to the experience of the personhood of a disabled child and of the motherhood of the woman who nurtures him or her? Are mothers selectively organizing the scattered events of their own and their children's lives in order to give coherence to what is in reality a chaotic lived experience? I suggest instead that mothers' lived experience of their child's disability is itself structured by the story they tell, a story of developmental delay, plasticity, and hope. Unlike the disfigured children of Israeli parents described by Weiss in the beginning of this chapter, these children are not "written *off*" and depersonalized; instead they are "written *into*" a story of struggle and progress, and thus of personhood as it is defined in American culture. Return of a child's vision, an increase in range of motion, the appearance of a smile, or an attempt at communication are not selected as desperate attempts to deny the reality of a diagnosis but rather experienced by mothers as developmental progress toward normalcy, often in spite of physicians who tell a different story (Landsman, 2003: 1957). Relentless determination and everyday acts of nurturance, intervention, and advocacy by mothers of young disabled children—children who in other times and places might be abandoned or segregated in institutions—are carried out within the meaning-laden context of the "overcoming disability" story whose ending mothers hope to realize.

It is precisely because actions and events are experienced by women in accordance with this plot that to miss an opportunity for one's child is to risk a "cloudy" ending to the story; to actively pursue opportunities to "rewire" a child's brain, on the other hand, is to move toward a happier outcome and to affirm full personhood. The broader cultural narrative of overcoming disability provides the plot of the stories mothers tell about their children and enables them, in a culture within which full personhood is incompatible with disability, to nevertheless experience the personhood of their disabled child. Mothers' own lives and actions are thus emplotted in a story of potential personhood in which they appear to endlessly give. And yet through the act of mothering over time, a different narrative may come to replace or to be held in tension with this story. The emerging narrative is one in which the child, rather than the mother, is the giver and in which a child's disability is both intrinsic to his or her self and compatible with full personhood. It is to this narrative that we turn.

5

THE CHILD AS GIVER

Mothers' Critique of the Commodification of Babies

I do not gift you with clever conversation, cute remarks to be laughed over and repeated. I do not give you answers to your everyday questions, responses over my well-being, sharing my needs, or comments about the world around me. I do not give you rewards as defined by the world's standards, great strides in development that you can credit yourself; I do not give you understanding as you know it. What I give is so much more valuable. I give you instead opportunities. Opportunities to discover the depth of your character, not mine; the depth of your love, your commitment, your patience, your abilities; the opportunity to explore your spirit more deeply than you imagined possible... If you allow me, I will teach you what is really important in life. I will give you and teach you unconditional love. I gift you with my innocent trust, my dependency upon you.

> (Excerpt from Anonymous, "I Am the Child,"
> reprinted in parent support group newsletters)

Mothers newly encountering a diagnosis of disability can assert their child's full personhood and reclaim their own motherhood through emplotting their children's lives in anticipation of a story ending in which disability is overcome. In doing so, they both accept a medical model that "defines disability as permanent biological impediment and positions individuals with disabilities as less able than those who can recover from illness or who are non-disabled" (Gilson and DePoy, 2000: 207–288) and reject the applicability of the model to their own child.

In other words, mothers may simultaneously view as deficient "the individual who cannot by 'fixed' by professional intervention" (Gilson and DePoy, 208) *and* envision the immediate or future removal of her own child from the category of disabled. Yet overcoming disability was not the only story within which mothers in this study emplotted their own and their children's lives. Also told, especially in the second round of interviews, were stories of personal transformation, stories in which the anticipated ending was not a temporarily impaired child valiantly struggling toward and reaching normative standards (i.e., "perfection") but rather a *woman's* own growth and a disabled child's *intrinsic* personhood. As the excerpt beginning this chapter implies, these are stories of gifts given and sometimes only reluctantly received.

What is the gift, and from whom does it come? The popular image of mothers of disabled children as special parents chosen by God to receive special children (discussed in Chapter 3) portrays the child itself as the gift and God as the giver. I have argued that this "bromide of distanced compassion" (Rapp, 1999a: xiii) reaffirms for the general public both the cultural devaluation of disabled children and the "specialness" (read abnormality) of their mothers. Mothers themselves generally reject the notion that they have been chosen and that a disabled child is itself a gift. "I don't deal with that saying too good because...He [God] had a brain accident that day when he sent Billy to me because I don't have the patience, and I think it entails an extremely large amount of patience," laughed Becky Romano. "I didn't want to hear one more person tell me that God chose me for this baby. I was like, then that's not a God I want to know" complained Donna Leiden bitterly; "Don't put that on God."

Mothers nurturing disabled children more often describe the gift they have received as a lesson or form of enlightenment; in their narratives, it is not God, but rather the *child*, who is portrayed as the giver. The newsletter of the national support group Mothers United for Moral Support (MUMS), for instance, publishes in each issue a section entitled "The Greatest Gift this Child Has Brought to Our Lives." As in my interviews with mothers, parents' published responses in this section most commonly cite the gift of knowledge of unconditional love, and it is on this gift that I later focus. The point for our purposes now is that in MUMS's column, as well as in narratives I collected, it is the child who brings the gift to its mother; the mother receives the gift, sometimes willingly, sometimes only with ambivalence or after long, hard struggle. In the words of one mother, "Megan has brought us the true meaning of patience and love. She has brought us so much joy. It isn't a perfect world and sometimes we don't like what's handed down to us, but we learn through patience, time, and love" (Meister, 1996). Diane Schur similarly presents her son as a giver: "He has brought our family closer, bridged gaps that would still be there, he's given us tremendous purpose in life" (1994: 10). Brenda Lommen explains that her daughter "has taught me patience, compassion, kindness and a love deeper than I thought possible. She brings out my softer side and my stronger side at the same time as my weakest side" (2003: 12). "Absolute unconditional love," writes Sarah Watson, "She has made me into a better person" (2002: 12). Other mothers describe the gifts bestowed by their children in similar terms: "Unconditional love. He has taught us to see life beyond materialistic point of view" (Gupta, 2002: 12); "He has given me the ability to never give up, the love and strength he has given us is priceless" (Wasia, 2002: 12); "I never felt or knew unconditional love until I had my son, Jeremiah. He has taught me and showed me so much I never thought could learn or see" (Michalale, 1999: 12).

The language of giving and getting has been analyzed as a means by which American women give meaning and value to their situations when their reproductive experiences, for reasons such as infertility or pregnancy loss, do not meet the cultural norm (Layne, 1999). Despite non-traditional routes to motherhood, in the cases of surrogacy (Ragoné, 1999) and open adoption (Modell, 1999), a woman acquires something of publicly acknowledged value, a much-wanted child. In these cases, gift rhetoric can mask the intertwining of surrogacy or adoption with the domain of commodity relations, which the financial transactions involved in those processes might otherwise bring to the fore. Representing more than just protection from the appearance of baby selling, gift rhetoric establishes social relationships and can equalize previously unequal relations.

A mother of a disabled child, however, neither gives nor receives anything of publicly acknowledged value. Her child is labeled "defective," its birth deemed a tragedy, and its very personhood diminished. Indeed, once aware of a pregnancy, all except one woman in the study had consciously taken steps to avoid birth defects and to bring into the world what she assumed would be a "perfect" or "normal" baby; each attempted to exert control through dietary choices such as eliminating caffeine and alcohol and by securing prenatal care from medical experts. Counter to their expectations, these mothers did not get what they worked for; the "product" is judged below standard. Yet, if a woman later redefines her child neither as a product in the commodity market nor as a gift from God but rather as a *giver* of gifts, she raises the value of her child beyond that of the "perfect" child she had once anticipated and strived to obtain.

Representation of the disabled child as giver is particularly subversive in American culture wherein the personhood of those with disabilities is diminished in large part because such individuals have been viewed not only as incapable of giving, but as relying upon the gifts of others. Portrayed in the media as impotent and dependent (Zola, 1985), disabled people in the United States have typically been understood "as helpless and incompetent" (Scotch, 1988: 161). The presumed dependency of disabled people is conspicuously exhibited in appeals by a vast array of charitable organizations, many of which feature children. The concept of the poster child has been widely adopted, "as the child selected for the year to represent the organization of a particular disability was always physically appealing, a symbol of vulnerability evoking sympathy" (Fleischer and Zames, 2001: 10). Historian Paul Longmore describes how the rhetoric of telethons symbolically defines three categories of persons: givers, takers, and the recipients of giving. "Takers" in American society are those who turn their backs on their duty to aid the helpless; givers' superior moral standing, on the other hand, is publicly validated by the compassion they show toward the "less fortunate." The third category, the disabled, necessarily fits into this model as those ritually defined as dependent on the moral fitness of nondisabled people (Longmore, 1997: 136).

Advocates of disability rights and the independent-living movement have countered this moral hierarchy. Claiming that impairment does not "naturally" or in itself create dependency, they argue that discrimination against people with disability *does*. The movement has worked toward changing the public stance toward disability from that of "helping" the unfortunate to that of guaranteeing civil rights. This shift is epitomized by the slogan on one disability rights poster, referring to the charitable

organization March of Dimes, the goal of which is the prevention of
birth defects: "You Gave Us Your Dimes. Now We Want our Rights."
The embattled Americans with Disabilities Act of 1990 also manifests
this shift in conception of disability, as it mandates accommodation to
differences rather than compensation for the losses supposedly posed
by disability. Many disabled adults have come to question the value
of telethons in particular, claiming, as does disabled journalist John
Hockenberry, that "Jerry's kids are people in wheelchairs on television
raising money to find a way to prevent their ever having been born"
(1995: 33); advocates argue that the primary "need of disabled children
is not the services to which telethons contribute, but rather a civil rights
movement" in which society's role in disabling people with impairments
is reduced (Fleischer and Zames, 2001: 11). The story of Mike Ervin, "a
renegade Jerry's Kid who took on the telethon" by organizing protests, is
portrayed in the 2005 documentary "The Kids Are All Right" by Kerry
Richardson (see also Johnson, 1994). Of particular concern to Ervin was
Lewis's portrayal of a wheelchair user as "half a person" (Lewis, 1990).

The "pity approach" of telethons has contributed to the American
public's view of disabled people as "childlike, helpless, hopeless,
nonfunctioning and noncontributing members of society" (Kemp,
quoted in Johnson, 1994: 120). As physical and economic self-sufficiency
serve as prerequisites to being moral agents in North American culture,
the consequences are by no means insignificant. The devaluation
of recipients of charity is indicative of a liberal political theory that
places autonomy in opposition to dependency. Ironically, giving to the
"less fortunate" as a display of superiority is largely made possible by
acquisition unfettered by the demands of others. Both moral moves in
North American culture—generous giving and boundless acquisition—
are assumed to be thwarted by dependency (Landsman, 1999: 149). For
theorists such as Rousseau and Smith, "to become dependent is to learn
how to act on behalf of others, not on behalf of the self. Dependent
people lose the ability to make judgments for themselves, and end up
at the mercy of others on whom they are dependent" (Tronto, 1993:
163).

The feminist movement is implicated as well in perpetuating the
devaluation of disabled people. Adrienne Asch and Michelle Fine
suggest that in adhering to an agenda involving the portrayal of

YOU GAVE US YOUR DIMES

NOW WE WANT OUR RIGHTS

Figure 5.1 This poster rejects charities' focus on cure and prevention, in favor of a minority group model of disability focused on civil rights.

women's strengths and competence, the feminist movement had long ignored disabled women precisely because of the cultural opposition of autonomy and dependence. Viewed as reinforcing "traditional stereotypes of women being dependent, passive, and needy" (Asch and Fine, 1988: 4), disabled women were deemed counter-productive to the feminist notion of women's agency. Dependency and full personhood are thus widely viewed as being incompatible, and the moral standing of "authentic" American men and women is intertwined with both the act of giving and the attribution of less than full personhood to those with disabilities.

> Putatively independent Americans thus have employed those they label "dependent" as a negative reference group against which to define themselves. Giving proves that the allegedly self-sufficient belong on the upper side of a great social divide that separates those designated autonomous from those branded dependent. Anyone resorting to public welfare or private charity is regarded as neither fully a person nor legitimately a citizen. The price of such societal aid in America is social invalidation.
>
> (Longmore, 1997: 151)

Shifting the representation of the disabled child from a pitiful and needy recipient of charity to a giver of gifts repositions the child on the "upper side" of the great American social divide, the very place from which its label of disability would seem to preclude it. As the quote prefacing this chapter makes explicit, mothers of disabled children may reverse the negative valuation of dependency: The child *gifts* the mother with its dependency upon her. By redefining as a "giver" an infant previously interpreted either as the just consequences of a mother's poor choices or as tragic misfortune she was chosen by God as strong enough to bear, a mother affirms the full personhood of her disabled child.

The Gift: "My Greatest Joy and My Greatest Sorrow"

In mothers' narratives casting the child as giver, the gift most often specified is that of knowledge of unconditional love. The narratives present the ability to love unconditionally as given by the child to its mother in one of two basic scenarios. As in Lily Beckett's description to me of her daughter's stay at Boston Children's Hospital, the child may be a *model* of unconditional love:

> She impresses me. I mean, I see what she goes through, and then turn around and be happy. When we were in Boston in June… (they were) putting her IV in, and they're having a really hard time, and I didn't go into the room…. and I could hear her screaming. Well, John…. heard her screaming and went in… He came out, and he said, "It's so hard because here they're hurting her," and they finally get it in, and he says, "We're all done, so we're going back to the room, say bye." She turned around with these tears falling down her cheeks and smiles and says, "Bye bye." I mean, she waves to them! And I'm like—like "these people just hurt me, but it's okay, and I'm not holding a grudge." You just—that kind of stuff just amazes me.

By facing adversity with love for others, the child is seen to teach his or her parents to love unconditionally as well. "I have now learned that you love someone no matter what. I have tried to apply this to my life also.…Tyler is just a remarkable child, no matter how bad he feels, he always manages to smile his sweet little smile," a mother writes in a parent support newsletter (Newman, 2002: 12). "She loves me unconditionally. I have never felt so loved as I have by her," writes a mother of a child with Rett Syndrome. "I can't believe I could love so incredibly much" (Schultz, 2000: 12). "It was through Jason that we learned to see the good in ourselves and in others, we learned to share what we have," writes another mother in the newsletter; "He has turned our lives around by giving freely and trusting implicitly" (Loos, 1999: 12). In these cases, the child is portrayed as setting an example of unconditional love for others to follow.

In the other scenario, disabled children may provide their mothers a unique opportunity to learn unconditional love by not meeting the normal developmental milestones by which American women commonly compare their children and mark their own successes as mothers. Tina Graham, whose child has mental retardation, tells this story in which she reinterprets an earlier quest in the light of her experience of mothering her disabled son:

> Years ago, this you may or may not relate to it, but I had asked the Lord to teach me unconditional love, and I think I wanted him to diffuse it into my brain—not have to go through any fiery experience and to burn it into me—but I just wanted to know what it was like to love people without putting expectations on them of performance and other things, and it really wasn't until six months later that we found out about Ryan... so this situation is invaluable in that way. I mean, certainly nothing I would have ever chosen. No way... A lot of expectations for our own kids that he wasn't meeting, you know what I mean, and even that rejecting-our-own-child-feeling, which almost every parent I've ever talked to who had a child with disabilities has struggled with... This is a lesson for everyone else to watch us... I learned about my own conditional love... and there never would have been a spotlight on it if it hadn't been for Ryan.

Pam Karcher, whose child has pervasive developmental disorder, describes a similar experience:

> I remember saying—praying one time, you know, in a little personal moment, it's like "Geez, I really wish I knew what unconditional love was." I have these relationships and I love them, *if* they're good, *if* they love me, *if* they give me cards, *if* they—it's like, I want to know what

that real unconditional love is. It's like, hello! Be careful what you ask for because you might just get it, you know.

Rather than a quality inherent to "special" women, knowledge of unconditional love is portrayed as a consequence of the experience of having a disabled child. It is often a lesson acquired through anguish or struggle; it emerges in the practice of mothering and is assumed to be shared by most others who have gone through such an experience. Women I interviewed often attributed this quality to *me* by virtue of my raising a child with a cerebral palsy. Tina Graham, for instance, commented in the interview, "I'm sure you've seen changes in yourself after having DJ and valuing all children and not just the elite award winners and those who are A+ students from nursery school on." Similarly, Lorraine Hamilton explained that when she first heard her child had agenesis of the corpus collasam, she and her husband "felt it was a tragedy;" at the time they couldn't know "what a delightful little boy, what a blessing he would be, and just so much excitement that he brings to our life." "I'm sure you know," she continued. By the same logic, the gift of unconditional love is assumed to be withheld from, or at least more difficult to attain by, those who have not had the experience of caring for a disabled child.

The pain often associated with accepting the gift of knowing unconditional love derives not just from physical and financial demands, though parents do refer to these difficulties, but from the belief that it comes at the expense of an innocent child. "I mean, it's like look at all the things he's taught me, patience, unconditional love.... I just hope that he doesn't have to suffer the rest of his life to teach me lessons," comments Pam Karcher. Similarly, Suzanne Dalton, mother of premature twins, one of whom has cerebral palsy, worries that "he's suffering and that some of us are getting better, being better people, but he's still suffering.... it's nice that other good things are coming from this. But I didn't want this at the cost of my child, you know." A mother can therefore believe that morally she is better off for having the gift *and* nevertheless long for, and strive toward, her child's being cured of disability; she can, and does, often wish she never received the gift.

A child's suffering may be described as a direct consequence of an impairment itself—pain caused by necessary life-saving heart surgeries for a child with Down syndrome or insertion of a shunt to drain fluid from around the brain for a child with hydrocephalus, for instance—but more commonly, it is portrayed as deriving from the social rejection a woman anticipates her disabled child will face in the future. Wondering whether her child will be accepted in the community, play with other children, have friends, get a job, date or eventually marry, brings anxiety and deep sadness. As giver, the child is established as morally superior to others, but recognizing the child as a giver of precious gifts to the mother in no way negates the emotional, physical, and/or financial strains a woman experiences from raising a disabled child. Gift rhetoric is not a romantic denial of sorrow, fear, or disappointment. Rather the rhetoric of the child as giver of the gift of unconditional love helps account for and unify what might otherwise appear as conflicting stories of hope versus resignation, anger versus joy, absurd and random injustice versus profound and ultimate meaning. As I stood to leave after our second interview, Peggy Hoffmeister, the mother of a boy diagnosed as autistic, reflected, "It's strange, you know. This is a gift. It's a gift I wish I didn't have. It's a gift I wouldn't wish on anybody else. But it really is a gift." "Even with all the hurt we have endured and with the things I have learned," writes Celeste Daniels, "I would not give up this experience for anything.... I owe my disabled daughter my life, she sent me on a better journey though she will probably never know this" (2003: 12). In the words of a mother of a child with chromosomal abnormalities, "She is my greatest joy and my greatest sorrow. She has shown me what is truly most important in life, uncompromising love" (Meyer, 1995: 12).

Unconditional love is, as anthropological research attests, far from a universal response to the experience of giving birth to and/or raising a child with a disability. Nancy Scheper-Hughes, for instance, describes the mortal neglect of sickly infants by desperately poor mothers in Brazil and claims that the practice of mothering there contradicts "the developmental and clinical literature on 'maternal bonding' understood as a universal script" (1992: 341). Hrdy reports on the persistence for centuries in medieval Europe of neonatal ordeals, such as subjecting newborns to ice-cold baths, as means to "let die, as not worth rearing, one that cannot bear the chilling" (Soranus, quoted in Hrdy, 1999: 464). As we have seen in the case of Israel, Weiss claims a high rate of abandonment of children with visible deformities at birth

(1994), and of territorial isolation of such children within the home
(Weiss, 1997). And the American mothers of disabled children that I
interviewed themselves recognize, and sometimes lament the fact, that
some mothers never accept their disabled children. They occasionally
comment on women who feel they must institutionalize their children
or give them up for adoption. Such mothers are not necessarily judged
harshly but may be viewed as somewhat less capable or open to the
important lessons of life; that is, as mothers who, having not yet
acquired knowledge of unconditional love, still interpret children as
defective commodities rather than as givers of gifts from which mothers
themselves will benefit.

Infants as Commodities

American mothers who choose to raise their disabled children suggest
they have been made aware of the pervasiveness of a North American
discourse in which infants are categorized as commodities. Their
encounter with this discourse in the context of mothering their own
child leads many mothers to develop a critique of the commodification
of babies that both converges and conflicts with the discourse of
disability rights.

Only some of the total range of things in any society are available
for marking as commodities (Kopytoff, 1988: 64). Those that are can
be exchanged in discrete transactions, the transaction itself signifying
that a counterpart has an equivalent value. Salability and the option to
exchange for other things thus suggests that an item has something in
common with other exchangeable items that, "taken together, partake of
a single universe of comparable values." To be saleable or exchangeable
is therefore to be common, as opposed to singular, unique, and therefore
not exchangeable for anything else (Kopytoff, 1988: 69).

In contemporary Western thought, Kopytoff explains, there exists a
common sense divide between commodities and non-commodities; it
takes form as the dichotomy between things and people. The universe of
commodities is understood to be comprised of things (physical objects
and rights in them), while at the opposite pole we place people, who
"represent the natural universe of individuation and singularization"
(1988: 64). The establishment of personhood is therefore critical for

defining a human being as outside the realm of commoditization. Human beings to whom personhood has been attributed are neither saleable nor exchangeable; each is unique and irreplaceable. Human beings who fall outside the category of full person—slaves, for example—are, in contrast, potentially replaceable.

As reproductive body parts and processes ranging from eggs and sperm to gestation are increasingly subject to sale in the marketplace, concerns about the body as a source of raw materials and babies as saleable products have become a topic of public concern. Where there is public acceptance of new reproductive technologies in contemporary Euro-American culture, some scholars suggest, it is linked to the use of naturalizing language (i.e., language that presents reproductive technology as simply lending nature a helping hand [see Franklin, 1997], enabling natural instincts for parenthood to be realized [Cannell, 1990; Ragoné, 1994] or, as in the case of gestational surrogacy, ensuring what is seen as the more natural, genetic relatedness of parents and child [Ragoné, 1999]). Such rhetoric diverts attention from the body fragmentation and financial exchanges involved in procreation under these circumstances. The use of technology for selecting specific traits of babies such as gender or compatibility for bone marrow transplantation has opened up new arenas for public controversy over the commodification of reproduction. An uneasy question emerges: Are we shopping for babies? A large feminist literature has focused our attention on just these issues (Corea, 1985; Hershey, 1994; Rothman, 1989, 1994; Rowland, 1992; Schmidt and Moore, 1998).

Yet regardless of any commercial arrangements made to bring a specific baby into a specific family, once there, the "normal" baby in contemporary North American culture is considered a person and is decommodifed; rather than being saleable, the child itself is now "priceless." Indeed, this very "pricelessness" of the child serves as the basis for both support and criticism of reproductive technologies. When a baby or young child is diagnosed with a disability, however, the cultural attribution of personhood is far from assured. Giving birth to and nurturing an anomalous child, as we have seen, reveals the presence of competing cultural categorizations; in some instances, children *do* fall within the domain of commodity exchange.

"Those Things Happen"

An American woman's consumption practices are publicly scrutinized and mark her as pregnant; signs in restaurants and bars proclaim that pregnant women should refrain from alcohol consumption, cereal boxes remind women of the need to eat folic acid, and pregnant drug users may be subject to arrest (Roberts, 1991; Biskupic, 2000). At the time of her pregnancy, a woman who complies with expert prenatal advice does not define herself as seeking to "buy" the perfect baby; rather, through her consumer choices, she is manifesting love for and responsibility toward the future child she carries. For this reason few women, *upon first hearing about their child's disability*, fail to reflect upon their behavior during pregnancy. As we have seen, women search their memories; it was the norm for women to ponder and even agonize over whether eating particular foods, working too hard or too late into the pregnancy, having an alcoholic beverage before knowing one was pregnant, or using an over-the-counter painkiller such as ibuprofen or acetaminophen might have caused the child to have a defect. However, as time went on, many of these same mothers themselves came to argue that compliance with recommended consumption practices, whether they be dietary rules or prenatal testing procedures, and living a responsible and moral life simply did not and could not produce the promises implied. Jenna Mosher talks about finding out a year earlier that her infant son had a chromosomal anomaly involving multiple disabilities, including profound mental retardation, vision impairment, speech delay, and severe motor impairments.

> All I could think of was, God, this is my first child. I did everything right during my pregnancy. I didn't have one cup of coffee. I ate all organic food, exercised. How come someone who doesn't take care of themselves and doesn't even want the kid, has a completely normal child? Yeah, I went through that. Why am I being punished, what did I do, I must have been really bad in a past life. Now do I ask myself why? I don't really.

Suzanne Dalton offers this commentary on women's control of a pregnancy's outcome:

Sometimes I'd like to go back (to her doctors) and get some answers from them, but I don't think there's any answers to be had. I understand first you blame yourself, then you blame your husband because he was hard on you or whatever. But there probably aren't any answers.... it's just one of those things that happen to good people who don't do anything wrong. It just happens.

Mother of a young boy with cerebral palsy, Angela Petrocelli tells of a conversation with her pregnant niece. "I said to her that, 'You know, you do have control quite a bit while you're pregnant, keeping yourself healthy. But there—it's also a lot that you have absolutely no control over what happens, and you learn to take whatever you get.'"

What many of the mothers' narratives revealed was a change in faith that a normal child could be guaranteed. Strategies that during pregnancy were imagined in terms of ensuring quality control or preventing birth defects have been revealed to be ineffective. Darlene Mulligan, for instance, is a married 36-year-old college graduate who works for the state government; the mother of a child with Down syndrome, she now finds herself angered by those who believe prenatal testing can predict "perfection."

The one girl in my office, her nursery was totally decorated, teddy bears. I mean, the kid had everything for a zoo. I did get a little annoyed with her. She was also older. She had the amnio done. She came back in, she kept telling me how she was going to have this perfect, healthy little boy, and she was going on and on, and finally, after I heard it for about the thousandth time, I said, "You know, the amnio only checks for three different genetic things. There is no guarantee that this child is healthy," and I think she kind of realized what she was saying, and she did stop that. She just started saying, she was having a boy, but it's like whatever they were testing for, they did fine, so in that sense, she will have a healthy child, but you can't say that; it's not guaranteed.

Mary Summers is a graduate of a high school vocational/technology program who now works in a deli; mother of a multiply disabled child, she too reflects on pregnant women's attitudes that they can be "safe" from the experience of disability:

Well, Peter used to be more cross-eyed than he is now, because he had eye surgery done on his first birthday and we were at the local—not Wal-Mart but another store that went out of business out here—and there was a little girl and the mother was expecting and the little girl looks at Peter and then towards her mother and said, "Mommy, will our baby look like that with his eyes?" And the mother said "No, the baby won't." And I turned towards my girlfriend and I said, "How dare her say that to her child?" She should have turned around and told her child we don't know until this child is born because we don't know what God has given out to us. That's another thing.... I mean you can be honest to a certain point with a child... you can just tell them we'll love this child no matter what way this child comes to be on earth. But there is a possibility that maybe your baby won't be perfect, but you'll love them regardless of what way he is or she. And that's what the biggest problem I have is facing people or hearing people say, "Your brother or sister won't ever be like that," because don't ever say that to me or my girlfriend or my mother, anyone who's with me. Don't ever say it won't happen to you, because you're the last person that will know it's happening to.

Connie Brown's infant son was born without a hand. When the boy was only three weeks old, she took him to her older son's karate practice. Two girls there, whom Connie presumes were about 7 and 10 years old, were intrigued by the baby.

They were like "Oh, look at the baby" and the younger one went "Ooohh!" and I saw her sister elbow her and I just started laughing and I bent down and I said "Oh, honey, that's okay." I said, "Yeah, he was born without a hand," and the other one said, "Yeah, sometimes little babies have that." And you know that was the best reaction I had received, better than any of the reactions I had ever gotten from adults: "Those things happen."

Having actively exercised choice during their pregnancies, many mothers in the study reflect upon what they *now* define as their prior assumption that babies, and specific qualities of babies, could be shopped for. They make the claim instead that there is no real control over what you get, no real choice. In the words of Denise Rivers, a married medical transcriber whose young daughter has cognitive and physical impairments due to hydrocephaly,

This is not my choice. This is not *your* choice. These are not our choices…. You never grow up in school saying, I'm going to grow up and have a handicapped child…. This is a whole new "here it is, take care of it, handle it" situation, you know.

Exchangeability: On "Lemons" and Persons

So what choices would a mother of a disabled child make if she could? Pregnancy in the United States is framed in terms of choice. When considering choices about prenatal testing, Rayna Rapp found that white middle-class women in particular expressed a preoccupation with selfishness and self-actualization. Such women melded the right to abort a disabled fetus with the right to plan an adult life; yet while reserving the right to choose what type of baby to bring into the world, they were nevertheless self-critical about their motives (Rapp, 1999b: 138). Some pregnant women may indeed perceive their use of prenatal screening technologies as "shopping" for babies. However, most describe themselves as doing so for reasons that are consistent with the theory of shopping expounded by Miller (1998); they see themselves as making choices *based on love* for existing or potential family members. A pregnant woman receiving a positive test result for a chromosomal anomaly, for instance, may conclude that regardless of her own personal desire to give birth, the quality of life would be unbearably low for the impaired infant, or the burden for other family members, especially siblings, would be too great. Reflecting upon her own capabilities, she may assess herself as not strong or "selfless" enough to give a disabled child a good life; indeed, she may believe that only "special" women are capable of such mothering (Landsman, 1999). Recent immigrant women, especially those from Central America, South America, and the Caribbean, act on concerns that a sick baby will be an obstacle to their family project of geographic and social mobility (Ginsburg and Rapp, 1999: 294). In all these situations, selective abortion as a means for exchanging a potentially disabled child for a hypothetical "normal" child to be conceived in the future can be portrayed concurrently as selfishness *and* as an act based on motherly love and commitment to family.

For the mother nurturing an *existing* child with a disability, however, the language of commodification is brought into play and applied to a specific, living child in her care. The very quality that disqualifies a human being from commodity exchange—full personhood—is in question for her child. In interviews, many mothers describe feeling that a woman is called upon to justify her continued investment in what is publicly perceived as a defective commodity.[1]

> I guess I get hurt by a lot of people saying that, "Why don't you just have another one?" like she doesn't count. You know, like that's the answer to everything, just have another one. You know, and I've had people say to me, "Well, you're not going to waste your life just devoting your whole life to her, are you?"
>
> (Lisa Hart)

> I did have a few people say things to me like, "Oh, I'm sorry," and trying to console you in some fashion or another and make comments like, "Well, you can always have more." You're like, well, I happen to love the one I've got now.… "Too bad you got this lemon." It sounds like that coming from some people almost, and we even had one woman say to us, she said, "Well, now you need to decide if you're going to sink your whole life into Ryan, or if you're going to have more kids and create a normal family environment."
>
> (Tina Graham)

In common usage, the metaphor of "getting a lemon" refers to the purchase of a defective automobile; it implies that one was cheated or didn't get what one paid for. Designed to protect consumers from continued investment in the maintenance and repair of hopelessly defective products, "lemon laws" have been enacted in all 50 states. New York's "lemon law" (General Business Law, section 198-a. Warranties) stipulates that if within a specified period a manufacturer or its agents "are unable to repair or correct any defect or condition which substantially impairs the value of the motor vehicle to the consumer after a reasonable number of attempts, the manufacturer.… shall replace the motor vehicle… or accept return of the vehicle from the consumer and refund to the consumer the full purchase price." California's lemon law (California Civil Code Section 1793.22) similarly requires that if a manufacturer cannot fix a vehicle to conform to the warranty within a reasonable number of repair attempts, the manufacturer may be required to replace the vehicle or reimburse the buyer for its purchase price. In essence, the laws state that as no amount of maintenance or repair will bring a "lemon" up to normal acceptable standards, such a product should be considered replaceable. The metaphor of a child as "a lemon" thus implies that the child is a permanently substandard commodity in which a parent's ongoing investment of resources, energy, and emotion is futile. No amount of medical treatment, rehabilitative therapy, special education, or mother's love will result in the child's reaching standards of normality; only the birth of a normal child in its place (physically and/or emotionally) can bring about "a normal family environment" (Landsman, 2004).

Patricia Marks adopted twin girls at high risk for cerebral palsy and numerous other disabilities as a consequence of their prematurity and very low birth weights. Well aware that the babies had been rejected by others and that she and her husband had moved up on the adoption list only because they were willing to adopt children with a poor prognosis, Patricia noticed her children being interpreted as potential "lemons." In this excerpt, she describes taking the babies to visit in her older son's classroom.

> One of the teachers in his grade came right up to me and said, "When are you going to know if they're okay?" And I said, "Not for years." "Well, what are you going to do then?" I knew what she was asking, and I said, "Whatever it takes." I had to bite my tongue and not say, "No, we are not sending them back. This was not a—we come with an exchange policy."

Mothers acknowledge that society's lower valuation of their child often makes it necessary for them not only to justify their parental investment (i.e., "sinking their whole life into the child") but possible for others, as well as mothers themselves, to envision replacing one child with another. "Right after Daniel was born," Jenna Mosher admitted, I wanted to have another child immediately. Because I just felt so gypped on my whole experience."

The following poem written by a birthmother who chose to give her disabled baby up for adoption, and recorded by Joanne Finnegan (1993), speaks to this very issue of not getting what one bargained for. Note how the "small life" is shifted by the writer from a state of personhood—a boy or girl—as a presumably normal fetus, into a commodity situation as a disabled baby.

> I feel so cheated.
> You were so perfect, my little one
> the small life inside of me
> my tummy still flat, I knew you were growing
> the first flutter
> then a kick
> A boy or a girl? We wondered
> But never would you be right
> the whole time you grew
> from pinpoint tiny to person-sized
> you were never right
> never perfect
> We rejoiced and planned
> we raised glasses to toast and
> cried tears of joy
> through autumn, then winter
> You kicked and stretched
> my tummy swelled
> But even then
> you were different
> even then
> you didn't look like us
> or think like us
> Precious as you were, a life we created
> you weren't the baby we'd waited for....
>
> (J.W.S. in Finnegan, 1993: 9)

Though the presence of a life is acknowledged in the poem, personhood is nevertheless rescinded; this was not the baby the parents had waited for, and like the twins Patricia is raising, it was given up for adoption. The poem leaves the reader with the understanding that there may yet be, at a later time, the right baby, one who "looks like us" or "thinks like us."

Contrary to the foregoing case, all mothers interviewed in the study kept and are raising their disabled children at home. They respond to the notion that children are exchangeable commodities in at least two ways. Though the two responses appear contradictory, they may nevertheless be expressed by the same woman at different times. As discussed in the last chapter, one response is to argue that the child is valuable because he or she has the potential to overcome disability. This is the claim that the child will not necessarily be disabled in the future, and it often appears in mothers' narratives in the context of interactions with physicians. Doctors interpreted by mothers as having "written off" their kids are common characters appearing in mothers' stories. This example is taken from an interview with Becky Romano, whose child has a chromosomal anomaly:

> … So the thing I was upset with Dr. Jones about is he had formed his opinion before he even walked into the room. He told us that. He said when I read the report, I knew this child was going to severely retarded. And I says, "Well, as you can see now, he's not." And he told me he would never be self-sufficient. He would never go to college. And you don't say "never" in my vocabulary!

Similar stories are told about doctors who reported a child might never live through the night, might never speak, never walk, and the like. As we saw in the last chapter, mothers incorporate examples of their child's having overcome past dismal predictions within a larger story that represents the child as currently experiencing a developmental delay that will eventually, with a child's perseverance and a mother's hard work, be overcome in the future. By leaving the future open to possibility, the concept of developmental delay here enables parents to retain hope that their child will not, in the future, be seriously disabled. The claim to full personhood is validated and nurturance justified in terms of the projected impermanence of the label "disabled."

However, though one response of mothers to the diminished personhood of their child is to emplot the child within a story that will presumably end in the child's attainment of normalcy, another is to reject the dominant discourse that disability and full personhood are incompatible. The narratives suggest that in the course of mothering a disabled child, women develop a critique of the commodification of infants through which they resist the diminishing of their child's personhood. Many mothers' narratives describe self-reflection on this point: Mothers claim that they themselves had once held views that put forth a single standard of value for children and that they have since rejected this perspective. That one's child is a valuable life as it is, regardless of whether or not the child "progresses," thus becomes another stance that mothers may take. The research suggests that this stance is *acquired*; through the process of nurturing children who fail to meet cultural standards, the commodification of infants in American culture is both highlighted for mothers and rejected by them. Many mothers, therefore, reinterpret their own behavior during pregnancy in just these terms. What a woman had understood during pregnancy as her efforts to do what was best for the baby and family she *now* represents negatively as "shopping" for the "perfect" baby. As Suzanne Dalton explains,

> I mean, of course, I always think, you know, when we had had those discussions earlier on in the pregnancy, what if the child had Down syndrome.... I mean, I wouldn't say punishment, but this is the answer that you wanted the perfect child. How selfish of you for wanting perfect children, you know. Children come in all different ways and I would have to say, if anyone asked, that I would say I have the perfect children.

Repudiating their public image as irresponsible producers of defective merchandise or duped consumers of flawed commodities in which they tragically, though perhaps nobly, continue to invest, these mothers now provide a critique of consumer culture. It is not only that there is no real choice or control over what you get that makes it impossible to "shop" for babies, they suggest, but that each child is singular and unique; unlike cars, children cannot be compared to one another according to a set standard of functional or aesthetic qualities. In telling their stories, mothers reposition themselves in opposition to the public discourse that would have a normal child replace a flawed one in a mother's life; in essence, against a cultural "lemon law" for defective children (Landsman, 2004).

"Before I knew Billy was handicapped, I still had that regret that it wasn't a girl," said Becky Romano. "Well, people ask me now and I said, I don't care if somebody handed me twin baby girls, infants, right now, to swap for Billy, I wouldn't." Pam Karcher's child has Asperger's syndrome, a disorder on the autistic spectrum. Talking to a friend who was pregnant and worried about her own ability to cope were the baby to be born with a defect, Pam offered reassurance in two forms, "Chances are you're going to have a healthy baby... But if you don't, I'm like 'look at him.... I wouldn't take it back,' and so no, I don't wish I didn't have him or you know, I'm like that's not even thinkable." "If my house burnt down tomorrow, I still have the people I love," Mary Summers recalls telling her boss at work. "That's just material things. I can always get more. But I can't replace my kids. That's how I feel. People look at me like 'yeah, right, you have two heads on your shoulders,' but I'm like, it's true." Tara Vernon, whose young daughter was diagnosed with autism, also reflects upon the irreplaceability of specific children. Apologizing for crying during the interview, she explains, "I think that's one reason I don't bring it up with people. It's because lots of times I do end up getting weepy, and I don't want them to think it's because I don't love Nicole, because.... If somebody said I could have a normal child, I would definitely say 'no.'" What is significant here is not only that these mothers claim they would not exchange their children but that they are, or imagine being, asked whether they would do so.

It was not uncommon for mothers to describe their own earlier failures to attribute personhood to their disabled infant, their own collusion in the devaluation of children with or at risk for disabilities. Jane Sawyer's baby was born prematurely with a very low birth weight and was subsequently diagnosed with cerebral palsy. Here Jane more fully relates the experience of first seeing her child in the NICU and of only later coming to recognize that this was indeed a person.

> I definitely looked at it as a tragedy. I mean, I didn't see one—I didn't see her as her, I didn't have the attachment to her. As a matter of fact, I think the first time I held her, I probably felt that, where I looked at her more than—I guess I saw her as a *baby*, and not as something that—a terrible thing that just happened.

Julie Sanders also describes only belatedly recognizing the personhood of her child. She spent months "being a basket case" while her son was

in the hospital after a birth injury causing permanent paralysis of his
arm. However, when he came home "it was so much better for me.
I had him there. I could love him and I could hold him and he was
home. So what he got one arm? He's my baby." Becky Romano sees her
experience as having helped her "to grow." She finds it "amazing that I
can go from feeling that this child was going to be this burden to me, to
I can't see life without him."

For Brenda Wilson, who had negotiated so fiercely with the developmental pediatrician for the definition of her daughter as developmentally
delayed rather than mentally retarded, there has also been profound
personal change. In her second interview a full year after the contested
doctor's evaluation of Lisa, Brenda explains that

> as time went on, it's like I've just accepted her for who she is and I wouldn't
> want her any—I mean, I wouldn't change her for the world. I mean, I
> would change what happened to her, but it's just like an acceptance with
> her now, you know… It's not hard anymore to say it or to even think it
> because she's alive. I guess I'd rather have—I said to my mom, I said, I'd
> rather have that label of mental retardation than to say my daughter's
> deceased…The neighbors and stuff, the people that I'm close to, I use
> that word openly—mental retardation…. That's what she is, but it's not
> a bad word anymore to me.

It was the threat of her daughter's death that also made the idea of
mental retardation now seem trivial for Lily Beckett:

> She was born on a Thursday, and Friday when they told us about the
> heart, we were just like "Take us back to Thursday and give us that
> Downs baby." There's no problems, and you were really sorry that you
> were upset about it to begin with.

In the form of a letter to her son on his first birthday, a mother of
a boy with cerebral palsy and microcephaly recalls her feelings at first
hearing the diagnosis. Questioning his very personhood, she recalls, "I
was very angry. We could see the little boy that should have been…where
was he?" The child's disability diminished her own motherhood as well.
"We were not parents, we were parents of a child with disabilities, a
group to which I did not want to belong. Did I really want to leave you
and your father on that day? I do not know. All I know is that I wanted

the pain to end." However in the end, it is the child, exerting his own agency, who transforms his mother. She writes,

> But I could not leave you. Your eyes demanded my presence. Your smile forced me to find hope. And things got better, somehow. Most of all, it was you. You defied them. You defied the odds. Your spirit was too strong. And now, I can look at you and not be overwhelmed by the fear, the pain. I am overwhelmed by love. For you know me, you know your father, and you love us. We are a family. My sweet baby boy, I would give anything to change what happened to you. But since I cannot, I will give you the only thing in my power to give. My love, now and forever, unconditionally, whatever your future brings. Happy Birthday, Little One! With All My love, Mother.
>
> (Bellcross, 1997: 5)

Mothers generally credit their reinterpretations of their pregnancies and of disability to love: both to the love they have for their child and for the "gift" of knowledge of unconditional love given to them by their child. Mothers of disabled infants and toddlers recognize and critique the discourse of commodity exchange of children in large part because it reduces the personhood of those they love; at the same time, they describe their acknowledgment of their disabled infant's personhood as a *consequence* of love. However, immediate and unconditional mother love, as scholars have shown (Hrdy, 1999; Scheper-Hughes, 1992; Weiss, 1994) and as these mothers attest, is not necessarily a universal script. Mothers throughout the world abandon disabled (and other unwanted) children, give them up for adoption, or let them die from neglect. "Scrutinizing newborn group members is a primate universal," Sarah Hrdy tells us. "But consciously *deciding* whether or not to keep a baby is uniquely human" (Hrdy, 1999: 463). Lorraine Hamilton explains how she came to make her decision:

> I remember when he was born wishing that I didn't love him, wishing I could just give him away and that we didn't have to bring him home. But it was too late. I was already—we were in the hospital for five days and had to stay a little longer because he was having feeding problems. But I remember just wishing I wish I didn't love him. But it was too late, I was already in love with him.

Jane Sawyer confesses that she now realizes that she never really thought of disabled children as people before having one of her own. She attributes the change to love.

> I would go driving down the street and there goes the bus with the handicapped kids and people and adults inside of it, and I'd be like, wow. And now I look at it so differently. I guess I look at them as human beings now, and I *thought* I did before…. Do you think they pick up on that? Because probably—maybe somebody wouldn't pick up on that and say, Oh, no, you were really nice to them, and it's not that I wasn't nice. What is it that was missing? You know what I mean, what *is* that? What is that? And how do you get that across to other people unless—I guess it isn't unless they're *in love* with a handicapped person, do you ever really sense that.

"Blessed With This Mess": Mothers' Transformations

Mothers are well aware that the socially acceptable plot within which to tell their child's life is that of overcoming disability. "I mean, some people have said, 'She'll be okay, right? You can fix it.' That's what they want," Charlotte Andretti observes. "'You can fix it, right?' She's not *broken*; she's deaf." When a child is not imagined as being on a track of progress, a process of healing in which hard work and struggle lead to eventual independence, both child and mother may be conceptualized as failures. However, as we have seen, mothers may recast a child's dependency as a mother's precious opportunity to receive the gift of knowledge of unconditional love. Layne (1999) suggests that for women who have experienced pregnancy loss, rhetoric of the gift becomes a means to reestablish a would-have-been mother as independent and thus as a moral person while simultaneously justifying her being a receiver. The quandary such women face is how to nurture, *to give*, in the absence of a child. For mothers of disabled children, however, the dilemma is that one is *always* giving, whether it be love, nurturance, time, money, or energy and commitment. And in a consumerist society, mothers' investments in "defective" children are constantly questioned; mothers report being openly advised not to "throw their lives away" in caring for a disabled child.

Similar rhetoric of investment is found in the public discourse about the education of disabled children. In a study of newspaper editorials over the course of 30 years, Rice (2006) notes the construction of special education as both a budget item and as a troubled system. As a devourer of resources, it is cast as not worth the money spent on it (Valle, Connor, and Reid, 2006).

Mothers of disabled children utilize gift rhetoric to transform the disabled child from a perpetual receiver into a giver; their child's projected dependency is morally elevated. The mother in turn redefines her sometimes sorrowful and often exhausting giving into an act of receiving. "I used to sit and think about this stuff and cry," reflects a mother of a child with Down syndrome, "but now, I mean, look at what I have got from it." While not what she originally "shopped" for, what she receives is now defined as even more valuable. This enables Tina Graham, mother of a child with mental retardation, to claim, "I really have been blessed with this mess, if you want to call it that. The *world* would say you have a mess."

The story being told here is not about the *child* changing but rather about those nurturing the child changing. The child in this story has intrinsic value from start to end, value that does not exist *in spite of* current disability and needs no validation through efforts to overcome disability; rather, value is enhanced *because of* disability. The story of developmental delay within which many mothers first emplot events of their child's life and which structures their own lived experience, anticipates an ending in which the child, after long struggle, approaches normalcy; the plot of the "child as giver" story, by contrast, documents not the *child's* journey but rather the *mother's*. It is a journey from prejudice and commodification to enlightenment and a profound redefinition of personhood. As we stood by the door saying good-byes after a long interview, Peggy Hoffmeister quietly reflected that for all its pain, the experience of mothering her autistic child was, after all, interesting, because "it's really put me in tune with what it means to be human."

Though mothers reflect on how the experience of mothering a disabled child brought them to recognize their own child's personhood, what is perhaps more significant is how many mothers generalized, claiming to now appreciate the personhood of others they once deemed to be less valuable human beings. Speaking first about raising her daughter with hydrocephaly and mental retardation, Denise Rivers moves on to describe the changes it has made in how she views other children as well. "You look at everything differently…. No matter how people look at her, she's still beautiful to you. And *every kid*, it doesn't matter." Becky Romano talks about how once she would have stared or been afraid of a child with deformities; having her own disabled child has changed her such that "where you would want to almost look at that child and run the other way because it would give you goosebumps, now I want to go over and you know, sit down and say 'Hi, sweetie.'" Judith Larson now understands that "if you look at a child in a wheelchair, you see a child in a wheelchair, but what it really is is another unique individual." She finds it "amazing how many children with disabilities there are, but they're still little kids, they're still little *people*."

For Kim Boland, the experience of mothering a child with Down syndrome and autism opened her eyes to the presence and injustice of other forms of social hierarchy:

> I was never really a prejudiced person, but I never really looked at how black people felt or whatever. You really think about it today and its all along the same lines. People judge how a black person is and that's not fair. I guess it's really opened up another world for a lot of people. My father is a prejudiced person, not to the point where he wouldn't talk to a black person, but I used to hear him say things when I was younger and now I think about it and I think that was really bad for him to say around us.

Similarly, Tina Graham surmises that as parents of disabled children, there is "more of a compassion in your heart, not only for disabled people, but for their loved ones, for everything. I mean, it just changes your whole heart. I mean it really kind of scrapes off some of the hard surface and just softens us to people."

Outside the norm, dependent, and permanently imperfect in a society in which perfection is deemed attainable and normal, the disabled child once appeared as less than a full person. In an era in which mothers' social worth resides in their association with valued children (McMahon, 1995: 190), the woman who gives birth to a disabled child may herself be less than a full mother. However, the child's gift of knowledge of unconditional love provides mothers a vocabulary with which to develop a critique of consumer culture as it has entered the domain of reproduction. Portraying their child as giver of a gift, not for which they were specially chosen but which they learned, through any normal mother's love, to receive, mothers reinstate their child's full personhood, situating it in opposition to the consumerism and social hierarchy that would devalue their children, their own motherhood, and indeed the lives of countless others.

6

ON MOTHERING, MODELS, AND DISABILITY RIGHTS

We're doing everything you'd do for a regular child, but maybe a little bit later. I say regular as opposed to normal. Somehow normal just doesn't— there is no normal.

(Darlene Mulligan)

My third child is now 15 years old. She is a bright-eyed, hard-working, usually cheerful, endearingly mischievous, and occasionally overly sensitive ninth grader with a keen appreciation for silliness and for a good (or even not-so-good) joke. Her name is "DJ" (for Dorothy Jean), and she has cerebral palsy. Nurturing her raised the questions that brought this book into being. So in the concluding chapter of this work, I very briefly return to the personal experience that served as its inspiration. In doing so, my intent is not to indulge in personal confession but to give life to the ambiguities and paradoxes inherent in the American experience of mothers encountering and living with a child's disability.

There was a time when I used to wonder, what if someone—a magician, a god, a doctor—were to say to me, "I have the power to remove your daughter's disabilities"? In spite of my great respect for—and theoretical agreement with—the disability rights position that discourages the quest for cures in favor of efforts to ensure a public policy of universal design and civil rights, I know that without a moment's hesitation I would respond, "Yes, please, give my daughter clear speech so that others could understand her thoughts and desires." If that wish were to be granted, I would unabashedly beg that she be given the ability to make her hands do whatever she bid them to do: eat with a spoon, call a friend on a cell

171

phone, dress herself, make her own peanut butter sandwich, hold a pen or type on a computer with ease. And if there were gifts still to be given, yes, I suppose I might even ask that she get out of her wheelchair and walk. And yet, paradoxically, I suspect that such a joyous day would also be one of profound loss for me. For all my ability to fantasize in other areas of life (world peace, a cure for cancer, having enough free time to read all the novels I want), I can no longer even imagine who my daughter would be without her disabilities. Is there a separate self, the "real" DJ who would emerge from being "trapped" inside a disabled body? Is she, in the language of one version of the North American disability rights movement, a "person first," someone with her own distinct personality who just happens to have a disability as one of her many characteristics but who would change little if her disability were to disappear? Or is who she is so intimately integrated with her body and its impairments and/or with her social experience of disability so as to be inseparable from them? Without the very impairments and disability I seek to eliminate, would she be someone else? Mothering a child who "departs from what is understood to be species typical" (Asch, 1998: 77) brings us to the very heart and soul of anthropological questioning: What is it that makes us human? What constitutes self and identity? What is unique and what the same about each of us? What sense can and should we make of profound differences within our shared humanity?

The perspective of mothers of disabled children on these issues is particularly appropriate for responding to the recent call for anthropologists to convey not only insights *about* but the insights *of* those we study into public policy debates (Anglin, 2002: 565). Often depicted as obstacles to disability rights—for perpetuating children's dependency, for relentlessly seeking cures, and/or for colluding in their public portrayal as self-sacrificing "saints" tending to pitiable disabled bodies—mothers may nevertheless be well positioned to contribute to public policy discussion and to the development of more complex conceptualizations of disability. "When someone depends on someone else to do physical things for them," disabled feminist researcher Jenny Morris has noted, " the more personal the task the greater the potential for abuse of human rights—and the greater the potential for the 'caregiver' to protect and promote human rights" (Morris, 2001: 14).

A goal of this chapter is to examine how mothers' experiences and interpretations position them in relation to models of disability in disability studies[1] and in relation to the discourses and politics of disability rights activism. The intent is to enable what women have learned from nurturing disabled children and debates now taking place within the field of disability studies to mutually inform each other. The ultimate challenge of this work is not to determine how what we know about mothers of disabled children can be used to help parents "adjust" to or "cope" with children's disability but rather to imagine how what mothers of disabled children have come to know can be used to further our understanding of humanity and to promote the expression and experience of full lives for all people.

The Medical Model

Contemporary American mothers nurturing disabled children have available contending models with which to interpret and make sense of disability and identity. Models themselves are not theories or explanations, nor can they be proven wrong through disconfirming evidence; rather they are representations in which one established and well-understood system is applied to a less well understood system (Llewellyn and Hogan, 2000: 157). Any model is therefore a social construction. In various settings from doctors' offices and shopping malls to family living rooms and Internet Web sites, mothers in the study interact with competing models, blending and reworking them in complex ways that provide insights into yet other possibilities for conceptualizing disability.

The medical model of disability portrays disability as a pathology located within the body or mind of an individual; the power to define and treat disabled people resides within the medical profession, and it is incumbent upon disabled people or their caregivers to seek expertise. This model structured the World Health Organization's controversial 1980 International Classification of Impairments, Disabilities and Handicaps (ICIDH), in which impairments were defined as abnormalities of body or organ structures and functions and disabilities defined as the reduction of a person's abilities to perform basic tasks as a consequence of such abnormalities (Simeonsson, et al., 2000). In their interactions with physicians, mothers often encounter the medical model in the form of doctors attributing labels that, in the absence of a cure, locate a child permanently outside the norm. Engaging with early intervention service providers such as physical or occupational therapists, mothers may experience the model in its rehabilitation variant; here disability may appear as temporary developmental delay with the goal being to approximate the norm or compensate for functional liabilities. Whether as permanent damage or temporary delay, in the medical model there is a "problem" which is understood to derive from the impairment itself.

The medical model has perhaps made its most controversial entry into public discourse with the recent disclosure of the "Ashley treatment," a specific combination of medical procedures performed at Seattle Children's Hospital on a profoundly disabled girl at her parents' request. Ashley's parents describe their daughter as a "Pillow Angel," a "beautiful girl whose body is developing normally with no external deformities" (http://ashleytreatment.spaces.live.com/blog/). She is, they write on their blog, a well-loved "sweet" child who stays right where they place her. Ashley is tube-fed and cannot keep her head up, roll or change her sleeping position, nor hold a toy or talk. Ashley's parents describe their concern that as their daughter got physically larger she would be more difficult to care for at home; in particular, she would be harder to transport, reducing her participation in family life. Ashley's mother sought and received for her daughter surgical and medical intervention to arrest Ashley's adult height and weight. The hospital's ethics committee formally approved the procedures.

In an article published in the fall of 2006 in *Archives of Pediatric and Adolescent Medicine*, the doctors involved described the growth attenuation treatment intended to improve Ashley's future quality of life. They argued that after proper screening and informed consent, the therapy should be a therapeutic option available to non-ambulatory children with severe, combined neurologic and cognitive impairment (Gunther and Diekema, 2006). The medical procedure entailed high doses of estrogen, which closed Ashley's growth plates and reduced her projected height by about 13 inches. Even more controversial, however, was the surgical removal of Ashley's uterus for the purpose of eliminating menstruation and its discomfort. (The hospital later acknowledged that in carrying out a hysterectomy on a developmentally disabled six-year-old without court authorization, it had violated Washington State law.) An additional and equally controversial part of the "treatment" was the surgical removal of the girl's breast buds; her parents claimed that Ashley was not in need of developed breasts as she would never breastfeed a baby and that they "would only be a source of discomfort to her," particularly in light of her maternal and paternal female lineage of large-breasted women.[2] In citing additional benefits of breast bud removal, Ashley's parents explain that "large breasts could 'sexualize' Ashley towards her caregiver, especially as they are touched while she is being moved or handled." Regardless of stated intentions, as a result of the procedures, Ashley could now appear to be a child, her parents' "Pillow Angel," forever.

Much of the ensuing debate revealed contestation over what constitutes being a good parent for a disabled child. For disability rights activist John Hockenberry (2007), the Ashley treatment both violates the personhood of the child and voids the parental relationship:

> I am not going to argue that Ashley's parents are immoral or unjustified in what they did. I will argue that they are no longer Ashley's parents. Regardless of their love and affection for their daughter their decision to remove her breasts and uterus and maintain her in a state of pre-puberty is not a parental decision. It is more the kind of control one might enforce on a pet to manage the relationship. It is something a farmer managing the productivity of his or her operation would naturally enforce on livestock. This would be done humanely, morally, and no-doubt with considerable tender affection and love for the subjects. There would be no outcry and no controversy, yet no one would confuse these acts of husbandry as parenthood.

In response to those who criticize the treatment as an affront to disabled people's dignity, physician Gunther tellingly posed a question: "Is there more dignity in having to hoist a full-grown body in harness and chains from bed to bath to wheelchair?" "Ashley," Gunther continued, "will always have the mind of an infant, and now she will be able to stay where she belongs—in the arms of the family that loves her" (quoted in Gibbs, 2007). While this appears as an affirmation of parental love, underlying Gunther's question is an assumption that the combination of adulthood and cognitive impairment is both incongruous and degrading.

Princeton bioethicist Peter Singer makes a similar argument, albeit by rejecting the very premise of the debate over dignity. Three-month-old babies, he argues, "are adorable but not dignified. Nor do I believe that getting bigger and older, while remaining at the same mental level, would do anything to change that" (Singer, 2007). Also weighing in on the issue is George Dvorsky, a member of the Board of Directors for the Institute for Ethics and Emerging Technologies on his blog Sentient Developments (2006), who was quoted by Ashley's parents: "The estrogen treatment is not what is grotesque here. Rather, it is the prospect of having a full-grown and fertile woman endowed with the mind of a baby."

In these latter arguments, a low level of cognitive function, particularly (but in Singer's case not exclusively) with an adult body, precludes dignity. Few would contest that in the United States as in much of the world, adults with profound mental retardation are not accorded great respect. However, when framed within a medical model, the solution for this problem is neither to challenge popular belief in the inherent indignity of mental retardation, nor to improve services to assist families caring for their mentally retarded children as they age but rather to surgically and chemically intervene in the individual child's body itself. Through the Ashley treatment, body and mind are made to appear consistent with each other, as that consistency is culturally constructed. Ashley's mind cannot be brought to an adult level, but in the next best approximation of normalcy, her body is medically altered to ensure its perpetual childlike appearance. The issue of why adult status is incompatible with dependency is an issue I will address later. The point for the moment is the medical model's positing of the individual as both the source of disability and as the site for intervention in the pursuit of normalcy.

Some have categorized medical and rehabilitation models together with the special education model as three variations of a deficit model.

> Each model specifies a deficit (health condition, employment condition, learning condition) which must be corrected to make the person with a disability "normal." Of course many of these conditions cannot be corrected (whatever that means) so that the person with a disability will never be allowed to be normal (whatever that means).
>
> (Pfeiffer, 2002: 3)

The medical model, historian Paul Longmore points out, "has dominated modern policy making, professional practice, and societal arrangements regarding people with disabilities" (Longmore and Umansky, 2001: 7). Critics have argued that it has advanced the agenda of professional interest groups, resulting in disabled people serving as a source of profit, power, and status for them (Longmore, 1995).

The medical model is the perspective on disability that most mothers in the study brought with them to their experience of having a child and the one into which they were shepherded by the early intervention system. Yet, as will be seen later, when brought to bear on a woman's own child, the model appears to be situationally anchored; women utilize the medical model but also actively negotiate with it.

Assuming a binary opposition between the categories of normal and disabled, the medical model has broad social implications. The historian Douglas Baynton suggests that this notion of disability may to a large extent underlie social hierarchy itself, in that disability has been used in the West to constitute a range of *other* cultural categories as well. Categories such as race and gender, for instance, have been shown to be constructed as binary oppositions with one side posited as the norm and the other as deviation, as in the "universal" male in opposition to the "deviant" female, the "normal" European American in opposition to the "abnormal" African, and the like. He points to how historically opponents of equality for women cited women's supposed physical, intellectual, or psychological deficits or deviations from the male norm, just as immigration laws at the turn of the century used disability to limit the entry of national or racial groups said to be prone to physical or mental degeneracy. "It may be that to some extent all social hierarchies rely upon culturally constructed and socially sanctioned notions of disability" (Baynton, 1997: 85). Elaborating on the degrading exhibition in nineteenth-century Europe of the African woman Saartje Bartmann as the "Hottentot Venus," Rosemarie Garland Thomson points specifically to ways in which the concept of disability has been used to cast what is normative embodiment in one cultural context as abnormal and inherently inferior; a culture's gender, race, and ability systems, she demonstrates, are intertwined (Thomson, 2004: 78).

In seeking their rights, members of denigrated social categories have themselves relied upon the binary opposition of normal and abnormal.

Woman suffragist Henrietta Briggs-Wall's poster "American Women and Her Political Peers," for example, depicts the Women's Christian Temperance Movement leader Frances Willard in the same legal category as Indians, criminals, "lunatics," and the mentally retarded, (Landsman, 1992: 270–272); it plays upon the viewers' sense of moral outrage at this political juxtaposition of normal, morally upright women and abnormal, deviant men. The assumption is neither that universal rights should be recognized nor that the dichotomy of normal and abnormal should be dismissed as inaccurate or artificial but rather that women of a particular social class are unjustly categorized with those (deviants) who may "justifiably" be denied full citizenship. The binary itself, as well as its grounding in disability, is maintained in this political stance; the debate is only over who should be placed in which category. "Oppressed groups do not challenge the basic construction of the hierarchy but instead work to remove themselves from the negatively marked categories, to disassociate themselves from those who 'really are' disabled" (Baynton, 1997: 86). On an individual level, many mothers first encountering a diagnosis of disability utilize the same strategy in regard to their child; in doing so, they justify the attribution of full personhood to their own disabled child in a culture in which personhood is diminished by disability (Landsman, 1997, 1998, 1999).

Upon first hearing their child diagnosed with a developmental delay or disability then, many mothers rejected the designation of their child as disabled (i.e., as "abnormal"). As we have seen in Chapter 4, mothers in the study told numerous "the-doctor-was-wrong" stories, in which they describe being given misdiagnoses and dismal predictions that were later proven wrong by a child. Overcoming past obstacles and/or predictions made during hospitalization (such as that a child would not survive or would be permanently blind, for instance), became incorporated into plot lines in which the child would continue to progress and ultimately disprove a doctor's label of permanent disability. Though in these stories these women rejected the authority of the physician to define their child, their resistance was not a rejection of the medical model itself but only of the accuracy of a particular medical professional's judgment in placing an individual in a specific category. This was particularly the case for mothers of children who were diagnosed through observation and clinical judgment rather than through laboratory tests such as chromosomal studies or brain scans, which were more often taken as authoritative. For example, Tara Vernon questioned whether her daughter fit the classification of autism.

> Sometimes she doesn't have all the characteristics; you're like, is she misdiagnosed, and because we're treating her in this fashion that she will show more symptoms?.... It's not something I focus on all the time, but you know, you watch these stories of a person who didn't have any psychological problems is put in a psychiatric ward, and all of a sudden they're—so it's not a cut and dry diagnosis. It's because of their characteristics that it's diagnosed. It's not like they did blood work and said, guess what, she's got Downs because of her chromosomes, you know?

In resisting an evaluator's placement of her child in a marked or stigmatized category, many mothers cite contradictory prognoses given by different physicians and therapists. Lisa Hart, the mother of a child diagnosed by a neurologist with cerebral palsy and mental retardation, describes being given the latter diagnosis:

> On the last report he sent us, on the end he had "mental retardation." Just threw down there. So, I called him. I said, "On what basis are you saying she's mentally retarded?" "Well, she has microcephaly and a lot of kids who have that end up having mental retardation and she's really far behind."…. Meanwhile all her reports from her therapists are saying that she's doing really well, and you know, it was just like he just added this on like it was like no big deal. I said, "And what test did you give her to come up with this assessment?" I was in the office. He said, "Well, none." I said, "Well, I think usually they give you a test before they just put that on there." He's like, "Well, it's the same as developmental delay but she's more than 10 percent behind so instead of it being developmental delay, it's mental retardation." I said, "I don't think so." So, it was funny. I went and I spoke with her pediatricians about it and they were like, "Oh, she's way too young to be labeled—you know, we certainly don't think she is from what we see, and he didn't even give her a test"…. It was always developmental delay and, you know—and her therapists were all like, "You know, we don't see that. We see her making good strides and she's very bright" and her new OT [occupational therapist] just thinks she's like a little whipper-snapper…

Mothers may accept medical categories, but they exercise agency in determining which medical experts to believe. Their narratives commonly involve the criticism that the doctors did not have enough time with a child to make an accurate assessment, that a child exhibits certain behaviors and capabilities at home but chose not to during the evaluation, or that the child was particularly shy or tired that day. Michelle White claims to have "pretty much dismissed the PDD," a diagnosis on the autistic spectrum. "You know I just don't think that for the short amount of time that Dr. Svenson was in the room watching Brittany, I was just very shocked that she came up with the diagnosis that quickly...." During an interview, Sara Anderson reminded me that at the evaluation, her daughter, diagnosed with microcephaly due to strep B infection, did not follow a red toy and that when she dropped her head she didn't show the reflexes to come back up; however, Sara counters that her daughter in fact does follow toys and have the reflex to come up when she is with her at home. Furthermore, she complained, "These doctors are seeing her when she's just taken that phenobarbital, and that phenobarbital has got her so worked up, she gets very aggravated after she takes it. He (doctor) doesn't see how she really is." Physicians and mothers here mutually rely on the medical model, agreeing that diagnoses label intrinsic abnormalities, which in turn predict a child's reduced life opportunities. Conflict between physicians and mothers center on what counts as evidence of disability, not in general but in the case of a specific child. At the risk of being labeled "in denial" or "not ready to face reality," a mother may in such instances declare *herself* as expert.

The medical model measures the child against a standardized norm, with disability appearing as a deficit to which a mother may respond by denying the applicability of a diagnosis to her child or resigning herself to the child's label and its culturally constructed implications. In either case, she is evoking a discourse of pity. Alternatively, she may seek to return the child to the track of linear progress that marks full personhood in American culture. In other words, she may engage in the socially approved project of "overcoming" disability. Yet this is tricky business; to obtain the tools necessary to move the child from disability to normalcy, a mother needs the doctor's documentation of disability or delay; his or her official evaluation opens or closes the gate to early intervention services. To be eligible for services, a child must receive a specific medical diagnosis of a disabling condition such as spina bifida, cerebral palsy, or Down syndrome, or be labeled with a measurable delay: 33% delay in one domain of development or 25% delay in two domains. The disabling condition or degree of delay provides the basis for the Individualized Family Service Plan (IFSP) that commits the services of early intervention providers: speech pathologists, physical therapists, special educators, and the like. Agreeing to these services by signing an IFSP, a mother literally "signs onto" the child's labeled deficit.

New York State's Early Intervention Program makes no promise of a cure and is rather broad in its family-oriented goals: the program's literature states that early intervention can help a parent learn the best ways to care for a child, support and promote a child's development, and include the child in family and community life (New York State Department of Health, 1998: 1). Nevertheless, the commitment mothers expressed to the Early Intervention program, as rendered in Lisa Hart's comments earlier, is largely predicated on their belief that mitigation or elimination of a child's disability is possible through a combination of early intervention services, the commitment of mothers, and the hard work, determination, and strong will of the child. Women across a wide range of educational backgrounds and ages express this belief. Recall that married, college-educated, part-time accountant Patricia Marks refers to herself as a "synapse-builder" who will work with her twin premature daughters to repair brain damage. Similarly, Jean Barbarino, a young, working single mother whose unemployed boyfriend rejected their son diagnosed with cerebral palsy, seeks more physical therapy for her child in the belief that "if it's something that he works with" every day, his body will change.

> They tell people who are paralyzed they're never going to walk. Why do they walk? Because it's just something they worked on every day, right? I mean, your mind is with it, you know, you have the motivation. This child has the motivation. He's got the determination. He wants to do it. Now he needs the help.

In taking this stance, mothers fit squarely within the medical model and its current imagery of the body as project. An extension of the late eighteenth-century notion that life is the raw material with which we are expected to do something, the "contemporary twist on the modern project of the self is that many of us moderns…. include doing things with our bodies among the ways to seek the unique point of our lives" (Frank, 2006: 72). With neoliberal medicine, sociologist Arthur Frank argues, the "flesh as God-given reality—for better or worse, this is how I am— gives way to the flesh as stuff to be worked with by various sorts of body workers…." (2006: 71). Among these body workers are not only the cosmetic surgeons and other physicians who form the focus of Frank's analysis but physical therapists, occupational therapists, special educators, and above all, "good" mothers.

Mothers and the Cure Debate

What are we to make of mothers' desires to help their children change? The passion with which parents seek a "cure" for disability and/or their linkage of a child's value to his or her valiant efforts to overcome disability have seemed to place parents and disability rights at cross purposes. Disability rights activists have long argued for and acted upon what has been called in the British context the "social model" and in the United States, the "minority group" or "civil rights" model of disability. The British social model offers a materialist perspective, focusing on the impact of the capitalist mode of production in the creation of disability, while the minority group model utilized more commonly by American disability scholars points to similarities between those with impairments and other oppressed groups. The different trajectories and divergent theoretical developments of U.K. and U.S. disability studies may be due to history, politics, space, place and the search for identity (Meekosha, 2004). Both disability models, however, locate impediments to a high quality of life *not* primarily within the body of the disabled person (such that the person should be cured, put out of his or her misery, or prevented from being born in the first place) but rather within the society that discriminates against disabled persons.

Central to the social model is the distinction between impairment and disability, perhaps first formally articulated by the Union of the Physically Impaired Against Segregation (UPIAS) in 1976. Impairment in this model refers to bodily dysfunction. Disability for both the social and minority group models, conversely,

is not a medical nor a health question. It is a policy or political issue. A
disability comes not from the existence of an impairment, but from the
reality of building codes, educational practices, stereotypes, prejudicial
public officials... ignorance, and oppression which results in some
people facing discrimination while others benefit from those acts of
discrimination.

(Pfeiffer, 1999: 106)

Impairment is not by definition disabling (Read, 1998: 287). Nor in
this model are the suffering of the family raising the disabled child or the
burden to society of having disabled people inherent consequences of
an individual's impairment or different functional abilities; instead they
are predominantly the result of "a society that fails to provide adequate
resources, and sees disabled people as a financial burden and a drain on
scarce resources" (Triano, 1999). As Dowling and Dolan (2001) argue,
the negative impact on families of caring for a disabled child—stress,
lower income, and the like—do not derive from the burdens of actual
caring but from the constant stream of appointments and therapies,
and the inflexibility of available jobs such that families must live on a
single income, and the like. The response to the Ashley treatment by
the Disability Rights & Education Defense Fund (DREDF), with its
explicit call to provide more services to families of children like Ashley
(see footnote 2), is an example of a political position emerging from a
social or minority group model of disability.

The development of the social and minority group models had a
profound relationship to disability rights movements in Britain and the
United States. They helped set the agenda of these political movements,
the goal becoming not cure but removal of barriers to full inclusion
and citizenship; the models also encouraged disabled people to think
of themselves in new ways, empowering them to take action to change
society rather than to change themselves (Shakespeare, 2001: 10–11).
Consistent with British social models of disability, Harlan Hahn's
(1994) minority group model specifically identified the role played by
public policy in shaping the physical and social environment; in the
U.S. minority group model, public policy is related to both the causes
of and the solutions to disability (Putnam, 2005: 189). The Americans
with Disabilities Act (ADA), passed in 1990 with wording crafted in

part by disability rights activists, represents the establishment in law of a narrative of civil rights and minority group politics (Haller, Dorries, and Rahn, 2006: 67).

Advocates of the social and minority group models of disability have actively criticized parental commitment to rehabilitative therapies designed to help eliminate or overcome impairment. Michael Oliver, for instance, interprets the popularity of "conductive education," an intervention for people with motor disorders, as

> a product of the ideology of the able-bodied individual, for its aim is to teach children with cerebral palsy to walk, talk and engage in all other activities in as near normal way as possible. No consideration is given to the issue of the ideology of "normality" nor to the idea that the environment could be changed rather than the individual.
>
> (Oliver, 1990: 55)

For advocates of the social model, parents are often seen as misplacing their efforts on correcting the impairment rather than on addressing the disabling conditions of society; in this view, rehabilitation therapies encouraged by mothers represent tyranny.

However, the parental goal of seeking a cure and/or of normalizing a disabled child is precisely the stance that is sanctioned by the larger society. It is the role that I, as a mother of a girl with cerebral palsy, am expected to take, and of all the efforts I make on behalf of my child, it is the one for which I am most likely to get credit. Support has been less forthcoming for my activism to get accessible buildings, transportation, and inclusive summer camp programs or for my efforts to negotiate a different work schedule to enable me to accommodate my daughter's daily needs.

Explaining why she, a former "poster child" later came to protest the Jerry Lewis Muscular Dystrophy Telethon, disability rights activist Laura Hershey reflects on the place of "the cure" in American society.

> But for all our progress in the areas of legal protection and accessibility, there's still this lingering attitude that what people with disabilities *really* need is to be cured. Society wants the problem to go away, so it won't have to accommodate people with long-term disabling conditions. It wants *us* to go away, or at least to "get better." One of my major

objections to the telethon is the way it reinforces that attitude.... The *cure* is a simple, magical, non-political solution to all the problems in a disabled person's life. That's why it's so appealing, and so disempowering. The other solutions we have to work for, even fight for; we only have to dream about the cure. The idea of a cure is at least in part an effort to homogenize, to make everyone the same.

Mothers' pursuit of cures is tempered by a deep desire to live a typical life in which women play with their children rather than schedule their lives around therapy appointments, and in which babies are not measured against a fixed scale of developmental milestones but treasured for the joy they bring to their families. Reflecting on mealtimes with her mentally retarded son Jacob, Jennifer Borden explains, "I know they want us to push, they want us to put different... types of foods in his mouth, you know, different consistencies, and... I hate doing it. He's doing this everyday.... You know, can't I just enjoy him?"

"It takes up a lot more energy to think about this," comments Suzanne Dalton. She compares her approach to toys and play with that of mothers of typically developing children. "You know, when baby sitters come and you tell them 'these are the play skills that we want them to follow,' no one else does that with their kid, you know.... When I'm searching in the stores for toys, I'm.... thinking, what kind of skills does he need now? How can I get these things so that it can help him pull and, you know, get good grasping skills? You know... there are periods of time when you think, wow, this is really all consuming!" But in an environment of competitive mothering, individual choice and mother-blame, the yearning to abandon attempts to repair a child's deficits are weighed against the belief that women cannot be good mothers unless their children show "progress." For this reason, some mothers feel the need to protect themselves from information that would divert them from this project.

Women who refused diagnostic tests explained that they did so because they fear that they will treat their child differently by virtue of knowing specific medically sanctioned information, and will thereby do damage to their child. Ironically, most often this is framed in terms of faith in intervention—a concern that if diagnostic tests prove definitive, a mother risks seeing the situation as futile and thus might give up on her efforts to "cure" or mitigate the impairment. The result might be to forego potential progress. A mother of a premature baby at risk for cerebral palsy thus reflects on the value of an undefined future. "I still have this belief that if I don't know, if no one can tell me, maybe I'll treat him differently and maybe he'll be better.... And I just always thank God that there's so many services available to him and we spend so much time with him and we just love him to death.... All these things put together will be as good as he can possibly be. So maybe he'll be just like a normal kid." And ever so tentatively, a mother of a ten-month-old child with severe brain damage challenges the doctor's prognosis during an office visit: "Okay, what if, I'm not saying it's going to happen, I'm trying to be in reality, but what if he do walk?.... He might walk, but I'm still in reality, but what if he do wake up one morning and decide he can walk?"

Mothers' resistance to medical authority and labeling of their child in these cases supports the medical model of disability in which disability is defined as a pathology located within the body and/or mind of an individual and in which disabled individuals are positioned as "less able than those who can recover from illness or who are non-disabled" (Gilson and DePoy, 2000: 207-8). As discussed in Chapter 4, not knowing the pathology leaves room for hope that a child may "overcome" his or her disabilities in spite of doctors' predictions.

Yet some mothers' narratives revealed another, perhaps darker, fear of believing the medical profession's prognosis of permanent disability: that the mother will herself look at her child as less valuable or less worthy of nurturance. Laurel Messerschmidt's comments, presented earlier, take on new meaning in this light. "One of the things that kind of surprised me is that there was like sort of a point where I wanted to push Ellen away," she explained.

> You know, it was sort of like, I felt like, I just sort of thought of the stuff we learned in school about when an animal perceives one of the pups is not going to make it, sort of push him away, and it was sort of like an unconscious thought that rose to the surface to a certain extent. And after a short time, it's sort of the—she's not perfect, so I'm not sure I want her, type of thing, and that was kind of a difficult couple of days.

"When was that?" I asked her. "It was after we'd been to the doctor, and we actually had a horror story," was the reply.

This interview excerpt represents an intriguing reflexivity, for it reveals a mother's awareness both of her child's inherent value and human rights, and of her own socialization in a culture in which personhood is diminished by the label of disability. In this context, "not knowing" becomes an act of preserving her child's status as normal not only for a woman's own psychological needs, as the concept of denial would suggest, but for purposes of shielding her child from discrimination, in this case discrimination by the mother herself. Mothers accept the medical model's authority to define disability as a deficit or defect of the individual, yet at the same time, reveal a belief in a *disablement process*, a fledgling recognition that disability may not only be about impaired bodies but about societal attitudes and politics as well.

Disability as Oppression

Indeed, when asked what their greatest concern for the future was, mothers consistently responded not in terms of their child's physical or cognitive impairment itself, but rather in terms of how the child would be treated by others. This concern was raised by mothers of all social classes and educational levels, and appeared regardless of the type of impairment.

> I laid awake and thought about it.... Is he going to get a prom date? Kids are going to make fun of it. This is going to be terrible.
>
> (Donna Leiden)

> I worry about kids maybe picking on him because he'll be the smallest. I worry about if he still has the flat spot on his head kids are going to make fun of him for that. I know kids can be pretty mean at times. Those are things I'm thinking about where I hope he doesn't have to deal with, but I don't really know.
>
> (Mary Jane Pickard)

> I worry that she's a girl, and that some boy's going to take advantage of her as she gets older because she's not going to be quite as with it as other

kids. And I worry about what other kids are going to say to her, and do to her, and all that kind of stuff.

(Mother of a girl with Down syndrome)

I don't know that this will answer your question but I'm going to say it anyway. My biggest fear for him is, I mean, I've heard people talk, you know, as I was growing up making fun of people, things like that, that's really my biggest. I don't want him to have to ever hear or deal with that. I know that to some extent he will and he's a very smart child no matter what the doctors are able to test for. And he knows. He knows what you're saying and that's my—really, I just hope he doesn't ever have to hear or listen to that.... He's, you know, still my little boy and not matter what he can or can't do...

(Lucy Baker)

I don't care what is wrong with her, but I don't want her to go to school and stuff, or go out on the street and people will pick on her. That's what angers me.... Because I see how people are, and how I sometimes see it, you know, people driving up the street in a wheelchair and you're like, "get out of the road or I'll hit you." I don't want people to pick on her.

(Sara Anderson)

I mean, what does the future hold for her? Do they get to have a family life or do they live singly by themselves? ....That part bothers me, I think, more than anything else. What happens when I die and she's left here by herself? Is she going to be by herself the rest of her life? Is she ever going to have a partner? I mean, that part, because that's normal, and that part is hard.

(Alice Brooks)

I worry about the first time he's in preschool or daycare. And the kids have to hold hands and how the kids are going to react to it. And then, everybody tells me, and I see it anyway because I'm a teacher, well kids make fun of each other anyway. Like this one's fat or that one's ugly or this one's stupid and that one's got a lisp. And I understand that. But that's something that everybody has to contend with. But then he's got this on top of that. He could turn out to be a *fat* kid with no hand, you know.

(Connie Brown)

I worry a lot about what people are going to think about her…. What her perception of other people's perception of her is, and that again, gets into the issue of school, and sometimes I do have images of her being ridiculed, and that's the hardest thing.

(Terry Johnson)

Although not conversant with the terms so central to the language of disability rights and the social/minority group models of disability, in conceiving their child's future, mothers over and over again distinguished between impairment and disability. Asked her concerns for the future, "Well, I don't know—how the world will treat him" was the reply of a mother of a child with cerebral palsy. Echoing the concerns raised by mother after mother in the study, she continued, "Not really how he'll be. He'll be fine, but how other people treat him…."

The rhetoric of the disability rights movement often appears accusatory of parents, charging them with attempting to "fix" or "normalize" their disabled children. This study suggests that this accusation is in itself valid, particularly for mothers whose children have been recently identified as disabled; however the study also reveals that the efforts at normalization may not necessarily preclude understandings consistent with the British social model or American minority model of disability. Like disability rights activists and proponents of the social and minority group models, mothers of newly diagnosed disabled children do, as the excerpts above reveal, believe that the greatest obstacles to a child's happiness and development are not a child's biologically based impairment, but rather the prejudice of the larger society. The most detrimental issue, they recognize and openly express, is not truly located within the child. Yet the narratives of mothers just encountering a prognosis of disability also reveal more faith that their *child* can be changed than that *society* can.

Amundson notes that when individuals try to hide their disability, their behavior has been interpreted patronizingly, "as evidence of the failure to accept one's limitations." He argues that such attempts at passing for non-disabled should instead be seen as a rational "recognition on the part of disabled people of a deep social prejudice against them" (Amundson, 2000). Many mothers denying a physician's diagnosis or engaged in efforts to "fix" their children may indeed be failing to accept their child's limitations; but they, like disabled individuals trying to "pass," may also be strategically assessing and acting upon the discrimination they know confronts those with impairments.

Mothers' analysis of disability is in this way not inconsistent with the social and minority group models developed within disability studies and the disability rights movement—disability is, for most mothers, understood to be caused by prejudice, oppression, and the denial of agency and autonomy. But the (immediate) *response* of mothers remains rooted in the individualized, medical model of disability. In the first round of interviews, women tend to describe their role as mothers as involving protecting their child from the discrimination they fear for them in the future. This role is generally not conceptualized in terms of political action but in terms of making sure that their child appears as "normal" or as consistent with American values as possible. This effort may address skills or knowledge, as in the case of Alice Brooks, a mother whose daughter has Down syndrome.

> It is very important to me that she speaks as normally as possible to the point that—see, that's going to be one of her stumbling blocks, I think. If she can't speak right, no one is going to want to listen to her, and they're going to shut off quicker. Her appearance is going to be part of it, but if she can't carry herself properly, then I am going to be in real trouble with her, and I don't want that. I want her to go to college. I want her to live as normal a life as possible that we can give her.

This same mother, a married, part-time waitress, also sought information about a special vitamin regimen for children with Down syndrome. Her goal was not to change her daughter's personality or intelligence level, but rather her physical appearance; it is on the basis of appearance, Alice and many other mothers believe, that society makes judgments that will determine employment and other opportunities in life. In this excerpt, Alice discusses not only her own daughter, but mine as well, predicting society's reaction to our children if intervention does not occur.

> She is what she is. I asked about the vitamin hoping that it would change her outward appearance, not her inside. It's more important for outward appearance because people judge you on the outside first, nothing inside.

Your daughter's probably very intelligent but no one's ever going to know that because they're not going to give her a chance, unfortunately. And that is sad. And that really, really bothers me a lot. Maybe she'll (daughter Susan) change people, I don't know. Hopefully, she can make a difference, and maybe people will look at her and say, gee, she has Down's, but she's intelligent. You know, gee, she doesn't have to sweep floors, she doesn't have to bag groceries. And that's not good enough for me and I won't accept that for her. You know, I wait tables because I choose to, not because I'm not intelligent enough.

Women may refer to their experience as mothers as helping them to see through the petty values of a consumerist society; nevertheless in the name of protecting their disabled children from discrimination, mothers claim to make an additional effort to ensure that their disabled child has the material goods that society associates with valued persons.

I said to Barbara, I said, "I make a point when we go out that they look spectacular." And I said, "without it being, you know, over-kill"… because I always want the first thing that they hear somebody say is "how pretty you look." Or "how pretty you are." I said, before you get the, "how come you've got those on your legs? or "why do you wear glasses?" or whatever… and I have encouraged other people to do that, especially folks who have had some bad experiences with their kids out in public. Because people pay attention to how the kid's dressed and, you know, this and that. And, I mean, even as babies; I had one lady, you know, point out to me one day that she didn't think that those socks and clothes went. And I just went, well, *I* did, you know; okay well, we'll not put this together in this combination again!

(Patricia Marks, mother of twin premature girls with cerebral palsy)

You know your kid gets picked on if he wears cheap sneakers, you know. You know they're going to get picked on if they look different, if they act different. That's one thing that we always say, that no matter what we have to do he's always going to have, like he has to wear glasses, and we kind of got him the style like yours. But when we first got him glasses we had Medicaid and all Medicaid wanted to cover was those big plastic, cat eye, ugly…I'm like why do they do that? This kid has enough problems without having to be picked on about his glasses. It only makes his problem worse. And we're always going to make sure that he has… well, he can only wear nice sneakers because his feet don't go in other ones, but we'll always make sure that he has at least the things that make him look the same as the other kids.

(Kim Boland, mother of son with autism and Down syndrome)

Mothers here clearly locate disability not within their child but within the external society; they appear to locate the "solution," however, in attempts to normalize their child either through image management (reducing the appearance of impairment) or through the search for a cure. Mothers' analyses of the limitations facing their children thus share with advocates of social and minority group models a rejection of the medical model with its "focus on impairment as the defining characteristic of life as a disabled person." They agree that "it is social barriers which create disability, and that the difficulties of living as a disabled person are due to discrimination and prejudice, rather than impairment" (Shakespeare, 1998: 670). Yet in seeking to prevent or mitigate the pain they anticipate their child experiencing from this discrimination, most mothers nevertheless act within the medical model's perspective "that the human being is flexible and 'alterable' while society is fixed and unalterable," and with the model's emphasis "upon adaptation to the environment" and individual effort (Llewellyn and Hogan, 2000: 158).

The bind in which mothers and children find themselves is exemplified in the experience of Jean Barbarino, a single mother whose own mother often cares for Jean's young son with cerebral palsy while Jean is at work. Jean resents the pressure to change her child, and is frustrated that the child's impairments, features of his anatomy, are assumed by most people to be transitory. Speaking of her boyfriend (the child's father) she says

I've got his father who insists…. "Gee, this kid ought to be walking. He ought to be doing this by now." "How much longer are they going to be doing the physical therapy on him?" [she mimics] Then I got my mother on the other side. "Boy, I hope this kid starts walking in the summertime. I don't know what I'm going to do if he doesn't start walking." EXCUSE ME, PEOPLE! HE MIGHT NOT WALK!

Nevertheless, Jean cannot bear to actually say as much to her mother, who she describes as a simple woman who wouldn't understand.

Jean is painfully aware of negative reactions to impairment. The day before our interview Jean had asked her live-in boyfriend, the boy's father, to sign Social Security benefits papers which indicated the child's diagnosis; it bothered him so much to admit that his son was disabled that he left home without signing the papers, and had not yet returned. Asked about whether she had sought respite services, Jean commented, "I don't need somebody to come in to help me out so I can get out. I just want to be able to take him with me." She seeks, in other words, to include her son in the social life of which she believes he should be a part. The obstacles to this goal are matters both of anatomy and prejudice, as well as of Jean's position in a class-stratified society. The child's body is so stiff that Jean is unable to separate his legs enough to carry him on her hip like most other children his age. Jean worries about the social exclusion she foresees for him. She talks at length about her current struggles to locate and afford a stroller that would accommodate her son's unique body so that he might participate in everyday outings; at the same time, she fights to get her county to pay for more physical therapy to help enable him to learn to walk. Thus to the outside world, including her own mother, she masks the permanency of her son's differences, while she simultaneously strives for societal change, her son's fair share of resources, and a biological cure through therapy.

"I see the situation disabled people are in," explains disabled writer and activist Cal Montgomery, "as unjust, not tragic. Created and sustained by society—which is to say, by all of us—and therefore potentially changeable." Writing in the online disability journal *Ragged Edge*, she explains "I'm not interested in changing myself into the sort of person society automatically enables; I'm interested in changing society so that it enables all its members." Yet by Montgomery's own admission, "the process of making the world better is not an easy one. Even imagining the kind of world you're shooting for is hard to do" (Montgomery, 2004). Through the experience of mothering a disabled child, many women do come to reject the medical model on the grounds that it denies full personhood to their child, yet ironically they appear to be acting on the medical model by seeking to have their child overcome or minimize disability, i.e., to change into the sort of person society enables. The goal of overcoming disability in this case may not exclusively be, as some disability rights advocates suggest it is, because mothers themselves still hold to a normative standard of development or because they struggle, as indeed many do, with limited resources; it may also be because mothers worry that their cherished children will face social ostracism and prejudice well before societal attitudes can be changed. "The process of making the world better," after all, "is not an easy one." To a woman striving to be a good mother, the promise of individual cure may sometimes appear more immediately realizable than does a welcoming society.

In representing a child as a "giver" a mother establishes the child as morally superior to others, but she nevertheless also believes that the gift her child has given may have come at the expense of the child's social acceptance. Caring for and publicly representing her child on a daily basis, she predicts that impairment will be an experience not only of bodily or cognitive limitation, but of social construction as the disabled "Other," in which her child will feel the pain of being out of place in the world. A mother can therefore simultaneously morally elevate her child's personhood to or beyond that of typical children, be truly grateful for having been given the gift of unconditional love, and still wish for, and work toward, her child being cured.

Mothers and Critiques of the Social Model Within Disability Studies

In understanding how mothers of children diagnosed with disabilities can hold this paradoxical position regarding their disabled children, it becomes necessary to address in a more nuanced manner the ways in which disability is caused by discrimination rather than anatomy. The Disability Rights Movement, with the social model as its "theoretical linchpin," has set as a major goal to remove restrictions and increase access to social contexts from which disabled people have been denied (Shuttleworth, 2002: 113). This has led to a focus on the removal of structural barriers in the public domain; in the United States, arenas such as employment opportunities and access to public facilities can, and in many instances, have, been addressed through legal means. The Americans with Disabiities Act (ADA) is perhaps the most significant example. But, as Shuttleworth argues, within other domains, such as in what in American culture are considered the private interactions of love and friendship, oppression is less easily amenable to change through public policy.

> In love, personal prejudices reflecting social attitudes toward disabled people, cultural meanings of disability and hierarchies of desirability are… given free rein. Access to this interpersonal context for disabled people thus cannot rely on the rule of law or public policy. As one man with cerebral palsy phrased it, "I don't give a flying fuck about the ADA because that's not gonna get me laid."
>
> (Shuttleworth, 2002: 113)

In movements predicated on civil rights, calls for geographical access to a community seem logical and appropriate. Interpersonal access to community, however, is another matter. "We consider it perfectly reasonable to demand that people put up with neighbors and classmates and coworkers that they might not want to include; but don't believe anybody has the right to demand that someone else be their friend" (Montgomery, 2004).

In revisiting the interview transcripts we see that it is precisely within the contexts of interpersonal relations, rather than structural access, that most mothers locate the most feared aspects of disability. Is she going to be alone the rest of her life? Will he get a date to the prom? Will another child hold his deformed hand? Will she be picked on and teased? Will people listen to her? In short, will my child experience love, friendship, and family? These are the questions that worry mothers. These worries derive from a focus on lived experience, the area critics within disability studies contend the social model has neglected. The "dominance of masculinist, anti-experiential perspectives in social modelist work has had the effect of privileging the 'restrictions on doing' dimensions of disability over its 'restrictions on being' dimensions," argues Carol Thomas (Thomas and Corker, 2002: 19). My research suggests that it is overcoming restrictions on *being* that underlies the efforts of mothers doing the work of nurturing disabled children.

The field of disability studies has successfully worked to demedicalize disability, defining disability as the outcome of oppression and discrimination, and portraying the medical control of disabled people as politically motivated and dangerous. The medical model "buys into the assumption that people with disabilities are more concerned with cures than rights, are more plagued with their condition than with discrimination" (Linton, et al., 1995: 8).

The social or minority group models of disability on the other hand, have been liberating in directing action toward social and political change, and in wresting agency from the hands of the medical profession. "Nothing about us without us," disability activists have argued in efforts to implement policy. And indeed, they have demonstrated that discriminatory practices and physical and institutional obstacles *can* be remedied (Asch, 1998: 78). In the United States, the Independent Living Movement redirected the medical model's focus on impairment to address restrictive environments and social attitudes; the creation of Centers for Independent Living helped to develop a cross-disability identity and enabled people with disabilities to become role models for contending with discrimination (Kasnitz and Shuttleworth, 2001: 24–25). But some claim that the very success of the social model in Britain is now its weakness (Shakespeare, 2001: 11). A powerful tool, the social model effectively became, Shakespeare claims, a "sacred cow," a litmus test by which disability activists are judged. In its strong version, the public presentation of the model is inconsistent with the real lives of disabled people. "Most activists concede that behind closed doors they talk about aches and pains and urinary tract infections, even while they deny any relevance of the body while they are out campaigning" (Shakespeare, 2001: 12). In *Disability Rights and Wrongs*, Shakespeare (2006) faults the British social model for its unsustainable distinction between impairment and disability, its claim that all disability can be removed by social change, and its downplaying of the role of impairment in the lives of disabled people. Like sex and gender within feminist analyses, in which sex refers to the biological and gender to social relations of inequality, the dichotomous framing of impairment and disability is now being challenged. Disabled people, Tom Shakespeare argues, experience the problems both of impairment and of disability, and a developed social theory of disability must encompass both aspects (1998: 671).

As scholars have more recently noted, while heavily reliant upon the medical model for its diagnosis, impairment may itself be socially constructed (Davis, 2002: 23). Shaken baby syndrome, for example, was identified as an impairment only after shifts in the pediatric field encouraged doctors to address developmental and behavioral issues of children; although child abuse has perhaps always been with us, the symptoms of this particular type of abuse was socially constructed as a medical syndrome in the United States during the 1970s (Evans, 2004: 161). Ilana Singh similarly argues that the medicalized categorization of behaviors as Attention Deficit Hyperactivity Disorder (ADHD) emerged within the context of patriarchal discourse and a specific culture of mother-blame. Diagnoses of and medication for ADHD remain a peculiarly American phenomenon (2004: 1193).[3] Similarly, dyslexia appears only in contexts of literacy. One might also argue that within the Chinese historical context the deformation of the natural foot, often including its paralysis, as a result of the practice of foot binding was the norm for wealthy women, and did not become an impairment until Westerners so defined it.[4] Other impairments that have also only recently been identified as such—including Asperger's syndrome—suggest we might want "to question the clear line drawn between the socially constructed 'disability' and the 'preexistent and somatic' impairment.... Is the impairment bred into the bone, or can it be a creation of a medical-technological-pharmaceutical complex?" (Davis, 2002: 23). In light of these cultural and historical analyses, the distinction between impairment and disability blurs.

To accent both the relationship of impairment and disability and the need for their analytic separation, Shuttleworth and Kasnitz (2004) have recently begun to utilize the term impairment-disability. In defining impairment as "a negatively construed, cultural perception of a bodily, cognitive, or behavioral anomaly in terms of function or some other ethnopsychological or ethnophysiological status," Shuttleworth and Kasnitz (2004: 141) imply that impairment, although referencing bodily or cognitive aberration, does not have an exclusively biological, pre-social existence.[5] Rather, impairment is always construed, experienced, and evaluated within a cultural context.

Acknowledging that articulating negative feelings about the experience of impairment may "play into the hands of those who feel that our lives are not worth living," feminist disability scholars have also contested the dichotomous framing of impairment and disability; in arguing that anatomy is not destiny, activists have too often "colluded with the idea that the 'typical' disabled person is a young man in a wheelchair who is fit, never ill, and whose only needs concern a physically accessible environment" (Morris, 2001: 9). Individuals who experience pain, or whose impairments result in a need for lifelong assistance with tasks such as eating or using the bathroom, may not easily recognize themselves in the social model. Nor do profoundly mentally retarded children, for whose lifelong care American parents feel they must plan, fit easily within this model. Regardless of accommodations, independence may not be a possibility for those with particular impairments; some people "could not survive, much less thrive, without constant and vigilant attention, without someone performing...nearly all the tasks of daily living" (Kittay, 2001: 566). Just as impairments may not exist solely in the realm of biology, not all disabilities are malleable social constructions.

I have earlier shown how American mothers just finding out about their child's disability have generally acted more to change their children than to change society—that is, they have directed their efforts toward impairment within the medical model vehemently opposed by disability rights activists. Yet I would like to suggest here that many mothers who have experienced nurturing a disabled child over a period of time have developed a discourse that may *converge* with the current efforts within disability studies to address issues of embodiment without losing the political agenda of human rights.

The problem with the current social model of disability, Hughes and Paterson have argued, is that like biomedicine, the social model treats the body as a "pre-social, inert, physical object, as discrete, palpable and separate from the self" (1997: 387). In this essentialist stance toward the body, impairment is presented as a private issue, devoid of public meaning, while disability is disembodied. Some disability scholars and activists therefore have called for "giving impairment a sociological agenda—as a culturally informed and meaningful quality of existence" (Paterson and Hughes, 1999: 602), for taking a "more nuanced view, simultaneously defending the moral value of disabled people's lives, but also recognising the differential impact of impairments" (Shakespeare, 1998: 670). As both caregivers for impaired bodies and advocates for their disabled children's full personhood within an unjust society, mothers of disabled children may be well positioned to contribute to this new understanding.

Disability scholars Kevin Paterson and Bill Hughes are particularly concerned to explain the *interconnectedness* of impairment and disability in the lived experience of disabled people. Following Leder's analysis of pain, they argue that in everyday life our experience is characterized by the disappearance of the body from awareness; however, in situations of disease or pain the body becomes present to us in a dysfunctional manner, it "appears as a thematic focus of attention, but precisely in a dys-state" (Leder, 1990: 84, quoted in Paterson and Hughes, 1999: 602). Instead of disappearing, in the context of pain the body "dys-appears." Applying this analysis to disability, Paterson and Hughes argue that in a disabling social environment, one in which there are physical barriers to accessibility or in which an individual faces prejudice, for example, the impaired body is brought to consciousness; there is a simultaneous recognition of both the external barriers and the internal body. In such settings "the body undergoes a mode of 'dysappearance' which is not biological, but social" (1999: 603). Impairment in this sense is an inherently intercorporeal phenonmenon. The authors illustrate this process using the example of speech impairment.

> The body of a person with speech impairment "dysappears" when faced with (socially produced) embodied norms of communication. Since these norms largely reflect the carnal information of nondisabled people, the relationship of disabled people to them is one of significant disadvantage. The "dys-appearance" of the impaired body is structured by this disadvantage. Exclusion from and disruption to communication is not therefore a matter of the ability of an impaired person to communicate, but about conventions and norms of communication, which are (*a priori*) hostile to non-conforming forms of physicality.
>
> (Paterson and Hughes, 1999: 603)

The criterion of time, in particular, makes the body of the speech-impaired person, in this case that of one of the authors, "dys-appear." Asked a question by someone during a ride in a lift (elevator), the author points out that the option to answer was not available to him, because the "duration norm" of the communication was not commensurate with (his) carnal needs" (606). Just as the architectural conceptions of space have been largely uninformed by the carnal information of wheelchair users, communication norms—codes of movement and timing—are primarily informed by non-impaired bodies; in such contexts, the body "dys-appears" in the experience of the person with speech impairment as a consequence of oppression.

Mothers of disabled children describe a similar phenomenon in relation to their experience of their children's impairments. In numerous interviews, mothers described how when alone, their child appeared to them (mothers) as "normal." "When I look at my daughter," the mother of a child with Cri du Chat syndrome (a genetic disorder) commented, "it's like, I don't see the strange, like 'what is this?' I see my daughter, you know, who's going to need a little extra help." Darlene Mulligan similarly no longer sees her child with Down syndrome as unusual.

> She is normal to me. She requires extra paperwork, she requires a lot of extra doctors that I've got to keep track of. I have to buy five more Christmas presents than I would normally have had to do. She is a high maintenance child, is what I would term her, but otherwise, she is normal.

Acknowledging that there may be contexts in the future in which her daughter's difference will be made to matter, Alice Brooks states that "until then, I'll live in my little fantasy world and enjoy her for what she is."

It was in two contexts that a child's impaired body "dys-appeared" to a mother. The first context involved encounters with typical children and their parents. This excerpt is from an interview with the mother of a young boy with cerebral palsy:

> It bothers me sometimes when I go to the grocery store and there's a kid that you can tell is about Peter's age, and is sitting independently in the cart, and you know, I've got him fastened in an infant carrier, you know, which is a *big* baby in an infant carrier. And I know that I get looks like I'm a crazy mother or an over-protective mom.... And he catches a lot of stares, and they'll say, "oh, isn't he adorable," but then, you know, when you say he's a year old, they'll look at you like, gee, he looks and acts like maybe six months old.

Ann Meadows, the mother of an autistic boy described her visit to an indoor playground with similar feelings.

I took him to Discovery Zone with my niece. She has a nine-month-old baby, and we just decided to go over one day, and there was another little boy there his age, and this little boy is running and jumping and saying, "watch this, mommy," and "no, I want to go here," and "I want to eat now," and Max, of course, isn't saying much anything, just screeching…. and, of course, I have to devastate myself. I had to ask how old he was, even though I knew. I knew it was going to be close. I was hoping she'd say he was three, he's just very small, and she said that he was like only a month older than Max, and then she asked, obviously, the next question is well, "how old is your son" and I told her, and she just kind of looked at him funny and like, gee, he doesn't say anything at all, and I just kind of took him and went the other direction, not trying to be obvious about it, but…

Jenna Mosher similarly talks about comparing her child to that of a neighbor:

It's still hard. Not as hard, but like there's a little boy…. he was outside running around with a little suit of armor on with a sword, and I couldn't believe that he was four. He was younger than Daniel, and that—it startled me more than it upset me—although for some reason the birthday party was hard.

The second context in which mothers describe their child's impairment as becoming more visible to them is that of the doctor's office. Becky Romano tells of hearing her son described by the doctor as the physician explains his chromosomal abnormality:

I mean, I think my son was so handsome and then he just ripped apart his face. He has all these dysmorphic features. His eyes are wide spread. He has no bridge in his nose. His ears are too low. He's got all the features of like a Down's child, but he doesn't have a Down's face…. He's got like what they call a shawl scrotum, and he's dwarfed in size, and all of that. I'm now sitting there absorbing all of this the first day that he tells me all of this and I'm like, "take me to Boston, please!" So I thought to myself— it was awful. The torment I went through. I felt like I wanted to wring my own neck because I would look at my son and find myself picking, oh, my God, he does look like that. It was awful. Then I would look at his portraits on the wall and I would say, oh, my. So every Christmas picture

I took after, I would say, he's got that look. I would look at him a certain way when he was sleeping at night, and I said, "Becky you've got to stop this because you can't let doctors say this to him."

In all of these cases, mothers describe their negative experience of their child's impairment not as deriving from an essential, pre-social feature of the child's body itself, but as an intercorporeal phenomenon. The impaired body, when cared for and nurtured by the mother on its own terms is normal, not brought to consciousness. "The impaired body 'dys-appears'," however, "as a consequence of the profound oppressions of everyday life. It is stunned into its own recognition" or in this case into recognition by the mother, "by its presence-as-alien-being-in-the world" (Paterson and Hughes, 1999: 603). This then helps explain mothers' apparently contradictory views toward their disabled children:

> My sister-in-law just had two twin boys, two twin boys perfectly normal, and you think, okay, everybody else in your family had normal, healthy children, why you, and then you say to yourself, "you're being foolish. You're just feeling sorry for yourself. Get on with it," you know what I mean? You do feel like sometimes, what did I do wrong? But then if you look at her, she is wonderful. She's, you know, she's happy and she's a normal child to me.
>
> (Alice Brooks, mother of a child with Down syndrome)

> I can handle Alexis when I really go in a broad spectrum and look down at everything and go what is life about? And there's different people, and so what. Alexis is different and your life is going to be a little different, and you look down on everything, and it's like all right, what's the end result? That we're supposed to love each other and take care of each other and help each other and help each other to have a good time and enjoy life, right? Generally, and then all the other things start coming when I get back down into my little, little area, and I start looking around and going, the Joneses, they go do this and they can go to the beach and they're doing this, and their kid is running around, why can't I do that, and poor Alexis, and then I get wrapped up in this poor little thing again, that I think instead of looking at what is the whole thing really about, I start looking at little things that I think are important, that even though

if I could have that one thing, there would be another thing. Do you
know what I mean?

(Jane Sawyer, mother of a daughter with multiple disabilities)

Intercorporeal encounters, Paterson and Hughes suggest, become
demands for disabled people to normalize themselves, to express
themselves carnally in a manner conditioned by ableist norms of
bodily comportment (1999: 608). The narratives I collected suggest
that mothers feel these demands, not only for their children, but for
themselves, as societal norms hold *them* accountable for their non-
conformist children.[6] In everyday encounters outside the home,
on neighborhood streets, in grocery stores and in doctors' offices,
impairment is produced as experience, albeit differently, for both
disabled child and mother.

Some mothers, particularly as they first experience a diagnosis
of disability, for their own comfort or in the hopes that their child's
mind or body can be changed to no longer dys-appear as alien in the
world, seek to intervene within the child itself; and/or they may attempt
to make the child appear "normal" by lying about the child's age or
dressing the child so as to hide orthotics or a child's drooling. Yet after
the experience of mothering a disabled child over time, most mothers
in the study claimed to have undergone profound changes in their own
understanding of personhood and disability. "If you were to say this
to me before I had Peter, or while I was pregnant that he would have
cerebral palsy, you know, he wouldn't be quite normal, I'd say 'oh, no,
I couldn't handle that,'" Angela Petrocelli reflects. "But now that you
see him, and you get an expression from him, he still smiles at you,
still has a favorite book, and he has a lot of things that normal kids,
it's okay now. You feel like you walk in a room in the morning and
they're smiling and, you know, I mean I can't change what happened,
and I—to me, he's fine. I mean, I know he's not, but he's, you know, he's
fine." Lucy Baker, mother of a mentally retarded boy remembers that
"for a long time, even after he was diagnosed, both my husband and I
almost didn't want to—almost admit to some people." Being able to talk
comfortably about it *now* is helpful to her " because that was the hardest
thing just knowing that it was something that you're almost ashamed
of, you know, not—not anymore, but, I mean, we definitely were—had

that feeling at first, you know, that it was something bad and that people would look down on us for it."

"Otherness" Paterson and Hughes argue, "is not an objective property of certain kinds of bodies, but rather the product of social processes that produce a hierarchy of identities" (1999: 609). Mothers in the study generally came to reflect on their own prior "othering" of disabled people, as well as on the existence of this hierarchy that devalues the identity of their child and their own identity as mother; many, claiming a transformation deriving from love for their disabled child, came to assert the full personhood of their child regardless of the permanence of disability, and to reject the hierarchy of identities as arbitrary or unjust. "I think we've basically come to the feeling Daniel's just sort of his own entity, his own person, and that's the way we have to think. You can't really compare him," concluded Jenna Mosher. As for Lucy Baker, when she looks at her mentally retarded son a year later "It's not a problem anymore, it's you know, that's just Scott."

Reflections on Normal

If these are, after all, just our children, what is the place of impairment and disability in their lives according to mothers? And what is the meaning of a cure in relation to a disabled child's identity? A common medical model discourse to which mothers are exposed is that their child's true identity has tragically been trapped by an impairment separate from the self. This message was exploited in the New York University Child Study Center's well-intentioned, but ultimately short-lived and demeaning 2007 campaign for public awareness about children's untreated psychiatric disorders. The ad campaign took the form of "ransom notes," in which disabilities were portrayed as kidnappers, holding children hostage. One ad ran "We have your son. We will make sure he will not be able to care for himself or interact socially as long as he lives. This is only the beginning." The note is signed "Autism." The text of another ad reads, "We are in possession of your son. We are making him squirm and fidget until he is a detriment to himself and those around him. Ignore this and your kid will pay.... ADHD." Yet another states "We have your son. We are destroying his ability for social interaction and driving him into a life of complete isolation.

It's up to you now.... Asperger's Syndrome" (http://thegimpparade. blogspot.com/2007/12/ransom-notes-campaign.html).

The ad campaign, discontinued in response to criticism from both disability rights and parents' organizations, had played on parents' fears and the broadly accepted notion that a normal child lies within or elsewhere, tragically trapped and in need of rescue through strategies that intervene to return the child to normalcy. As Penny Richards comments on the blog "The Gimp Parade," similar "replacement thinking runs through a lot of parent-support-group chatter—as in 'I want my life back' (no, this is still your life; you might wish it was running closer to your expectations, or just closer to the average, but that's a different complaint), or age-normed ideas such as 'he's sixteen, he would have been driving now if not for...' (well, maybe, maybe not—a driver's license isn't a universal birthright)" (http://thegimpparade.blogspot.com/2007/12/ransom-notes-campaign. html, retrieved December 24, 2007).

The experience and ambiguity of mothering has led some of the women in the study to openly challenge the medical profession's binary categorization of normal and abnormal. "We're doing everything you'd do for a regular child, but maybe a little bit later," comments the mother of a girl with Down syndrome. "I say regular as opposed to normal. Somehow normal just doesn't—there is no normal." A mother of a girl identified with cerebral palsy similarly complains, "I think the hardest thing is when you go to the doctor and so many doctors will use the term abnormal or not normal. What is normal, you know?.... You can call her atypical or whatever, but you don't use the word normal because what's normal to you isn't normal to somebody else." Teenage mother Maria Peters, whose son is blind, mentally retarded, and has cerebral palsy, reflects that as this is her first child, "it's just like I got used to it.... You know what I'm saying? This is normal. To me. And maybe not normal to anybody else who has a kid."

Kim Boland complains that because her mother-in-law hasn't been around kids with Down syndrome, "she doesn't really know, but she'll say things like 'those kids.' Well what exactly is 'those kids?' He's a little boy." It is specifically through the experience of mothering children whose bodies are not typical and having family life informed by their non-typical carnal needs, that the opposition of normal and abnormal is revealed not only as oppressive to those who don't fit the mold, but also as an arbitrary construction. The term normal, these mothers argue, should either be discontinued, or expanded to include those currently excluded from the domain of full persons. There are, they argue, many ways to be normal.

In taking this stance, mothers, though labeled as being in "denial" about their children's abnormalities, are nevertheless reassessing the concept of the normal in a manner consistent with biologists and anthropologists' revisions to the concept of race; that is, in which race is no longer seen as a natural, biological category. Functional determinists make the claim that "functions take place in a uniform mode at a relatively uniform performance level by a statistically distinctive portion of the members of a species. These are the normals" (Amundson, 2000). But, Amundson claims, "like the concept of race, the concept of normality is a biological error. The partitioning of human variation into the normal versus the abnormal has no firmer biological footing than the partitioning into races. Diversity of function is a fact of biology" (Amundson, 2000). Examining current scholarship in physiology and anatomy, he concludes that the concept of species normality should be replaced by a concept of individual normality or responsiveness. The concept of responsiveness, he suggests, represents individual normality, and replaces the statistical and comparative basis of normality with an assessment of the relation between individual performance and needs. "There is no need for a species design" (Amundson, 2000).

It is this idea that some mothers claim to have learned from nurturing a child whose body or behavior, when measured by a universal standard, falls outside the statistical norm. Children, they argue, cannot be compared, nor can the experience of mothering. What's normal to one person, is not normal to another. Both articulating that "there is no normal," and acknowledging that the concept of normality is oppressively linked to both social opportunity and cultural valuation, mothers' acquired knowledge can contribute to a new ethics which would incorporate disability rights within a broader conception of personhood and human value. This is a point to which I will shortly return.

The medical model functions, and children are monitored, labeled, and deemed eligible for intervention services, within a statistical paradigm developed in Europe in the nineteenth century. Over the last one hundred fifty years, people have been "encouraged to strive to be normal, to huddle under the main part of the curve" (Davis, 2002: 105). Yet a number of mothers in the study describe a personal transformation in terms not only of rejecting the binary of normal/abnormal, but of embracing the very qualities in their child that are labeled by society as abnormal. The child's impairment is in this interpretation not relegated exclusively to a biology separate from the self, but rather is understood as integral to the child and infused with meaning. Reflecting on her child's impairment (agenesis of the corpus collasum), Lorraine Hamilton asks " You have this child that you love so much and if they didn't have that, who would he be?" A cure would in this case be the equivalent to the replacement of one child with another; to love this particular child is thus to love the impairment-disability, for they are inseparable. As Peggy Hoffmeister comments about her autistic son during her second interview,

> Rather than think about what would he be like if he didn't have this, I just accept that, well, he does have it and this is the way he is, and this is—and it's not as if he has a disorder that could be magically lifted away to reveal some different boy because that's not—that's a part of his personality. This isn't something like your hair is dyed green, but it will grow out and your own self will be revealed. This is him. I mean, his hair is green. Well not really, but anyway…

Pam Karcher describes an event that epitomizes the endearing qualities of her son Mac, qualities she understands to be inextricably linked to Asperger's syndrome and are the origin of his nickname of "Wacky Macky,"

> I mean, all children do cute, strange things and everyone thinks their child is the best, but … he really does do the strangest things that just crack me right up. I mean, we are just hysterical. We have him on tape. He has this little rubber pretzel.… It's a teether, but he wanted it on his head. Now this is when I was first suspecting something, but now I think that this is part of that trait within him, but he wanted it on his head and it wouldn't stay on his head. And we have this like on tape. And he's getting all mad and he's really getting mad, and we're cracking up at him in the car. We're driving up to Niagara Falls and he's trying to get this pretzel to stay on his head. It keeps falling off. And we have the whole thing on tape. I'm like, "we should send this in to 'Funniest Home Videos'" because I've

seen much less funny things win $10,000, I'll tell you right now. And he finally gets it up there and he's like—he's staring at it like this, his eyes are crossing, and it's almost like "okay, nobody move!" And he just stayed like that and then he looks at you and he's like—he was just so proud of himself because he got the—and then every now and then he'd check to see if it was still up there and it was just so funny. And I'm like, that's like just little, weird little Mac stuff that makes him like so unique.

In these conceptualizations, a self that is intimately integrated with impairment is also linked to social value and to the uniqueness, rather than exchangeability, that characterizes individuals as full persons. Here "anomaly presents as originality rather than deviance" (Silvers, 2002: 240). Full personhood, rather than "otherness" is thereby extended to a broader range of humanity. In these mothers' conceptualization, the performance of independence in meeting needs is irrelevant; a condition of complete dependence is acknowledged as within the range of normal.

Let me give a concrete example of such a redefinition of normal as it played out in the interaction of my teenage disabled daughter with two non-disabled friends who had come to spend the night. I had set up air mattresses and sleeping bags on the living room floor, got DJ washed up and in her pajamas, and given the girls the movies we had rented for the weekend. At 1 a.m. I peeked in on them, was promptly kicked out, and went up to bed. I awoke the next morning to find DJ dressed. "How did she get dressed?" I asked the girls. "She woke up and said she had to go to the bathroom, so we put her on the toilet" was one girl's casual response. "Then she said she wanted to get dressed, so we got her dressed, but we couldn't find her bra." "Oh," I said, trying to sound casual myself, "It's in her white set of drawers." "I *told* you to look in there!" exclaimed one girl to the other triumphantly. For these girls, as well as for DJ herself, it is obvious that impairment causes difference; her impairment precludes DJ going to the bathroom by herself for instance, in turn setting up different practices of modesty and intimacy. Yet it's very true that with the same body in a different context, with different friends or with children who are not close friends, DJ would have been much more disabled than she was in this context.

The interesting question is what enabled these girls to respond this way? Here we are in the realm of policy *and* attitude, structural access *and* being. Few American adults have grown up with friends who would have put us on the toilet as if it were no big deal. What do these kids know that growing up, my friends and I didn't? Although none of them would describe the situation in these terms, the relation of impairment to disability here hinges on all three girls' concepts of normal. That is, DJ and her friends define her as different, but as normal for *her*. By extension, they too are both different and normal: if you are friends with DJ, it is normal for you to assist her in translating her speech, using the bathroom, and eating. It is also normal for you to get to park closer to the movie theater using the handicapped parking tag, to get out of study hall to have lunch with DJ, and to look forward to having access to her parents' adapted wheelchair van when you get your driver's license. Implementation of a public policy of inclusion had provided *some* children, at least, the opportunity to redefine the meaning of normal, as has mothers' daily participation in the care of their disabled children.

Mothers' descriptions of how they have come to understand and value their unique children articulate a position consistent with a "cultural model" of disability, in which impairment is both human variation interacting with environmental obstacles *and* socially mediated difference that lends identity and phenomenological perspective (Snyder and Mitchell, 2006: 10). Snyder and Mitchell distinguish this model from the British social model, which is more committed to the dichotomous representation of impairment as a designator of biological difference and disability as social process. Instead, Snyder and Mitchell suggest that social obstacles and biological capacities both impinge on the lives of disabled people, with the result that these differences have significant bearing on how disabled people experience their lives (2006: 6). They give a reading of the Oedipus Rex story in which the limping Oedipus can answer the sphinx's riddle precisely because of his experience with mobility impairment. In the cultural model they propose then, embodiment is critical as a source of meaningful materiality. Social obstacles and children's biological capacities have significant bearing as well on how women in this study come to experience motherhood and give meaning to disability.

As I have discussed elsewhere (Landsman, 1998, 1999), mothers who have nurtured disabled children over time describe their children as both their greatest joy and greatest sorrow. They do not portray them as passive gifts, as in the common phrase "God gives special children to special parents" which keeps intact the categories of normal and special, ensuring that the speaker remains safely entrenched in the category of normal and free from the Other's "tragedy"; but rather as active givers, most often of the gift of knowledge of unconditional love. To accept the gift is often described by mothers as a long and sometimes reversible process, an ongoing physically, emotionally and financially painful struggle. But to do so is also to allow, in the life of the mother, exactly that which Paterson and Hughes claims disablism prevents: for impaired carnality to make its mark on the design of social space and time.

Conclusions: Mothers and Disability Rights

The implications of having impaired carnality make its mark, not only in the home of the disabled child but in the larger society, are not lost on mothers. In practical terms for parents, it means for instance that the work place would accommodate mothers' and fathers' schedules of personal assistance to their disabled children. Denise Rivers, mother of a child with hydrocephalous, explained that she lost her job as a medical transcriber at a local hospital because she missed too many days at work. "I don't think the system is set up right for mothers." she states. "You know, I had eight years in this place and because my child—I happen to have a sick child and I lose my job, where somebody else had a, you know, normal child, they wouldn't have lost their job." It might mean as well that mothers' work as nurturers of disabled children would be valued as much as that of those who nurture children without impairments. "You know, I've had people say to me, 'well you're not going to waste your life just devoting your whole life to her are you?'" complains a mother of a child with cerebral palsy in her second interview. "I don't think that's a wasted life.... I think people who haven't been there don't know what to think so therefore they say stupid things."

Many people "who have been there," this research suggests, identify meaning in subtle actions that are unintelligible, and indeed often undetectable, to those attuned exclusively to communication norms informed by "normal" carnality. A shift in the tone of a cry, the relaxation of a muscle, a cock of the head or a glint in the eye:

mothers have learned to read such behaviors as a child's expression of self. Such wisdom, gleaned from intimate experience in non-typical encounters, is not routinely recognized as knowledge; rather, mothers report that it is dismissed as wishful thinking, as denial. Personhood, as anthropologists know, is a reflection not of inherent qualities, but of cultural valuation. Engaged in everyday acts of caring and experiencing protocols of communication informed by impaired carnality, mothers not only come to discover, but to establish, their child's personhood. As we have seen in the previous chapter, mothers often redefine a child's dependency as a source of reciprocity. In this way, mothers and disabled children are engaged in relations of mutual giving and interdependence. The disabled child's personhood, largely negated by society, emerges in relationship with the mother, and so too a mother's transformed self emerges in relationship with the child.

If others had the benefits of their experience, these mothers suggest, impaired bodies of all types would not "dys-appear," but rather be incorporated into a less judgmental world in which each person had his or her valued place. Speaking of the personal impact of her experience raising a mentally retarded son, a mother states,

> I try and have it make me more understanding of not even just other children and other parents that have gone through this, but really everybody. You know, everybody has something whether it is a disability or really—it just seems like everybody has some sort of disability. You know, it may not be necessarily be a physical one, but something, so it's—we just try and be—it certainly doesn't always work but—more understanding and more compassionate of everybody, you know, whether it's a crabby neighbor or, you know.

Ann Meadows is a mother whose child has pervasive developmental disorder, on the autistic spectrum. She tells a similar story in which her experience mothering a child with a non-normative mode of interaction has been generalized to affect her understanding of other children and beyond that, to other people:

> People have to realize that not every child is perfect, and that even the children that aren't perfect, still have things about them that are great, no matter what. No matter how bad a child is. I was telling you about the

friend that I just met and she brought her son over, and he came into the house screaming and ran from end to end, but he's gorgeous, and he was just so adorable, you know, and I guess maybe if it hadn't been for knowing Max and understanding that some children are different, I don't know if I would've been able to see that. I would've just looked at him and go, "oh, God, how do you deal with it?" but I looked at him and I saw that he was an adorable little boy, and then he calmed down and I got to see that there is something in there besides the problem, and that people have to look past what's wrong with the child to find out what's right.... I think that people just have to learn to—and even not only children, but other adults, too. You have to decide that everybody has something. Well, okay, maybe not everybody; there's mass murderers out there. But most people have something that's really great about them, and you have to learn to find it.

Mothers' experiences of their children's bodies as alien in the outside world have led some to attempt to change those bodies, to normalize them. In so doing, these women participate in the medical model of disability even as they interpret disability as the consequence of oppression. While seeking to change the protocols of intercorporeality that provide the basis for judgments about their child's performance within the context of physician evaluations, many mothers feel powerless to change those protocols *outside* the doctor's office, in the larger society. The medical model these mothers uphold presents the impaired body as trapping the real child; here the impaired child is always an unfinished product requiring medical expertise to become fully human (see Dreger, 2004: 125). But caring for, knowing intimately, and loving deeply their children's differentially impaired bodies has led many mothers to envision a future in which *no* type of body would be alien in the world; all would have a place and none be made to "dys-appear." As Kim Boland explained in an excerpt presented earlier, "if everyone in the world had one person in their family that had a problem, that had Downs's syndrome or you know cerebral palsy, or whatever, people wouldn't be so quick, the world wouldn't be such a mean place...." Describing how her experience as a mother of a disabled child led to a broader understanding of racism and prejudice in general, she continues, "You really think about it today and it's all along the same lines.... I guess it's really opened up another world for a lot of people."

What is this world to which mothers are opened up? And to what vision could the experience of mothering disabled children contribute? Can mothers' experiences move beyond the domain of inspirational stories of "special parents for special children" and be made to speak to challenges posed by scholars of disability studies and activists for disability rights? Might they contribute to possibilities for engagement of disabled people in valued domains of love and friendship? The power behind the concept of disability, Lennard Davis proposes, is that it "presents us with a malleable view of the human body and identity" (Davis, 2002: 26). He uses the term "dismodern" to describe the new perspective to which disability studies scholarship can and should lend itself. "The dismodern era ushers in the concept that difference is what all of us have in common.... That technology is not separate but part of the body. That dependence, not individual independence, is the rule" (Davis, 2002: 26). Many disability rights activists are themselves now publicly claiming that independence is a deception, interdependence the reality.

"We all need each other to live well," writes Bill Rush (Interdependent Living), a journalist and peer counselor with cerebral palsy, as he exposes the interdependence that belies any American's claim to self-sufficiency: the use of manufactured goods, food purchased in grocery stores, indoor plumbing, and the like. Acknowledging this broad interdependency, Tom Shakespeare's critique of the social model (Shakespeare, 2006) claims that biological limitations will nevertheless affect some people such that they will always remain dependent in every context, unable to reciprocate equally. We need to have a model of disability that addresses *this* difference without denying value and dignity. In their statements that there can be no standard by which to judge children, that all forms of oppression or hierarchy based on physical or mental markers are invalid, and that mothers are indeed gifted by their child's dependency and the knowledge of unconditional love it brings, mothers of disabled children come close to expressing the ideal that "aims to create a new category based on the partial, incomplete subject whose realization is not autonomy and independence but dependency and interdependence" (Davis, 2002: 30).[7]

Whether pursuing cures, attempting to minimize visible markers of disability, utilizing early intervention services, or crying as they describe their fears and hopes to a researcher, mothers in the study expressed a desire to have their disabled child, one they themselves once might have interpreted as "other," participate in social life. The social life they envision is itself specifically American. Yet in reconceptualizing the normal, or in rejecting the concept altogether, they also critique American values.

In the new way of thinking toward which Davis argues disability studies should move, "We are all nonstandard" (Davis, 2002: 32). Rather than an American minority group, disability may thus be understood as a form of human variation (see Asch, 2004; also Colligan, 2004), "the most human of experiences, touching every family and—if we live long enough—touching us all" (Thomson, 2004: 76). This is not to suggest that a universal biological condition of frailty and vulnerability become the basis for citizenship. The latter, Hughes argues, may constitute a theoretical means of ameliorating the existential negativity associated with being disabled," but it does so "at the expense of disability identity" (Hughes, 2007: 673). It is not the disabled body, but the "normative, invulnerable body of disablist modernity that is the problem" disability studies needs to address (Hughes, 2007: 681). In a movement based on such understandings, might not the beliefs of mothers of disabled children both that their children are profoundly different and that "there is no normal," find a home? Paterson and Hughes among others have asked us to examine not only how structural barriers produce oppression, as the social model has been so effective in explicating, but also how oppression "is manifest in corporeal and intercorporeal norms and conventions, and can be read in and through the ways 'everyday encounters' can go astray" (1999: 608). It is here that mothers' knowledge—not inherent, but acquired through the intimate experience of nurturing non-typical, different, dependent children in everyday encounters—may begin to converge with the perspective of this more nuanced disability scholarship and with activism to promote justice for all people.

Epilogue: Personal Reflections

It is my daughter DJ's last day of school before summer vacation. This morning I watch her maneuver her bright yellow power wheelchair with its joystick control toward the special lift-equipped public school bus that pulls into our driveway, as she listens to a CD of a currently popular rock band on Sony Discman headphones that rest over her fashionably pierced ears. (The iPod, so much in vogue, requires too much manual dexterity for her to control). She and her father have already had today's obligatory disagreement over the volume of the music. Hanging off the back of the wheelchair, her pink backpack bulges with her laptop computer, splint, the notebook used for communication between me and her aide, algebra and English books to return, and a yearbook for friends to sign; her Dynavox, an augmentative communication device, also hangs somewhat precariously on the overburdened chair. I move in quickly to grab a kiss; having raised two kids before her, I know how fleeting are such opportunities. As the bus aide follows protocol to secure the wheelchair, I look through the bus window; I watch DJ's jerky movements, her arms "flapping" and her body rocking in joyous response to music, temporarily oblivious to the world outside that created by the headphones. And I ponder, what is the role of impairment and disability in the making of this very unique, yet very American girl?

Later that day, I will contain my anger and hold back the tears as I argue with the administrator of a summer youth program at a local college who proposes a refund of my deposit because while DJ's one-on-one aide is welcome and her adaptive computer keyboard is compatible with their system, there is no way to get DJ into the science building where her chosen courses are scheduled. Apparently eight steep concrete steps are to prevent her participation. Too bad, but it's an old campus. In an environment constructed in accord with conventions informed by non-disabled carnality, she is simply to be excluded; what then of her chances in the domains of friendship and love? But I press on. "My experience has been that when reasonable people of good will put their heads together, they can find a way to make things work out," I patiently explain to the administrator. Meeting resistance, I continue, "and if not, maybe the New York State Office of the Advocate for Persons with Disabilities can help come up with some ideas for how you can comply with the law." I ask about other entrances to the building, other available rooms, the instructors' lists of required items, all the while thinking to myself, Is DJ really the first person with cerebral palsy ever to be on that campus? Will she ever *not* be a pioneer? A couple hours and countless phone calls later, there is a breakthrough: It seems that most classes can, after all, be switched to accessible rooms; all will be fine. The voice on the phone leaves no doubt that I am to be grateful for what is seen as their extraordinary efforts to accommodate her. I am annoyed—enraged, actually—but comply and say, "Thank you," well aware that anger at me can be taken out on my daughter. Now I can move on to hope that DJ will have fun and to worry about whether the other kids will listen carefully and long enough to her impaired speech to recognize her wit and sense of humor. Before bed, DJ and I have a talk about the ADA.

And I ponder: What is the role of impairment and disability in the making of my *own* life and my experience of motherhood? If you had asked me before I gave birth to DJ, my third child, would I *choose* to have a child with multiple disabilities, I am sure I would have said, "No." But if you had asked me before my *first* child was born, would I want to raise a "normal" child who as a teenager would be disrespectful, experiment with underage drinking, have friends I don't particularly like, and not live up to her potential in school, I suppose my answer would also have been no. Yet both happened, and both daughters, as well as my athletic and academically high-achieving, middle-child son, have enriched my life immensely. All evidence now suggests that each of them will become a compassionate, caring, and accomplished adult; engaging their own particular skills and passions, each will make contributions to their communities. Contrary to my earlier certitude, I can now find no criteria to determine which child was more appropriate for me as a parent to bring into the world, or which one's care "oppressed" me more as a woman. Some would claim that my feelings are irrational, the product of an inherently "special" mother's love I could—and perhaps should—have been spared; I suggest they derive from new knowledge I acquired through the experience of mothering.

In my desire to have my daughter overcome her disabilities through the various physical and speech therapies that have become part of her weekly routine, I may offend some in the disability rights movement and seem to support mainstream, medical-model perspectives that locate a problem within my daughter's "defective" body. From this perspective, my simultaneous passion for my daughter's right to be who she is and to be included in the social life of the community *as* she is, seems paradoxical, my inability to even imagine my daughter without impairment lending itself to claims of resignation. I would propose instead that my stance represents not defeat, a once-resisted "acceptance" of that which I tragically cannot change, but rather my own growth and transformation.

Appendix: Profiles of Interview Participants

The following list provides brief biographical profiles of those women who were interviewed as part of the study. Except where noted otherwise, individuals interviewed are white. Pseudonyms have been assigned to all participants and their families.

Katie Allen

Katie is 19 years old and unmarried. She dropped out of high school after the tenth grade and later enrolled in a GED program, which she quit when her baby was born prematurely. She is now a full-time homemaker living on public assistance. She was not raised in any religious tradition. She and the baby, Justin, live in an apartment in a city housing project. Justin was premature; he had a grade IV bleed and was hospitalized in the neonatal intensive care unit. A computed tomography (CT) scan showed severe brain damage, and the doctor's prognosis includes cerebral palsy.

Sara Anderson

Sara, 22, is a high-school graduate who had worked as a nurse's assistant; currently she is on public assistance and living in an apartment near her parents in an urban neighborhood. As a child, she had briefly gone to a Salvation Army church but was not brought up in any religious tradition. A single mother, Sara had her first child, a boy, at 19. Her second child, Jeannette, was born three years later. An infection of group B strep meningitis resulted in severe brain damage. At the baby's first visit at Newborn Followup at about four months of age, Sara was told that Jeannette has microcephaly and profound mental retardation; at a later visit, Jeannette was diagnosed with cerebral palsy and epilepsy as well. At that time, Sara was also told that Jeannette would never walk. She is fed by a g-tube. The children's father is a college student; he does not live with the family and is relatively uninvolved in their care and support.

Charlotte Andretti

Charlotte is 27 years old. She and her husband both have degrees from two-year colleges and live in a suburban home. She was raised Protestant but became Catholic so that the family would practice the same religion. Charlotte worked in the accounting field until shortly before her daughter, Cindy, was born. Cindy was first diagnosed with tracheomalacia (a collapsing trachea, which affects her breathing and her ability to eat). More recently, Cindy was also diagnosed as being profoundly deaf.

Lucy Baker

Lucy is in her early twenties and is a high-school graduate with a year of college. She had worked in a drug store, but at the time of the first interview was a full-time homemaker. Her husband is a salesman. Lucy occasionally now does part-time cleaning at night. Her son, Scott, was first diagnosed with mild mental retardation at the age of 2, but by the time of the second interview, he had tested in the low-normal range for cognition; his speech, however, is still delayed, and he is being taught some simple sign language. The family lives in a single-family home in a city. Lucy is a practicing Catholic.

Jean Barbarino

Jean is a single mother living in an apartment in an urban neighborhood. She is employed full-time as a medical claims examiner and gets babysitting help from her mother. She comes from an Italian Catholic family. Her boyfriend is unemployed and does not provide her or the child any financial assistance. Jean had given birth to premature twins; one child died. The surviving twin, Anthony, had a grade IV bleed while hospitalized in the neonatal intensive care unit. He has been diagnosed with cerebral palsy.

Lily Beckett

Lily, 33, is Catholic. She and her husband live in a single-family home. She has a degree from a community college and works at a local factory placing print ads. Her daughter, Alicia, was born with Down syndrome, a diagnosis that took a backseat to her life-threatening heart defect. Shortly after Alicia's birth, her parents were told not to expect the child to survive. She has had two major heart surgeries and will require a third as she grows. Such surgeries are risky; Lily feels that they will not have Alicia with them long. By the time of the second interview, Lily had given birth to a second child, Charles.

Cheryl Benedetto

Cheryl is a single, 22-year-old woman. She had been a nursing student when she got pregnant, and she is a practicing Catholic. Cheryl and her son live with her parents in a city neighborhood. Cheryl's fiancé is unemployed and is active in the care of their son. Austin was born with a diaphragmatic hernia, life-threatening complications of which led him to be placed on a heart-lung machine for a process known as extra-corporeal membrane oxygenation (ECMO). ECMO entails a high risk for stroke, and indeed Austin suffered a cranial bleed that left him severely impaired. He has been diagnosed with cortical blindness, general low muscle tone with spasticity on his right side, and mental retardation. Austin is fed with a gastric tube, and he had seizures, which by the time of the second interview were under control with medication. At that time, Cheryl was also pregnant with a second child.

Kim Boland

Kim is 23 years old and married. She dropped out of school in the tenth grade. She earned a cosmetology license but is not employed outside the home now. Her husband is a truck driver, and the family lives in a trailer in a rural trailer park at the outskirts of a small city. She is Methodist.

Her son, Steven, was diagnosed with Down syndrome. Kim noticed some behavioral traits that concerned her, and she brought him to Newborn Followup for an evaluation, where he was given an additional diagnosis of autism.

Jennifer Borden

Jennifer has a newborn girl and a two-year-old son, Jacob. After the birth of the second baby, she quit her job as a nurse and became a full-time homemaker. Jennifer's husband is a firefighter. At the end of her pregnancy with Jacob, no fetal movement was detected, and labor was induced; the child had to be revived, and Jennifer and her husband were told not to expect him to live more than a few hours. Jacob, however, survived. He has severe mental retardation and an undiagnosed seizure disorder. The family is Catholic and lives in a suburban home.

Chloe Bridgeford

Chloe, 21, dropped out of school in the ninth grade but later completed her GED; she is married. She has worked as a hotel housekeeper, a factory laborer, and a home health care aide but now is a full-time homemaker. Her husband works as an auto body mechanic. Brought up Catholic, Chloe does not go to church or practice any particular religion now. She lives in a suburban neighborhood in the northernmost part of the state and traveled to the Newborn Followup Program after years of being told by pediatricians that there was nothing really wrong with her two children. At the Newborn Followup Program, orthopedic abnormalities were noted, and she was told that further testing would be required to determine whether the children had a muscle disease.

Alice Brooks

Alice is a part-time waitress and the mother of two children; her husband is a postal worker. The family lives in an apartment in a city neighborhood. When she was pregnant with her youngest child, Alice had an ultrasound that detected a serious heart defect in the baby; at that time, Alice was told to expect the child to only live a couple of hours after birth. Susan survived, however, and was diagnosed with Down syndrome. She has a speech delay, motor delays, and mild mental retardation.

Connie Brown

Connie, 31, has held a variety of jobs since graduating from college, including kindergarten teacher, special education teacher, waitress, and running her own hot dog truck. She is married and has two sons. The family is Catholic and currently lives in a suburban apartment complex, but they own in another city a house that they are trying to sell. The youngest son, Travis, was born without one hand.

Ashley Burkart

Ashley, 30 years old, is a married college graduate with an R.N. degree. Her husband is a graduate student; they live in an apartment in a small city but were planning to move once her husband completed his degree and started the new job he had recently accepted. Ashley was working as a nurse when she gave birth to her son, Theodore. The infant has spina bifida, which could potentially result in multiple physical or cognitive disabilities (or both).

Suzanne Dalton

Suzanne is the mother of premature twins, born at just under 25 weeks' gestation. She is a 33-year-old college graduate who works as an alcohol counselor for a managed health care company. Her husband is a teacher. Raised as a Catholic, Suzanne defines her religion now as only "loosely Catholic." At the time of the first interview, her twins, one male and one female, had no definitive diagnosis but were considered at risk for cerebral palsy and learning disabilities. Matthew's course in the neonatal intensive care unit had been the more difficult, as he had a grade IV brain bleed. By the time of the second interview, Louise had been evaluated as having normal development; Matthew was diagnosed with cerebral palsy and low normal cognition. The doctor noted concern with

Matthew's brain growth and predicted language and reading problems in the future in addition to his motor impairment.

Katherine Douglas

Katherine has a Ph.D. and holds a position as a college professor. She was raised a Presbyterian. Katherine is divorced and lives in an urban neighborhood near her work. Her two older children had been adopted out of institutions, and both have disabilities. At the time of the interview, Katherine was in the process of adopting her third child, an infant girl named Janine. Janine's birth mother was in prison, and Janine had been in protective custody; Katherine was aware that the baby had had intercranial bleeding and was at risk for future disabilities, such as cerebral palsy. At her visit to Newborn Followup, Katherine was told that the girl would probably also have mental retardation.

Amy Garrison

Amy is in her early twenties, has a high-school diploma, and is married. She was brought up Lutheran. She has lived on public assistance and has also been a child care worker and a home health aide; she is now a full-time homemaker with hopes of someday becoming a cosmetologist. She recently moved from an apartment to a single-family house in a suburb. Amy has a preschool-age child from a previous relationship. Her second child (her husband's first) was born prematurely at 25 weeks' gestation. Philip was diagnosed with vision impairment, cerebral palsy, and possible mental retardation.

Marilyn Graber

Marilyn, 27, left high school in the tenth grade and later earned a GED. As a teenager, she worked as an aide for disabled people, then took some classes and got jobs doing secretarial work. Her husband is a correctional officer; she is now a full-time homemaker, and they live in their own house in a small town. She had gone to a Baptist Church as a child, and as an adult has been to various churches, believing that "any Christian religion is fine." She describes herself as having had a learning problem in school. At Newborn Followup Program, her older daughter, Elaine, was evaluated as having mild mental retardation.

Tina Graham

Tina, 30, has a high-school diploma and some college experience. She was raised Catholic but is now a born-again Christian, as is her husband. They live in a house in a suburban neighborhood. Her husband has his own small business and does snowplowing on the side. Up until the early part of her pregnancy Tina had worked on her parents' flower farm; she is now a full-time homemaker and also does volunteer work in a hospital. Her son, Ryan, has mental retardation and vision impairment. At the time of the second interview, Tina was pregnant again.

Bonnie Hagstrom

Bonnie, 31, is married and has two children. A high-school graduate, Bonnie worked in fast-food restaurants but quit when her mental illness became too debilitating; many years later she was diagnosed with bipolar disorder. She is a full-time homemaker. The family had been receiving public assistance but is currently supported by her husband who works two part-time jobs as a restaurant dishwasher and as a manual laborer at an arena. They live in an apartment in a small city. Bonnie's youngest child, Sandy, was diagnosed at the Newborn Followup Program with pervasive developmental disorder, a disorder on the autistic spectrum.

Lorraine Hamilton

Lorraine, 33, lives in a house in a suburban neighborhood. She is Baptist. Lorraine has a college degree and is a full-time homemaker. By the time of the second interview, her husband was just starting a new business out of his home, and Lorraine plans to work for him part-time. Lorraine's third child, Thomas, was born with agenesis of the corpus collosum; he is missing the part of his brain that connects the right and left hemispheres. This birth defect has resulted in multiple disabilities, including profound mental retardation and visual impairment. At

Newborn Followup, he was also diagnosed with autism, but this diagnosis was contradicted by physicians at a different hospital.

Francine Hanson

Francine was 33 years old at the time of the interview. As a single parent, she had been on public assistance for a time; however, she is now married and lives with her husband and her three children in a house at the end of a dirt road in a rural area. She had been employed at a leather factory but is now a full-time homemaker. After having her fears about her infant son's lethargy dismissed by various medical personnel, Francine pursued her concerns with a cardiologist who diagnosed a life-threatening congential heart defect. Brett has undergone surgery. He also has a speech delay and receives both speech therapy and physical therapy.

Karen Harmon

Karen recently moved to the area; her husband is in the Navy, and they live in an apartment in a small city. She is in her early twenties. Karen got married right out of high school and worked briefly as an office clerk before giving birth to premature twins. Joey and Carol both had serious brain bleeds while in the neonatal intensive care unit, and each have multiple disabilities, including cerebral palsy and vision impairment. Both children have shunts to prevent further damage from hydrocephalus; both had to be tube-fed for a time. Karen was not raised in any religious tradition and does not believe in God.

Lisa Hart

Lisa is in her thirties and lives in a single-family house in a city neighborhood. She has a degree from a two-year college and worked at a law firm before her baby was born. Her husband works for the state government. They are Catholic. Daughter Samantha was conceived through in-vitro fertilization. At birth, Samantha aspirated meconium and was hospitalized with complications in the neonatal intensive care unit. She had seizures and no sucking reflex. When Lisa brought

Samantha home from the hospital, doctors had not yet given a definitive prognosis. By the time of the second interview, Samantha had been diagnosed with cerebral palsy; she is fed through a g-tube.

Peggy Hoffmeister

At the time of the first interview, Peggy was 39 years old and had a Master's degree. She had worked as an administrator at a college, a position she gave up to stay home with her children. Her husband is employed by the state. Daniel is her second child. He was first diagnosed with pervasive developmental disorder, a term that refers to being on the autistic spectrum. By the time of the second interview, Daniel had been diagnosed with "full-blown" autism, and Peggy had also given birth to a new baby girl. The family lives in a suburban single-family home. While she had been exposed to Catholic teachings, Peggy describes herself as an atheist.

Terry Johnson

Terry is in her early thirties and has a M.S.W. degree; at the time of the first interview, she was working as a social worker for a state agency, but she later lost her position owing to budget cuts. Her husband works for the state, and they live in a house in a small town. Terry was raised in the Greek Orthodox tradition; her husband is Methodist. Their second daughter, Colleen, was born with Hirschprung's disease, a disorder of the colon requiring colostomy surgery. Colleen also had developmental delays that Terry hoped were the temporary consequence of Colleen's medical problems. By the time of the second interview, however, Colleen had undergone chromosomal testing that revealed she had Cri du Chat syndrome; this syndrome involves mental retardation, motor delays, and some behavioral abnormalities. At the time of the second interview, Terry had also given birth to her third child, a boy, and was applying for a new job.

Pam Karcher

Pam is a 35-year-old single mother of two boys. After graduating from high school, Pam attended a business institute for a year and then worked, sometimes full- and sometimes part-time. She now lives in a trailer park and works part-time as a waitress. She was raised Catholic but "faded away" and has been looking into other churches, the latest being Methodist. Her son, Mac, was diagnosed with Asperger's syndrome, a neuropsychiatric disorder on the autistic spectrum characterized by an inability to understand how to interact socially, by social withdrawal, and by poor motor skills.

Judith Larson

Judith, 28, lives in a house she and her husband have fixed up themselves in an urban neighborhood. Judith graduated from high school and has not worked outside the home since her marriage. Her husband has a job with the state. Judith has twin daughters who were developing at different rates. At the time of the first interview, Tiffany had been diagnosed with a seizure disorder and had developmental delays that Judith attributed to the seizures. Her expectation at that time was that Tiffany would "catch up" once her seizures were controlled with medication. By the time of the second interview, however, Judith had received a new diagnosis. Tests determined that Tiffany has Prader-Willi syndrome, the symptoms of which include mental retardation, motor delays, and serious obesity brought on by hyperphagia (a need to eat an extraordinary amount of food).

Donna Leiden

Donna, 32, has a college degree and is a part-time student in elementary special education. Her husband runs his own printing business in their suburban home. She is Catholic but less religious since the birth of her second child. Keith has a radial club hand; he is missing the thumb and radius on one hand and has a deformed index finger. He was also evaluated as having some gross motor delays and is receiving physical therapy.

Barbara Mangino

Barbara, 28, currently works as a babysitter. Previously she had been an administrative assistant in a bank. Her husband works two jobs to help pay the mortgage on their home. Barbara has two years of college and is Episcopal. As an infant, her son, Richard, had difficulties digesting food. He has since been evaluated as having a speech delay.

Pauline Marino

Pauline, 36, is married and has a college degree. She had been employed by the state government doing accounting and computing but is now doing accounting from her suburban home. She has a seven-year-old daughter and a four-year-old son, Zachary. Zachary has developed no speech at all, and Pauline struggled for a long time to get a firm diagnosis. He was labeled with hypotonia (low muscle tone) and attention deficit disorder in addition to his serious speech disorder. At the visit at the Newborn Followup Program, Zachary was given a diagnosis of dyspraxia with dysphasic characteristics. Zachary was later diagnosed with a sensory integration disorder as well.

Patricia Marks

Patricia had given birth 11 years earlier to a very premature boy, Samuel. Unable to conceive again after Samuel's birth, Patricia and her husband decided to adopt. After waiting a number of years and experiencing some bitter disappointments, they were asked whether they would consider adopting premature twin girls. They took Danielle and Erika, weighing 1 lb. 5 oz. and 1 lb. 11 oz, respectively, into their home. Both of the girls have been diagnosed with cerebral palsy. Tests have shown varying results for Danielle's cognitive abilities, ranging from normal to low normal. Erika has been declared legally blind. Patricia disagrees with the label of mental retardation given for Erika. A business major in college, Patricia had worked as an accountant but quit work after the adoption. She is now in her thirties. She and her husband are both Catholic. The family lives in a single-family home in a small city.

Jane Martin

Jane is the 32-year-old mother of three girls. She has a college degree and had previously worked for the state. Her husband is a dentist, and the family lives in a duplex home in a suburban neighborhood. The middle child, Andrea, has a history of ear infections and was diagnosed with a hearing loss; she also has a speech delay and is sensitive to textures.

Diane McDonald

Diane is in her thirties and has a college education. She had worked as a medical technologist but is now at home full-time. Her husband is an engineer, and the family lives in a single-family home in a rural-suburban area. At the time of the first interview, her son, Ryan, had a speech delay and was evaluated as having a very low cognitive ability. No cause was identified. By the second interview, Ryan's speech and performance on cognitive tests had improved to the point where he had been "declassified"; he no longer qualifies for special education services.

Ann Meadows

Ann, 31, was a photographer before she had her youngest child, Max. Now she is a full-time homemaker, though she is considering going back to school to become a special-education teacher. She has two older children, ages 11 and 7. Her husband manages a golf club, and the family lives in a house in a city neighborhood. Ann is Catholic. Max was diagnosed with pervasive developmental disorder, a disorder on the autistic spectrum.

Laurel Messerschmidt

Laurel is a 38-year-old married mother of three. She has a Master's degree and is employed full-time in a social service agency. Her husband is an engineer, and the family lives in a house in a suburban neighborhood. She is Methodist. Laurel's second child has a speech delay and was already receiving speech therapy services at the time that

Laurel brought her youngest child, Ellen, to Newborn Followup for an evaluation. Ellen was diagnosed with mild cerebral palsy.

Sharon Miller

Sharon is a 24-year-old African-American single mother. She grew up with the religious traditions of African Methodist, Baptist, and Episcopal churches. Sharon had served in the Army but is now an undergraduate college student planning a career in social work. She conceived her son, Robert, while using birth control, and for the first three months of the pregnancy was unaware that she was pregnant. Her child's father is a young artist who does not live with her but does help out with childcare. At the time of the first interview, Sharon was sharing a house with a friend and the friend's child; later she moved into her own apartment.

Jenna Mosher

Jenna is a high-school teacher, as is her husband. They live in a house in a city neighborhood. Jenna is Unitarian. Her son, Daniel, was born with a chromosomal anomaly (a translocation of the 7th and 9th chromosomes), resulting in multiple disabilities including profound mental retardation, vision impairment, speech delays, and severe motor impairments. Jenna has been told that Daniel will never walk. At the time of the second interview, Jenna had a newborn baby girl and was staying at home full-time.

Darlene Mulligan

Darlene, 36, is married and lives in an apartment in an urban neighborhood. She has a college degree in computer programming and a job with the state government. She is Catholic. Her husband is currently unemployed. While pregnant, Darlene had amniocentesis, which showed that she was carrying a child with Down syndrome. Faced with this information, she and her husband decided to carry the baby to term. Patty has a heart defect associated with Down syndrome and will need surgery.

Nancy Papagallo

A 23-year-old high-school graduate, Nancy has held jobs doing laundry and housecleaning. She now stays home full-time and is on public assistance. Nancy was not brought up in any religious tradition. She is a single mother and has an ongoing relationship with her baby's father, whose name the child bears. Nancy and infant, Christopher, live in an apartment in a small city. Hours after Christopher's birth, Nancy was told that he had "a hole in his heart." He has had one heart surgery and will need another. Christopher is on oxygen and was diagnosed at Newborn Followup with developmental delays. Tests also indicated that Christopher was exposed to lead.

Maria Peters

Maria, 19, was born in Puerto Rico and grew up in a community outside of New York City. She has a high-school diploma. She had recently moved to the capital district to be with her boyfriend, who is attending college in the area. Maria was enrolled for a semester in a different college but had to quit when her baby was born. Under the terms of his financial aid, Maria's boyfriend must live on the college campus; Maria and her son, Tim, live in an apartment in an inner-city neighborhood. She currently lives on public assistance. Maria's mother was Pentecostal and her father Methodist. Her boyfriend's family is also Pentecostal, and they have taken their son to church when visiting there, but Maria herself does not practice any religion now. The baby was born at 27 weeks' gestation. He has been diagnosed with cerebral palsy and is blind.

Angela Petrocelli

Angela, 35, comes from a large, Italian family. She is Catholic. She went to college for a degree in medical technology but ended up working in the insurance industry. Angela is now a full-time homemaker, and her husband works for a utility company. They live in a house in a suburban neighborhood and have a teenage daughter as well as their son, Peter. Angela experienced complications in her pregnancy with twin boys.

They were delivered prematurely by C-section, and one son was stillborn. The surviving son, Peter, was sent to the neonatal intensive care unit. He was diagnosed with spastic diplegia, a form of cerebral palsy primarily affecting his legs. By the time of the second interview, magnetic resonance imaging had confirmed minor brain damage.

Mary Jane Pickard

Mary Jane, 30, is a married, Catholic, college-educated woman living in a suburban home. Until the birth of her baby, she worked as an accountant. Mary Jane had experienced fertility problems and then a difficult pregnancy. When it was determined that the fetus was not growing, Mary Jane and her husband had to make a decision of whether to let it die or deliver the baby early by C-section. They made the choice to deliver the baby, and Brent spent three months in the neonatal intensive care unit. Upon evaluation, Brent was found to have minor developmental delays and a slightly misshapen head, most likely caused by resting his head continuously in the same position owing to poor head control.

Maureen Quinlan

Maureen is a married, 36-year-old mother of three children. Her husband is an auto mechanic, and they live in a trailer in a suburb. Maureen took some college courses but stopped after becoming pregnant with her first child, a daughter. She has not worked outside the home since then. The family is born-again Christian. Her older son was diagnosed with pervasive developmental disorder, and when Maureen saw her two-year-old displaying similar symptoms, she brought him to the Newborn Followup Program for an evaluation. There he was also diagnosed with pervasive developmental disorder, a disorder on the autistic spectrum.

Janet Ramirez

Janet spent the early part of her life in the Dominican Republic before moving to New York City. She is 38 and married and has four children.

Janet has a college degree; she had worked as an elementary school teacher but is now a full-time homemaker. Her husband works as an occupational therapist and paramedic. The family is Catholic and recently moved to the area in the hopes that they would find better services for their third child, Betty, who has Prader-Willi syndrome (including mental retardation). They brought in their youngest child, Mitchell, for an evaluation. Mitchell has a speech delay and possible attention deficit disorder.

Elena Rivera

At the time of the first interview, Elena's third child, Adam, had just been diagnosed with autism. The family was temporarily living with Elena's mother; later they moved to a small trailer park at the outskirts of a city. Elena has two teenage children by a previous marriage; these children sometimes live with her and sometimes with her ex-husband. Her husband works as a carpenter; Adam is his first child. Elena has an associate's degree and had been employed as an accountant, but at the time of the first interview, she was staying home full-time with her two young children. A year later, she had begun doing some part-time tax work. The family is Catholic. In addition to his primary diagnosis of autism, Adam has asthma.

Denise Rivers

Denise, 28, is the mother of two daughters. At the time of the first interview, she was working as a medical transcriber at a local hospital but was experiencing problems with her boss, problems that she felt stemmed from the hospital's unwillingness to give her time off to care for her youngest daughter. At 16 months of age, Paula was diagnosed with hydrocephalus. She required a permanent shunt placed in her head to drain excess cerebrospinal fluid and to relieve pressure on the brain. As a consequence of the hydrocephalous, Paula has developmental delays, including cognitive, speech, and motor delays. Denise is married. The family is Catholic and lives in an apartment in an urban neighborhood. In the period between the first and second interviews, Denise gave birth to a boy who also experienced serious medical problems, and Denise was fired from her job at the hospital.

Laura Robertson

Laura, 25, has a college degree and works as a special-education occupational therapist. She is married to a firefighter. They live in a single-family home in an urban neighborhood. Laura's only child, Monica, has a seizure disorder and developmental delays. The first seizure occurred shortly after the infant was immunized, and Laura believes her daughter's disabilities were caused by an allergic reaction to the vaccine. Laura was raised as a Catholic but is no longer religious.

Becky Romano

Becky is 30 years old and married. She has had some college experience but did not graduate and now holds a part-time clerical position with a state agency. She lives with her husband and two sons in a suburban home; the family is Catholic. Becky's second child, Billy, was born with a chromosomal anomaly that she was told could result in mental retardation and motor impairments. At one point, Becky was told by a doctor that her son would never walk. Nevertheless, the boy did learn to walk and has been tested as having normal intelligence. At a visit to the Newborn Followup Program, Becky was told that Billy was showing evidence of having attention deficit disorder.

Linda Rubenstein

Linda is married and in her 30s. She has a college degree; she had worked in the business field, but is now a full-time homemaker. Linda's first child was premature and has multiple disabilities, including mental retardation and motor impairments. She came to the Newborn Followup Program to have her second child evaluated. This infant son, Richard, was also premature. However, his course in the neonatal intensive care unit was not as difficult as his older brother's, and the doctor's optimistic prediction was for only minor (and perhaps temporary) developmental delays. The family lives in a single-family home in a suburban neighborhood.

Julie Sanders

Julie, 36, is single and lives with her four sons in a trailer in a rural area. She is a Jehovah's Witness. The boys' father left her; he does not provide financial support for the children, though he and his brothers provided the labor to bring electricity and running water into the trailer. Julie is a full-time homemaker and currently receives public assistance. Her youngest son, Randy, was injured during a difficult delivery. As a result, he has Erb's palsy, a paralysis of the shoulder, arm, and diaphragm. Though he had surgery on his diaphragm, his arm and shoulder remain paralyzed.

Jane Sawyer

Jane has a college degree and has worked as a special-education teacher. She is currently a full-time homemaker but plans to return to work. Her husband has a position in state government. They are Catholic and live in a house in an urban neighborhood. Their daughter, Alexis, was born prematurely at 24 weeks' gestation and spent many months in the neonatal intensive care unit. Alexis has been diagnosed with cerebral palsy; in addition to severe gross and fine motor impairments, Alexis is speech-impaired. Her inability to communicate has made it difficult to ascertain her level of cognitive functioning.

Phyllis Smith

A 26-year-old married mother of three children, Phyllis had recently moved to the region from Florida. She has a high-school degree and is a full-time homemaker. She lives in a small house in a suburban neighborhood. Faith, her middle child, is deaf and visually impaired. Depressed over problems in her marriage, Phyllis drank alcohol while pregnant with Faith; though she has been told her child does not have fetal alcohol syndrome, she nevertheless worries that her drinking caused her daughter's disabilities. Phyllis was raised a Catholic and is now a practicing born-again Christian.

Sonya Somich

Sonya was a married, stay-at-home mother of two when she gave birth to a premature infant girl. Katrina was born at 23 weeks' gestation, weighing only 1 lb. 5 oz. Katrina had a rocky course in the neonatal intensive care unit during her five-month hospitalization. At the time of her release from the hospital, the infant was still on oxygen and was at risk for a variety of disabilities. At a later visit to the Newborn Followup Program, Katrina was diagnosed with only a minor speech delay. The family is active in the Ukranian Orthodox Church.

Kelly Strathmore

Kelly is married and 39 years old. She has a degree from a junior college and works as a seamstress out of her home in a city neighborhood. She was raised Catholic but does not practice any religion now. She has two children. Her son, Brendan, does not speak and was given a diagnosis of verbal apraxia, a speech-programming disorder.

Mary Summers

Mary is 25 years old. She is a graduate of a vocational-technology program at her high school and now works in a deli. Mary was raised as a Methodist and continues to practice her religion. She lives with her husband and two children in a trailer park in a rural area. Mary's daughter, Joanne, is 6. Her son, Peter, is two years old; he had first been diagnosed with cerebral palsy and later was labeled as having mental retardation as well. Peter is fed with a g-tube and does not walk or speak.

Tara Vernon

Tara lives with her husband and two daughters in a single-family home in a suburban area. She has a college degree and is a nurse but now works only on weekends. Her husband is an engineer. Tara reports that she is not religious. At first her younger daughter appeared to be developing normally but later began to lose the words she had once spoken. By 18 months of age, Nicole was diagnosed with autism.

Michelle White

Michelle is 33 years old and married for the second time. She is Episcopal and lives in an apartment in an inner-city neighborhood. Her husband does manual labor as a roofer. Michelle had worked as a bookkeeper right out of high school, but after Brittany was born, she decided to get a less stressful job and became a hairdresser. Michelle had experienced fertility problems and conceived Brittany through the use of fertility drugs. Brittany was born prematurely at 27 weeks' gestation, had respiratory distress syndrome, and spent three months in the neonatal intensive care unit. At seven months of age, Brittany developed meningitis, and a CT scan showed brain atrophy. She has been diagnosed with speech and cognitive delays and attention deficit disorder; Michelle was also told that Brittany showed some signs of pervasive developmental disorder.

Brenda Wilson

Brenda is a college graduate in her late twenties. She is married to a salesman and was a full-time homemaker at the time of the first interview. A year later, she was working part-time as a cashier in a liquor store and planning to get pregnant with a third child. The family lives in a duplex in a suburban neighborhood. She and her husband are Catholic. Her daughter, Lisa, is her second child. At the age of five months, Lisa came down with a life-threatening respiratory virus known as RSV and had to be transferred to a hospital in Buffalo. There she underwent a process known as ECMO. While on ECMO, Lisa had a stroke. She had been declared legally blind, but her vision did improve over time. At Newborn Followup Program, she was diagnosed with motor delays and mental retardation.

Dawn Woodward

Dawn had her first child at 19; now 23, she has two daughters. She completed a GED and then earned an associate's degree. She has worked as a secretary but is now at home full-time with her children. Dawn was brought up Catholic but now considers herself an atheist. Her husband is in the Navy, and the family lives in a Navy housing project in a small city. Her youngest child, 18-month-old Rebecca, was diagnosed with a form of muscular dystrophy.

Notes

Chapter 1

1 Anthropological analyses of reproduction "gone awry" (Jenkins and Inhorn, 2003) have recently highlighted the illusory nature and problematic consequences of such representations; in this vein, scholars have addressed such experiences as infertility (Becker, 1997, 2000), positive prenatal screening results (Rapp, 1999a, 1999b), childhood disability (Landsman, 1998, 2000, 2003), and pregnancy loss and stillbirth (Layne, 2003). An international conference on reproductive disruptions was held at the University of Michigan in 2005, and many of the contributions appear in a volume of the same name (Inhorn, 2007). Furthermore, medical and statistical literature indicate that in spite, and perhaps because, of advances in neonatology, the prevalence of children in the United States with disabilities has in fact risen (Kaye et al., 1996; Lorenz et al., 1998; McElrath, 2002; Watts and Saigal, 2006). Among other issues such studies remind us that, to put it simply, things don't always work out as expected or planned.

2 This is not to say that every evaluation I observed resulted in a doctor's giving what was considered "bad news." These instances in which a child was determined to be "normal" in themselves proved revealing, both in how mothers reacted to such news and in how medical staff were affected.

3 This is not surprising. In spite of statistics indicating that most American mothers are now in the workforce, Rannveig Traustadottir suggests that "these new and expanded boundaries of women's lives are very fragile. As soon as there is an increased demand for traditional women's work within the home—such as caring for a child with a disability—the boundaries shift and women come under tremendous pressure to leave the public arena and go back into the home" (1991: 225). For low-income women, the need to stay home to care for a disabled child is no less great than for mothers in the middle or upper income levels. However, according to Litt (2004), maternal work requirements of Temporary Assistance for Needy Families "devalues the family care-giving of poor women" (638). As a result, their ability to provide adequate care is compromised.

4 For instance, Traustadottir found that all of the mothers in her study of American families with disabled children had the main responsibility for providing the care necessary to keep the child within the family (1991: 218). "Caring is seen as women's responsibility, and the division of labor assigns far more responsibility for caring to women than to men" (1991: 216);

such care includes both traditional caring work, and the work of searching for and coordinating any services a child might receive. For a review of the literature on allocation of responsibility for family work, see Home (2002); she argues that the replacement of public responsibility for disabled individuals by community and family care has not been matched by changes in resources, leading to increased caring burdens for mothers of disabled children. Analyzing data from three studies in Canada, McKeever and Miller (2004) similarly find that the shift of the site of care away from institutions is associated with an increasingly disproportionate responsibility for disabled children's care, much of it technologically sophisticated, being borne informally by women.

5 For a history of professional research on family reactions to a child's disability, see Ferguson, 2002. Ferguson notes that during the long period from about 1920 to 1980 professional analyses of parental adaptation presented parents alternatively as being driven to neurotic or dysfunctional behavior or as experiencing perpetual sorrow and suffering. "The challenge for research was to catalogue and sequence the evidence of parental damage and to argue for the efficacy of this or that therapeutic intervention" (Ferguson, 2002: 125). More recent analyses address social context and parental resiliency. See Landsman and Van Riper, 2007.

6 The term *family-centered* refers to a set of principles and practices for enhancing child development and learning. These include:

> individualized, flexible, and responsive practices... family choice regarding any number of aspects of program practices and intervention options; parent–professional collaboration and partnerships context for family-program relations; and the provision and mobilization of resources and supports necessary for families to care for and rear their children in ways that produce optimal child, parent, and family outcomes. (Dunst, 2002: 139)

Chapter 2

1 This closely matches the experience of women in Australia, where ultrasound has transformed women's embodied experience of pregnancy such that "the fetus, once 'seen,' becomes a separate entity for which the woman is responsible. She becomes morally (and perhaps legally) culpable for damage that may ensue from a failure to exercise microregimens of care..." (Harris, Connor, Bisits, and Higginbotham, 2004: 41).

2 There is a clear association of heightened risk for disability with conditions of poverty. Recent longitudinal estimates indicate a significant increase in the rate of childhood disability in the United States over the period of 1983–1996, with the increased risk for disability located among constituencies defined by poverty and by single-parent headed families (Fujiura and Yamaki,

2000: 187). Children living in poverty are more vulnerable to, among other conditions, low birth weight.

3 This is consistent with the findings of Markens, Browner, and Press (1997: 351–371). Their focus was on prenatal diet; they found no significant differences by ethnicity or social class in women's attitudes toward prenatal care or prenatal care practices.

4 No studies have shown damage caused by *an occasional* drink or cigarette (Malone, personal communication, 1998). There is consistent evidence for an association between smoking during pregnancy and low birth weight, the latter putting infants at greater risk for disabilities including cerebral palsy (see Oaks, 2001: 6–9); Oaks points out, however, that the

> "scientific facts" on the risks of smoking are population-based estimates and predictions that cannot be applied with precision to an individual's experiences. Medical experts cannot in good conscience tell any individual pregnant woman who smokes that her fetus or baby certainly will be adversely affected; they can only warn her of this chance. (Oaks: 13)

5 The mechanism for the protective effect of folic acid is not clear. Some research has shown an increased number of spontaneous abortions (embryonic and fetal death) among women who take the recommended amount of folic acid (Hook and Czeizel, 1997). This had led to speculation that folic acid might work to prevent neural tube defects not by reducing their development in fetuses but by stimulating the miscarriage of fetuses that would otherwise develop into babies born with neural tube defects. In suggesting that the protective effect of folic acid may work by terathanasia, a term used to describe agents that may diminish the rate of birth defects by selectively inducing abortion of affected conceptuses, Hook and Czeizel recognize that those who find abortion ethically unacceptable might have a reasonable objection to routine pharmacologic use of folic acid (1997: 514). Judith Hall takes up this issue in her response to Hook and Czeizel, suggesting that their paper, "if taken to extremes, could interfere with a very important public-health opportunity for primary prevention of congenital anomalies" (1997: 1322).

6 The March of Dimes now encourages expectant fathers to quit smoking because of the impact of second-hand smoke on a fetus and to set an example.

7 The position of these authors (or of myself) should not be construed as a stance against women's reproductive freedom or the morality of abortion; on the contrary, the authors support a woman's right to choose whether or not to have a baby at a particular time, but caution against social pressures on women to choose what *type* of baby to have. Such pressures may lead to new eugenic consequences. As Joan Rothschild points out, in promoting genetic testing for individual women, the medical profession shapes genetic

outcomes; decisions are cumulative in their effects, she argues, and "each decision marks the imperfect fetus" (2005: 109).

8 See Wang (1992) for a discussion of the stigmatizing impact of injury prevention campaigns.

Chapter 3

1 Bogdan and Taylor (1992) make the argument that sociologists' focus on the rejection of people with disabilities has led them to ignore or discount instances of acceptance of people with disabilities as full persons. They take the position that "the definition of a person is not determined by either the characteristics of the person or the abstract social or cultural meanings attached to the group of which the person is a part, but rather the nature of the relationship between the definer and the defined" (276). Conflating the terms *human* and *person*, Bogdan and Taylor examine the perspectives of non-disabled caregivers who attribute qualities of "humanness" to their disabled partners. That the caregivers are exceptions in doing so speaks to the more general cultural interpretation of people with disabilities as less than full persons. But it does suggest a means by which mothers, when they are caregivers to their disabled children, come to redefine personhood.

2 Morgan cites Montagu's research on the Arunta of Central Australia, among whom a premature infant is interpreted as being the young of some other animal, such as a kangaroo, that mistakenly entered the body of the woman (Morgan, 1996b: 25). Among the Punan Bah, twins are not considered human (Nicolaisen, 1995). Among the African Nuer studied by Evans-Pritchard, twins were believed to be birds; when they died, and most did, they were said to have returned to the air (cited in Scheper-Hughes, 1992: 375).

3 Conklin and Morgan acknowledge that the "all or nothing" quality of American personhood is open to dispute; they frame their discussion in terms of a shift from individualistic to relational definitions of personhood that may occur as families experience making decisions at the "early margins of life." Such decisions include whether or not to terminate a pregnancy or to prolong the lives of imperiled infants. However, by focusing on temporary decision making at the beginning and end points of human life rather than on the ongoing definitions of living individuals (such as those with disabilities), as I later argue, Conklin and Morgan miss the gradations of personhood that are a *regular* feature of North American culture.

4 As Layne points out however, acknowledging the existence of something worth grieving need not automatically accede the inherent personhood of fetuses unless one accepts the anti-abortion view in the first place (1997: 305).

5 It may be at the heart of the everyday experience of disabled people as well. However, my focus is on the impact of this diminution of personhood on the

mothers who give birth to and nurture such persons. The disability rights literature has not addressed this issue from the perspective of parents. In part this may stem from parents' efforts to cure children of their impairments, an attitude about which the disability-rights literature is critical; in part it may stem from concern that parents have been paternalistic and detrimental to the attainment of autonomy of disabled individuals. See chapter 6.

6 For discussion of the impact of visual imaging technologies on concepts of fetal personhood see Duden, 1993; Hartouni, 1991, 1993; Rapp, 1997; Stabile, 1992; and Taylor, 1998. Gerber (2002) compares the understanding of the fetus by women using RU486 with understandings drawn from ultrasound imaging. See Mwaria (1990) for a discussion of differences in the medical criteria used to determine a diagnosis of persistent vegetative state and Joralemon (1995: 340–341) and Lock (2002) on controversy over redefining death as the absence of cerebral or brainstem activity in the context of organ donation.

7 Murphy (1995) has employed the anthropological concept of liminality to describe the personhood of those who have acquired disability; this term has also been applied to the lives of those who have entered a persistent vegetative state (Mwaria, 1990). In both of these instances, a person is between statuses, having been divested of one status, but having not yet attained another. The concept of liminality describes the ambiguity of disabled babies, but what sets the children in this study apart from the cases of acquired disability or persistent vegetative state described by Murphy and by Mwaria is that when the diagnosis is made at birth, the child's status as person has never been established; the child is therefore not *between* statuses. It is the doctor who often appears to either assign or withhold the status of person to someone who has not yet been granted that status. The term *liminality* is also problematic in that it implies that a transition to a new status will take place, while in the case of disability it may not.

8 Keisha Sellers is an African-American mother whose child was evaluated at the Newborn Followup program but who was not interviewed. Therefore her name does not appear in the Appendix.

9 The quote from the transcript was included in a paper I wrote, which later appeared as Landsman (2000). I gave copies of the paper to the physicians and nurses at the Newborn Followup Program, and it was chosen for discussion at the monthly Developmental Pediatrics Journal Club. It was during the Journal Club discussion that the physician referred to in the quote gave a response.

10 While the mother was still taking care of some paperwork with the office secretary, I left the medical staff in the conference room to say goodbye and to thank the mother. I walked with her across the room. By the time the woman had reached the outside door, she had begun to cry. I could report back that indeed, the mother had gotten it.

11 Some of what follows appears in a different version in Landsman (1999).

12 For a discussion of changes in perceptions and treatment of disabled individuals, see Polloway, Patten, Smith, and Smith (1996). They track the development of three "paradigm shifts" relative to mental retardation and developmental disabilities, from a facility-based paradigm, through a services-based paradigm, to the current supports-based inclusion paradigm; the latter, they claim, may now be "merging with the new thrust toward concern with empowerment" (1996: 8).

Chapter 4

1 The root of discrimination against people with disabilities in the United States has been the subject of much speculation. Avi Rose hypothesizes four central views in the Judeo-Christian religion that together have influenced the assumptions and prejudices operating in the broader society: disability as a sign of punishment or evil incarnation, disability as challenge to divine perfection, disability as object of pity and charity, and disability as incompetence (Rose, 1997: 397). Those drawing on historical materialism, such as Oliver (1990) and others, find the "foundations of present-day disablism in the historical emergence and developmental stages of capitalist relations of production (Thomas and Corker, 2002: 19). In their analysis of the cross cultural literature on disability, Whyte and Ingstad (1995) suggest that in a society in which achievement is highly valued, as is the case in the United States, the attribution of full personhood to people with disabilities is less likely. Frank also notes that where status derives from one's level of performance of a specific task in a competitive labor market, such as is the case in advanced capitalist societies, individuals with impairments are most likely to be devalued and excluded (2000: 47). Morris (1991) and Wendell (1996) similarly argue that an overvaluation of independence and autonomy result in a denigration of people with disabilities and point to the arbitrariness of cultural definitions of independence and dependence: "Few people in my city would consider me a 'dependent' person because I rely on others to provide me water out of the tap, electricity to heat and light my home, run my computer, and wash my clothes, and food and clothing in markets where I can buy them instead of producing them myself" (Wendell, 145–146).

2 According to Jordan, "for any particular domain several knowledge systems exist, some of which, by consensus, come to carry more weight than others, either because they explain the state of the world better for the purposes at hand (efficacy) or because they are associated with a stronger power base (structural superiority) or both" (Jordan, 1997: 56). That which carries more weight is authoritative.

3 It's interesting to note that official dicta contradicted the opinions of both practicing professionals and nonprofessional American adults in this regard (Goodman, 1989: 315). Citing definitions put forward by the American Association of Mental Retardation, the International Classification of

Diseases, and the American Psychiatric Association's 1987 Diagnostic and Statistical Manual of Mental Disorders, Goodman claims that "according to the major professional organizations, mental retardation means subaverage functioning without regard to etiology or prognosis" (1989: 313). Nevertheless, surveys of pediatricians and parents of normal children have shown that "substantial numbers do not believe mental retardation could be reversed," and "adults have acquired an excessively pessimistic view of mental retardation (biologically determined and unmodifiable)" (1989: 315).

4 See also Landsman, 2000.

5 Though some see Down syndrome as placing a cap on the child's development, many mothers of children with Down syndrome do not.

6 Briskin and Liptak (1995), for instance, see denial as a stage in the process of grieving the ideal child of one's dreams. "Denial serves to buy the grieving individual the time to find the inner strengths and the external supports necessary to prepare for the major changes that eventually must be made in the person's life" (Briskin and Liptak, 263).

7 Kearney similarly notes that in her research in Australia, parents had realistic understandings of their child's diagnosis, but seemed to be denying the "verdict" or "defying the implications" medical staff gave to such diagnoses (1999: 339). Like the American mothers in this study who felt that to deny doctors' dismal predictions enabled them to work with their child to make developmental progress, Australian parents found that such hope was necessary for parental advocacy and determination without which, Kearney claims, a child might otherwise fulfill the professionals' predictions of hopeless futures" (339).

Chapter 5

1 The position of disability-rights advocates and scholars on the divisive issue of selective abortion following prenatal screening is expressed in just these terms—the devaluation of life with an impairment. Tom Shakespeare, for example, notes that women are encouraged to abort fetuses diagnosed with Down syndrome,

> so that they and society in general are saved the cost of this value-less life.... While the literature distinguishes abortions for social reasons from abortions for reasons of medical abnormality, the latter are often in fact decisions about the former. Foetuses with genetic abnormality are terminated because our society places no value on disabled lives, and because the social and economic costs of having an impairment in a disabling society are considerable. (Shakespeare, 1998: 679)

Similarly, in a public discussion with bioethicist Peter Singer, who proposes infanticide of newborns with severe disabilities, disabilities scholar and activist Adrienne Asch argues that "the reasons that people wish to terminate the lives of disabled newborns, the reasons that physicians have given for withholding treatment, the reasons that many people choose abortion of their diagnosed fetuses, flow from many of the same views that Singer holds and they are misguided views: assuming that there is only one standard of what makes a life valuable" (Asch, 1999). Rothschild (2005) holds physicians partially accountable for the ranking of some lives as more valuable than others. Noting the cumulative effect of decisions to abort certain types of fetuses, she argues, "As the numbers of diagnostic decisions ratchet upward, imperfections, and undesirable fetuses, are inevitably selected and ranked. In this way, physicians' individual professional actions contribute to framing a genetically based health hierarchy of birth" (109–110).

Chapter 6

1 For examples of discussion of models of disability, see among many others, Asch, 2004; Barnes, Oliver, and Barton, 2002; Gilson and DePoy, 2000; Gabel and Peters, 2004; Hughes and Paterson, 1997; Humphrey, 1999; Johnston, 1997; Kasnitz and Shuttleworth, 2001; Linton, Mello, and O'Neill, 1995; Llewellyn and Hogan, 2000; Overboe, 1999; Paterson and Hughes, 1999; Pfeiffer, 2002; Scotch, 1988; Shakespeare, 1994, 2005, 2006; Shakespeare and Watson, 1997; Sheldon, Traustadottir, Beresford, Boxall, and Oliver, 2007; and Tregaskis, 2002.

2 Not surprisingly, the Ashley Treatment was condemned by disability rights groups, including ADAPT, Not Dead Yet, Feminist Response in Disability Activism (FRIDA), and the Disability Rights Education & Defense Fund (DREDF). The latter group issued a statement dated January 7, 2007 portraying the treatment as a violation of human rights for people with disabilities. DREDF posted the statement on their Web site (www.dredf. org/news/ashley.shtml). While empathizing with parents facing the often daunting task of caring for children with severe physical and cognitive disabilities, DREDF portrayed Ashley's medical treatment as a violation of a sacrosanct and non-negotiable principle of personal and physical autonomy for persons with disabilities. If Ashley's parents were unable to get the assistance they need to adequately care for their child as she is and would be, then "it is all our duty to change the system so it works rather than find novel ways to modify people so that they will more easily 'fit' a flawed system." This latter statement is a clear refutation of the medical model. In a rare position statement, entitled "When the Slippery Slope Becomes a Mudslide," Exceptional Parent Magazine also took a public stance in opposition to growth attenuation treatment for children with disabilities (http://www.eparent.com/newsletter/StatementToOrganizations.htm). Linking this treatment to the announcement of Switzerland's Supreme Court's ruling that assisted suicide for persons with serious mental illness

is acceptable, and of the "Groningen Protocol" that physicians in The Netherlands are encouraged to follow in order to sanction the euthanizing of infants born with disabilities, including Down syndrome, Exceptional Parent (EP) decried the public acceptance of threats to people with disabilities. Embracing the rhetoric of human rights, EP's Position Statement argued that "The utilitarianism" creators of these procedures "promote in the name of compassion is nothing other than new language and new ideas designed to encourage the systematic denigration of those with disabilities, stripping them of the basic human right to life and dignity." A powerful repudiation of the Ashley Treatment also comes from Anne McDonald (2007), in a newspaper column subtitled "Been there. Done that. Preferred to Grow." McDonald documents her own experience as a child with cerebral palsy who has motor skills of a three-month-old. Left to live in a state institution in Australia for 14 years, her growth and secondary sexual characteristics attenuated owing to malnutrition and neglect. Her life changed when at the age of 16 she was provided a means of communication; two years later, through spelling, she instructed the lawyers who fought the habeas corpus action that enabled her to leave the institution.

3 Singh discusses this in terms of the rising incidence of diagnoses of attention deficit/hyperactivity disorder (ADHD) and the debate over treatment with the drug Ritalin (Singh, 2004).

4 Thanks to Huhana Hickey for making this point in a work in progress she generously shared with me.

5 Compare this to the definition articulated by the Union of the Physically Impaired Against Segregation (UPIAS) in 1976 and widely accepted by British social model theorists, in which impairment is "the lack of a limb or part thereof or a defect of a limb, organ or mechanism of the body" (quoted in Tremain, 2002: 33).

6 For discussion of how mothers feel that they are accountable, or are held accountable by others, for their child's disability, see Landsman, 1998.

7 See also Longmore (1995). In what Longmore has called the second phase of the movement of disabled Americans, the disability experience has become the source of values and norm. Many people with disabilities now "declare that they prize not self-sufficiency but self-determination, not independence, but interdependence, not functional separateness but personal connection, not physical autonomy but human community" (Longmore, 1995: 6).

Bibliography

Abrams, E., & Goodman, J. (1998). Diagnosing developmental problems in children: Parents and professionals negotiate bad news. *Journal of Pediatric Psychology, 23*(2), 87–98.

Alexander, D. (1998). Prevention of mental retardation: Four decades of research. *Mental Retardation and Developmental Disabilities Research Reviews, 4,* 50–58.

Anglin, M. (2002). Lessons from Appalachia in the 20th century: Poverty, power, and the "grassroots." *American Anthropologist, 104*(2), 565–582.

Anspach, R. R. (1993). *Deciding who lives: Fateful choices in the intensive care nursery.* Berkeley: University of California Press.

Asch, A. (1998). Distracted by disability. *Cambridge Quarterly of Healthcare Ethics, 7,* 77–87.

———. (1999). Comments made at Ethics, Health Care and Disability Forum, Princeton, NJ: Princeton University, October 12, 1999.

———. (2004). Critical race theory, feminism and disability: Reflections on social justice and personal identity. In B. Smith & B. Hutchinson (Eds.), *Gendering disability* (pp. 9–44). New Brunswick, NJ: Rutgers University Press.

Asch, A., & Fine, M. (1988). Introduction: Beyond pedestals. In A. Asch, & M. Fine (Eds.), *Women with disabilities: Essays in psychology, culture and politics* (pp. 1–37). Philadelphia: Temple University Press.

The "Ashley Treatment." Towards a better quality of life for "pillow angels." Retrieved on June 25, 2007, from http://ashleytreatment.spaces.live.com/blog.

Aylward, G. (2002). Cognitive and neuropsychological outcomes: More than IQ scores. *Mental Retardation and Developmental Disabilities Research Reviews, 8,* 234–240.

Barnes, C., Oliver, M., & Barton, L. (Eds.) (2002). *Disability studies today.* Cambridge: Polity Press.

Baynton, D. (1997). Disability as a useful category of historical analysis. *Disability Studies Quarterly, 17,* 81–87.

Becker, G. (1997). *Disrupted lives: How people make meaning in a chaotic world.* Berkeley: University of California Press.

———. (2000). *The elusive embryo.* Berkeley: University of California Press.

Begley, S. (1997, Spring/Summer). How to build a baby's brain. *Newsweek* [Special issue], 28–32.

Begley, S., & Wingert, P. (1997). Teach your parents well. *Newsweek 129*(17), 72.

Bellcross, C. (1997). A letter to Connor on his first birthday. *The Matchmaker: MUMS National Parent-to-Parent Network Newsletter, 68,* 5.

Bettleheim, B. (1967). *The empty fortress: Infantile autism and the birth of the self.* New York: Free Press.

Bhusan, V., Paneth, N., & Kiely, J. (1993). Impact of improved survival of very low birth weight infants on recent secular trends in the prevalence of cerebral palsy. *Pediatrics, 91,* 1094–1100.

Bierman-van Eendenburg, M. E. C., Jurgens-van der Zee, A. D., Olinga, A. A., Huisjes, H. H., & Touwen, B. C. L. (1981). Predictive value of neonatal neurological examination: A follow-up study at 18 months. *Developmental Medicine and Child Neurology, 23,* 296–305.

Biskupic, J. (2000). "Crack babies" and rights: Court to review public hospital tests on pregnant women. *Washington Post,* 29 February, A03.

Blakeslee, S. (2001 [1995]). In brain's early growth, timetable may be crucial. In N. Wade (Ed.), *The New York Times Book of the Brain* (pp. 158–163). Guilford, CT: Lyons Press.

———. (2001 [1997]). Studies show talking with infants shapes basis of ability to think. In N. Wade (Ed.), *The New York Times Book of the Brain* (pp. 1152–1157). Guilford, CT: Lyons Press.

Blumberg, L. (1998). The bad baby blues: Reproductive technology and the threat to diversity. *Ragged Edge, 19*(4), 12–16.

Bogdan, R., & Taylor, S. J. (1992). The social construction of humanness: Relationships with severely disabled people. In P. Ferguson, D. Ferguson, & S. J. Taylor (Eds.), *Interpreting disability: A qualitative reader* (pp. 275–294). New York: Teachers College Press.

Bombeck, E. (1993, May 22). Perfect moms best for disabled kids. *Albany Times Union,* C-2.

Briskin, H., & Liptak, G. (1995). Helping families with children with developmental disabilities. *Pediatric Annals, 24*(5), 262–266.

Browner, C., & Press, N. (1995). The normalization of prenatal diagnostic screening. In F. Ginsburg & R. Rapp (Eds.), *Conceiving the new world order: The global politics of reproduction* (pp. 307–322). Berkeley, CA: University of California Press.

Browner, C., & Press, N. (1997). The production of authoritative knowledge in American prenatal care. In R. Davis-Floyd & C. Sargent (Eds.), *Childbirth and authoritative knowledge* (pp. 113–131). Berkeley: University of California Press.

Browner, C., Preloran, H. M., & Cox, S. J. (1999). Ethnicity, bioethics, and prenatal diagnosis: The amniocentesis decisions of Mexican-origin women and their partners. *American Journal of Public Health, 89*(11), 1658–1666.

Brucker, B. (1998). Recent discoveries of central nervous system plasticity and the future of biofeedback. Keynote address at the Twenty-Ninth Annual Meeting of the Association for Applied Psychophysiology and Biofeedback, Orlando, FL, April 1998.

Bruder, M. B., & Staff, I. (1998). A comparison of the effects of type of classroom and service characteristics on toddlers with disabilities. *Topics in Early Childhood Special Education, 18*(1), 26–37.

Bruner, J. (1991). The narrative construction of reality. *Critical Inquiry*, *18*, 1–21.

Cannell, F. (1990). Concepts of parenthood: The Warnock Report, the Gillick Debate, and modern myths. *American Ethnologist*, *17*(4), 667–686.

Carlson, L. (2001). Cognitive ableism and disability studies: Feminist reflections on the history of mental retardation. *Hypatia*, *16*(4), 124–146.

Casper, M. (1998). *The making of the unborn patient*. New Brunswick: Rutgers University Press.

Cho, S.-J., Singer, G., & Brenner, M. (2000). Adaptation and accommodation to young children with disabilities: A comparison of Korean and Korean American parents. *Topics in Early Childhood Special Education*, *20*(4), 236–249.

Coker, S. (1989). *Developmental delay and mental retardation*. New York: PMA Publishing Group.

Conklin, B., & Morgan, L. (1996). Babies, bodies, and the production of personhood in North America and a native Amazonian society. *Ethos*, *24*(4), 657–694.

Connolly, K. (2007). The rolling exhibition: Artist statement. Retrieved January 11, 2008, from http://therollingexhibition.com/statement.php.

Corea, G. (1985). *The mother machine*. New York: Harper and Row.

Corker, M., & Shakespeare, T. (2002). *Disability/postmodernism*. London and New York: Continuum.

Cott, N. (1987). *The grounding of modern feminism*. New Haven, CT: Yale University Press.

Cushing, P. (2006). Anthropology. In G. Albrecht (Ed.), *Encyclopedia of disability* (pp. 104–112). Thousand Oaks, CA: Sage.

Damman, O., & Leviton, A. (2006). Neuroimaging and the predictions of outcomes in preterm infants. *New England Journal of Medicine*, *355*(7), 727–729.

Daniels, Cynthia (1997). Between fathers and fetuses: The social construction of male reproduction and the politics of fetal harm. *Signs*, *22*(3), 579–616.

———. 1999. Fathers, mothers, and fetal harm: Rethinking gender difference and reproductive responsibility. In L. Morgan & M. Michaels (Eds.), *Fetal subjects, feminist positions* (pp. 83–98). Philadelphia: University of Pennsylvania Press.

Daniels, Celeste (2003). Letter. *MUMS National Parent-to-Parent Network Matchmaker*, 93.

Darling, R. B. (1979). *Families against society: A study of reactions to children with birth defects*. Beverly Hills: Sage Publications.

Davis, L. J. (1995). *Enforcing normalcy: Disability, deafness, and the body*. London: Verso.

Devlieger, P. (1995). Why disabled? The cultural understanding of physical disability in an African society. In B. Ingstad & S. R. Whyte (Eds.), *Disability and Culture* (pp. 94–133). Berkeley: University of California Press.

Drotar, D., Baskiewicz, A., Irvin, N., Kennell, J., & Klaus, M. (1975). The adaptation of parents to the birth of an infant with a congenital malformation: A hypothetical model. *Pediatrics*, *56*(5), 710–716.

Dubowitz, L. M. S., Dubowitz, V., Palmer, P. G., Miller, G., Fawer, C.-L., & Levene, M. I. (1984). Correlation of neurologic assessment in the preterm newborn infant with outcome at 1 year. *The Journal of Pediatrics*, *105*(3), 452–456.

Duden, B. (1993). *Disembodying women: Perspectives on pregnancy and the unborn.* Cambridge, MA: Harvard University Press.

Dunst, C. (2002). Family-centered practices: Birth through high school. *The Journal of Special Education, 36*(3), 139–147.

Dvorsky, G. (2006). Helping families care for the helpless. Retrieved June 26, 2007, from http://sentientdevelopments.blogspot.com/2006/11/helping-families-care-for-helpless_06.html.

Early Intervention Coordinating Council. (1999). *Early intervention annual report on the status of the early intervention program.* Albany: Author.

Eisenberg, A., Murkhoff, H., & Hathaway, S. (1991). *What to expect when you're expecting,* 2nd ed. [revised]. New York: Workman Publishing.

Evans, H. H. (2004). The medical discovery of shaken baby syndrome and child physical abuse. *Pediatric Rehabilitation, 7*(3), 161–163.

Family Planning Advocates of New York State. (1993). The key to reducing late abortion (making it illegal is not the answer). Albany: Author.

———. (1996). "mis"informed consent for abortion. Albany: Author.

Ferguson, P. (1996). Mental retardation historiography and the culture of knowledge. *Disability Studies Quarterly, 16*(3), 18–31.

———. (2003). Winks, blinks, squints and twitches: Looking for disability and culture through my son's left eye. In P. Devlieger, F. Rusch, & D. Pfeiffer (Eds.), *Rethinking disability* (pp. 131–148). Antwerp and Apeldoorn: Garant.

Ferguson, P., Gartner, A., & Lipsky, D. (2000). The experience of disability in families: A synthesis of research and parent narratives. In E. Parens & A. Asch (Eds.), *Prenatal testing and disability rights* (pp. 72–94). Washington, DC: Georgetown University Press.

Finnegan, J. (1993). *Shattered dreams – lonely choices: Birthparents of babies with disabilities talk about adoption.* Westport: Bergin and Garvey.

First, L., & Palfrey, J. (1994). The infant or young child with developmental delay. *The New England Journal of Medicine, 330*(7), 478–483.

Fleischer, D., & and Zames, F. (2001). *The disability rights movement: From charity to confrontation.* Philadelphia: Temple University Press.

Fost, N. (1981). Counseling families who have a child with a severe congenital anomaly. *Pediatrics, 67*(3), 321–324.

Frank, A. (2006). Emily's scars: Surgical shapings, technoluxe, and bioethics. In E. Parens (Ed.), *Surgically shaping children* (pp. 68–89). Baltimore: The Johns Hopkins University Press.

Frank, G. (2000). *Venus on wheels: Two decades of dialogue on disability, biography, and being female in America.* Berkeley: University of California Press.

Franklin, S. (1991). Fetal fascinations: New medical constructions of fetal personhood. In S. Franklin, C. Lury, & J. Stacey (Eds.), *Off-centre: Feminism and cultural studies* (pp. 190–205). London: Harper Collins.

———. (1997). *Embodied progress: A cultural account of assisted conception.* London and New York: Routledge.

Freund, H.-J. (1996). Remapping the brain. *Science, 272,* 1754.

Fujiura, G., & Yamaki, K. (2000). Trends in demography of childhood poverty and disability. *Exceptional Children, 66*(2), 187–199.

Gabel, S., & Peters, S. (2004). Presage of a paradigm shift? Beyond the social model of disability toward resistance theories of disability. *Disability and Society, 9*(6), 585– 600.

Geertz, C. (1973). *The interpretation of cultures.* New York: Basic Books

Gerber, E. (2002). Deconstructing pregnancy: RU486, seeing "eggs," and the ambiguity of very early conceptions. *Medical Anthropology Quarterly, 16*(1), 92–108.

Geronimus, A. (2003). Damned if you do: Culture, identity, privilege, and teenage childbearing in the United States. *Social Science and Medicine, 57*(5), 881–893.

Gibbs, N. (2007, January). Pillow angel ethics. Retrieved April 4, 2007, from *Time Magazine Online.*

Gillon, R. (1991). Human embryos and the argument for potential [Editorial]. *Journal of Medical Ethics, 17,* 59–61.

Gilson, S. F. & DePoy, E. (2000). Multiculturalism and disability: A critical perspective. *Disability and Society, 15*(2), 207–218.

Gimp Parade. (2007). The "ransom notes campaign." Retrieved December 24, 2007, from http://thegimpparade.blogspot.com/2007/12/ransom-notes-campaign.html.

Ginsburg, F. (1989). *Contested lives: The abortion debate in an American community.* Berkeley: University of California Press.

Ginsburg, F., & Rapp, R. (1995). Introduction: Conceiving the new world order. In F. Ginsburg & R. Rapp (Eds.), *Conceiving the new world order* (pp. 1–17). Berkeley: University of California Press.

———. (1999). Fetal reflections: Confessions of two feminist anthropologists as mutual informants. In L. Morgan and M. Michaels (Eds.), *Fetal subjects, feminist positions* (pp. 279–295). Philadelphia: University of Pennsylvania Press.

Glascoe, F., Byrne, K., Ashford, L., Johnson, K., Chang, B., & Strickland, B. (1992). Accuracy of the Denver-II in developmental screening. *Pediatrics, 89*(6), 1221–1225.

Goffman, E. (1963). *Stigma.* New York: Simon and Schuster.

Goldenring, J. (1985). The brain-life theory: Towards a consistent biological definition of humanness. *Journal of Medical Ethics, 11,* 198–204.

Good, M.-J., Munakata, T., Kobayashi, Y., et al. (1994). Oncology and narrative time. *Social Science and Medicine, 38*(6), 855–862.

Goodman, J. (1989). Does retardation mean dumb? Children's perceptions of the nature, cause, and course of mental retardation. *Journal of Special Education, 23*(3), 313– 329.

Gottlieb, A. (1998). Do infants have religion? The spiritual lives of Beng babies. *American Anthropologist, 100*(1), 122–135.

Greenwald, J. (1999). Retraining your brain. *Time, 154*(1), 52–53.

Gupta, S. (2002). Letter. *Matchmaker: MUMS National Parent-to-Parent Network Newsletter, 90,* 12.

Hack, M., Taylor, H., Drotar, D., Schlucter, M., Carter, L., Wilson-Costello, D., et al. (2005). Poor predictive validity of the Bayley Scales of Infant Development for cognitive function of extremely low birth weight children at school age. *Pediatrics, 116*(2), 333–341.

Hack, M., Taylor, H., Klein, N., Eiben, R., Schatschneider, C., & Mercuri-Minich, N. (1994). School-age outcomes in children with birth weights under 750 g. *New England Journal of Medicine, 331*(12),753–759.

Hall, J. (1997). Terathanasia, folic acid, and birth defects. *The Lancet, 350,* 1322.

Haller, B., Dorries, B., & Rahn, J. (2006). Media labeling versus the US disability community identity: A study of shifting cultural language. *Disability & Society, 21*(1), 61–75.

Haraway, D. (1986). Primatology is politics by other means. In R. Bleier (Ed.), *Feminist approaches to science* (pp. 77–118). New York: Pergamon.

——. (1997). *Modest_witness: Second_millenium. FemaleMan_meets_OncoMouse: Feminism and technoscience.* New York: Routledge.

Harris, G. (1989). Concepts of individual, self, and person in description and analysis. *American Anthropologist, 91*(3), 599–612.

Harris, G., Connor, L., Bisits, A., & Higginbotham, N. (2004). "Seeing the baby": Pleasures and dilemmas of ultrasound technologies for primiparous Australian women. *Medical Anthropology Quarterly, 18*(1), 23–47.

Harris, S. (1987). Early detection of cerebral palsy: Sensitivity and specificity of two motor assessment tools. *Journal of Perinatology, 7*(1), 11–15.

Harry, B. (2002). Trends and issues in serving culturally diverse families of children with disabilities. *The Journal of Special Education, 6*(3), 131–138.

Hartouni, V. (1991). Containing women: Reproductive discourse in the 1980s. In C. Penley & A. Ross (Eds.), *Technoculture* (pp. 27–56). Minneapolis: University of Minnesota Press.

——. (1993). Fetal exposures: Abortion politics and the optics of allusion. *Camera Obscura, 29,* 131–49.

——. (1999). Epilogue: Reflections on abortion politics and the practices called person. In L. Morgan & M. Michaels (Eds.), *Fetal subjects, feminist positions* (pp. 296–304). Philadelphia: University of Pennsylvania Press.

Hastings, R., Allen, R., McDermott, K., & Still, D. (2002). Factors related to positive perceptions in mothers of children with intellectual disabilities. *Journal of Applied Research in Intellectual Disabilities, 1,* 269–275.

Hedderly, T., Baird, G., & McConachie, H. (2003). Parental reaction to disability. *Current Pediatrics, 13,* 30–35.

Hershey, L. (1994). Choosing disability. *Ms., 5*(1), 26–32.

Hillyer, B. (1993). *Feminism and disability.* Norman: University of Oklahoma Press.

Hockenberry, J. (1995). *Moving violations: War zones, wheelchairs, and declarations of independence.* New York: Hyperion.

——. (1997). Walking with the Kurds. In K. Fries (Ed.), *Staring back* (pp. 22–36). New York: Plume.

——. (2001). The next brainiacs. *Wired*, *9*(8), 1–7.

——. (2007, February 23). Straight on till mourning. Posted on The Gimp Parade: *Slumgullion #29*. Retrieved on June 29, 2007, from http://thegimpparade. blogspot.com/2007/02/saturday-slumgullion-29.html.

Holland, A. (2004). Commentary: Plasticity and development. *Brain and Language*, *88*, 254–255.

Home, A. (2002). Challenging hidden oppression: Mothers caring for children with disabilities. *Critical Social Work*, *2*(2), 88–103.

Hook, E., & Czeizel, A. (1997). Can terathanasia explain the protective effect of folic-acid supplementation on birth defects? *The Lancet*, *350*, 513–515.

Hrdy, S. (1999). *Mother nature: A history of mothers, infants, and natural selection*. New York: Pantheon Books.

Hughes, B. (2007). Being disabled: Towards a critical social ontology for disability studies. *Disability & Society*, *22*(7), 673–684.

Hughes, B., & Paterson, K. (1997). The social model of disability and the disappearing body: Towards a sociology of impairment. *Disability & Society*, *12*(3), 325–340.

Inhorn, M. (2007). *Reproductive disruptions: Gender, technology, and biopolitics in the new millennium*. New York: Berghahn Books.

Irvin, N., Kennell, J., & Klaus, K. (1976). Caring for parents of an infant with a congenital malformation. In M. Klaus and J. Kennell (Eds.), *Maternal-infant bonding* (pp. 167–208). St. Louis: C.V. Mosby.

Ivry, T. (2003). The ultrasonic horror picture show: Obstetrical ultrasound in Israeli public spheres. Paper presented at the Annual Meeting of the American Anthropological Association, Chicago, IL.

——. (2006). At the back stage of prenatal care: Japanese ob-gyns negotiating prenatal diagnosis. *Medical Anthropology Quarterly*, *20*(4), 441–68.

Jenkins, G., & Inhorn, M. (Eds.). (2003). Reproduction gone awry: Medical anthropological perspectives theme issue. *Social Science and Medicine*, *56*(9), 1831–2008.

Johnson, M. (1994). A test of wills: Jerry Lewis, Jerry's Orphans and the Telethon. In B. Shaw (Ed.), *The Ragged Edge: The disability experience from the pages of the first fifteen years of the Disability Rag* (pp. 120–130). Louisville, KY: The Advocado Press.

Johnston, M. (1997). Integrating models of disability: A reply to Shakespeare and Watson. *Disability & Society*, *12*(3), 325–340.

Johnstone, B. (1990). *Stories, community, and place: Narratives from Middle America*. Bloomington: Indiana University Press.

Joralemon, D. (1995). Organ wars: The battle for body parts. *Medical Anthropology Quarterly*, *9*(3), 335–356.

Jordan, B. (1993). *Birth in four cultures*. Long Grove, IL: Waveland Press.

——. (1997). Authoritative knowledge and its construction. In R. Davis-Floyd & C. Sargent (Eds.), *Childbirth and authoritative knowledge* (pp. 55–79). Berkeley: University of California Press.

Kamm, K., Thelen, E., & Jensen, J. (1990). Dynamical systems approach to motor development. *Physical Therapy*, *70*(12), 763–775.

Kang, Y.-S., Lovett, D., & Haring, K. (2002). Culture and special education in Taiwan. *Teaching Exceptional Children*, *34*(5), 12–15.

Kasnitz, D., & Shuttleworth, R. (2001). Anthropology and Disability Studies. In L. Rogers & B. Swadener (Eds.), *Semiotics and disability: Interrogating categories of difference* (pp. 19–41). Albany: State University of New York Press.

Kaye, H., LaPlante, M., Carlson, D., & Wenger, B. (1996). Trends in disability rates in the United States, 1970–1994. *Disability Statistics Abstract* No. 17. Washington, DC: U.S. Department of Education, National Institute on Disability and Rehabilitation Research.

Kearney, P. (1999). Connecting the personal with the professional. *Disability Studies Quarterly*, *19*(4), 337–344.

Kittay, E. (2001). When caring is just and justice is caring: Justice and mental retardation. *Public Culture*, *13*(3), 557–579.

Konner, M. (2002). Weaving life's pattern. *Nature*, *418*, 279.

Kopytoff, I. (1986). The cultural biography of things: Commoditization as a process. In A. Appadurai (Ed.), *The social life of things: Commodities in cultural perspective* (pp. 64–91). Cambridge: Cambridge University Press.

Kushner, T. (1984). Having a life versus being alive. *Journal of Medical Ethics*, *10*(1), 5–8.

Lach, J. (1997, Spring/Summer). Cultivating the mind. *Newsweek* [Special issue], 38–39.

Landsdown, G. (2001). It's our world too! *A Report on the Lives of Disabled Children for the UN General Assembly Special Session on Children.* London: Disability Awareness in Action.

Landsman, G. (1988). *Sovereignty and symbol: Indian–White conflict at Ganienkeh.* Albuquerque: University of New Mexico Press.

——. (1992). The "Other" as political symbol: Images of Indians in the woman suffrage movement. *Ethnohistory*, *39*(3), 247–284.

——. (1998). Reconstructing motherhood in the age of "perfect" babies: Mothers of infants and toddlers with disabilities. *Signs*, *24*(1), 69–99.

——. (1999). Does God give special kids to special parents? Personhood and the child with disabilities as gift and as giver. In L. Layne (Ed.), *Transformative motherhood* (pp. 133–166). New York: New York University Press.

——. (2000). "Real" motherhood, class, and children with disabilities. In H. Ragoné & F. Twine (Eds.), *Ideologies and technologies of motherhood* (pp. 169–187). New York: Routledge.

——. (2003). Emplotting children's lives: Developmental delay vs. disability. *Social Science & Medicine*, *56*, 1947–1960.

——. (2004). "Too bad you got a lemon": Peter Singer, mothers of children with disabilities, and the critique of consumer culture. In J. Taylor, L. Layne, & D. Wozniak (Eds.), *Consuming motherhood* (pp. 100–121). East Brunswick, NJ: Rutgers University Press.

Landsman, G., & Krasniewicz, L. (1990). A native man is still a man: A case study of intercultural participation in social movements. *Anthropology and Humanism Quarterly, 15*(1), 11–19.

Landsman, G., & Van Riper, M. (2007). Incorporating children with disabilities into family life. In E. J. Sobo & P. S. Kurtin (Eds.), *Optimizing care for young children with special health care needs* (pp. 83–113). Baltimore: Paul H. Brookes, Publishing.

Layne, L. (1996). "How's the baby doing?": Struggling with narratives of progress in a neonatal intensive care unit. *Medical Anthropology Quarterly, 10*(4): 624–656.

———. (1997). Breaking the silence: An agenda for a feminist discourse on pregnancy loss. *Feminist Studies, 23*(2), 289–315.

———. (1999). "I remember the day I shopped for your Layettte": Consumer goods, fetuses, and feminism in the context of pregnancy loss. In L. Morgan & M. Michaels (Eds.), *Fetal subjects, feminist positions* (pp. 251–278). Philadelphia: University of Pennsylvania Press.

———. (2003). *Motherhood lost: A feminist account of pregnancy loss in America.* New York: Routledge.

Leiter, V. (2004). Parental activism, professional dominance, and early childhood disability. *Disability Studies Quarterly, 24*(2). Retrieved May 5, 2004, from www.dsq-sds.org.

Lenhard, W., Breitenbach, H., Ebert, H., Schindelhauer-Deutscher, H., & Henn, W. (2005). Psychological benefits of diagnostic certainty for mothers of children with disabilities: Lessons from Down syndrome. *American Journal of Medical Genetics, 133A*, 170–175.

Lewis, J. (1990, September 22). What if I had muscular dystrophy? *Parade Magazine.* Retrieved May 19, 2008, from www.cripcommentary.com/parade.html.

Linton, S. (1998). *Claiming disability.* New York: New York University Press.

Linton, S., Mello, S., & O'Neill, J. (1995). Disability studies: Expanding the parameters of diversity. *Radical Teacher, 47*, 4.

Litt, J. (2004). Women's carework in low-income households: The special case of children with attention deficit hyperactivity disorder. *Gender & Society, 18*(5): 625–644.

Llewellyn, A., & Hogan, K. (2000). The use and abuse of models of disability. *Disability & Society, 15*(1), 157–165.

Lock, M. (2002). *Twice dead: Organ transplants and the reinvention of death.* Berkeley: University of California Press.

Lommen, B. (2003). Letter. *Matchmaker: MUMS National Parent-to-Parent Network Newsletter, 93*, 12.

Longmore, P. (1995). The second phase: From disability rights to disability culture. *Disability Rag and Resource*, Sept/Oct. Internet publication URL http://www.independentliving.org/docs3/longm95.html

———. (1997). Conspicuous contribution and American cultural dilemmas: Telethon rituals of cleansing and renewal. In D. Mitchell and S. Snyder (Eds.), *The*

Body and Physical Difference: Discourses of Disability (pp. 134–158). Ann Arbor: University of Michigan Press.

Longmore, P., & Umansky, L. (2001). Introduction: Disability history: From the margins to the mainstream. In P. Longmore & L. Umansky (Eds.), *The new disability history* (pp. 1–29). New York: New York University Press.

Loos, M. (1999). Letter. *Matchmaker: MUMS National Parent-to-Parent Network Newsletter, 78,* 12.

Lorenz, J., Wooliever, D., Jetton, J., & Paneth, N. (1998). A quantitative review of mortality and developmental disability in extremely premature newborns. *Archives of Pediatric and Adolescent Medicine, 152,* 425–435.

Luker, K. (1984). *Abortion and the politics of motherhood.* Berkeley: University of California Press.

MacKenzie, D. (1981). *Statistics in Britain 1865–1930: The social construction of scientific knowledge.* Edinburgh: Edinburgh University Press.

March of Dimes. (1994). *March of Dimes birth defects foundation catalog of public health education materials.* White Plains, NY: March of Dimes Birth Defects Foundation.

Markens, S., Browner, C.H., & Press, N. (1997). Feeding the Fetus: On interrogating the notion of maternal-fetal conflict. *Feminist Studies, 23*(2), 351– 372.

——. (1999). "Because of the risks": How US pregnant women account for refusing prenatal screening. *Social Science & Medicine, 49,* 359–369.

Marteau, T., & Drake, H. (1995). Attributions for disability: The influence of genetic screening. *Social Science & Medicine, 40*(8), 1127–1132.

Martin, E. (1987). *The woman in the body.* Boston: Beacon Press.

Mattingly, C. (1998). *Healing dramas and clinical plots: The narrative structure of experience.* Cambridge: Cambridge University Press.

McConachie, H. (1995). Critique of current practices in assessment of children. In P. Zinkin & H. McConachie (Eds.), *Disabled children and developing countries* (pp. 110–130). London: Cambridge University Press.

McCubbin, M. A., & McCubbin, H. I. (1993). Families coping with illness: The resiliency model of family stress, adjustment, and adaptation. In C. Danielson, B. Hamell-Bissell, & P. Winstead-Fry (Eds.), *Families, Health and Illness: Perspectives on Coping and Intervention* (pp. 21–63). St. Louis: Mosby.

McDonald, A. (2007). The other story from a "Pillow Angel." *Seattle Post-Intelligencer.* Retrieved June 17, 2007, from http://seatlepi.nwsource.com/opinion/319702_noangel117.html.

McElrath, T. (2002). Management for neonatal survival at the limits of viability. *Contemporary OB/GYN, 47,* 43–71.

McKeever, P., & Miller, K.-L. (2004). Mothering children who have disabilities: A Bourdieusian interpretation of maternal practices. *Social Science & Medicine, 59*(6), 1177–1191.

McMahon, M. (1995). *Engendering motherhood: Identity and self-transformation in women's lives.* New York: The Guilford Press.

Meekosha, H. (2004). Drifting down the Gulf Stream: Navigating the cultures of disability studies. *Disability & Society, 19*(7), 721–733.

Meister, R. (1996). Letter. *Matchmaker: MUMS National Parent-to-Parent Network Newsletter, 66,* 12.

Meyer, L. (1995). Letter. *Matchmaker: MUMS National Parent-to-Parent Network Newsletter, 62,* 12.

Michalale, A. (1999). Letter. *Matchmaker: MUMS National Parent-to-Parent Network Newsletter, 78,* 12.

Miller, D. (1998). *A theory of shopping.* Ithaca: Cornell University Press.

Mitchell, D., & Snyder, S. (1997). Introduction: Disability studies and the double bind of representation. In D. Mitchell & S. Snyder (Eds.), *The Body and Physical Difference: Discourses of Disability* (pp. 1–31). Ann Arbor: University of Michigan Press.

Modell, J. (1999). Freely given: Open adoption and the rhetoric of the gift. In L. Layne (ed.), *Transformative motherhood* (pp. 29–64). New York: New York University Press.

Montgomery, C. (2004). Harry Potter and the allure of separatism. *Ragged Edge Online.* Retrieved June 3, 2004, from http://www.ragged-edge-mag.com.

Moore, H. (1994). *A passion for difference.* Bloomington: Indiana University Press.

Morgan, L. (1996a). Fetal relationality in feminist philosophy: An anthropological critique. *Hypatia, 11*(3), 47–70.

———. (1996b). When does life begin? A cross-cultural perspective on the personhood of fetuses and young children. In W. Haviland & R. Gordon, *Talking about people* (pp. 24–34). Mountain View, CA: Mayfield.

Morgan, A., & Aldag, J. (1996). Early identification of cerebral palsy using a profile of abnormal motor patterns. *Pediatrics, 9*(4), 692–697.

Morris, J. (1991). *Pride against prejudice.* Philadelphia and Gabriola Island, BC: New Society Publishers

———. (2001). Impairment and disability: Constructing an ethics of care that promotes human rights. *Hypatia, 16*(4), 1–16.

Morrow, J. (2000). Making mortal decisions at the beginning of life: The case of impaired and imperiled infants. *MSJAMA, 284,* 1146–1147.

Mull, D. D., & Mull, J. D. (1987). Infanticide among the Tarahumara of the Mexican Sierra Madre. In N. Scheper-Hughes (Ed.), *Child survival* (pp. 113–134). Dordrecht: D. Reidel Publishing.

Murphy, R. (1987). *The body silent.* New York: H. Holt.

———. (1995). Encounters: The body silent in America. In B. Ingstad & S. R. Whyte, *Disability and culture* (pp. 140–158). Berkeley: University of California Press.

Mwaria, C. (1990). The concept of self in the context of crisis: A study of families of the severely brain-injured. *Social Science & Medicine, 30*(8), 889–893.

Nash, M. (1997). Fertile minds. *Time, 149*(5), 48–56.

Nelson, K. B., & Ellenberg, J. (1982). Children who "outgrew" cerebral palsy. *Pediatrics, 69*(5), 529–536.

New York State Department of Health. (1998). *The early intervention program: A parent's guide.* Albany: New York State Department of Health.

Newman, D. (2002). Letter. *MUMS National Parent-to-Parent Network Newsletter 87*, 12.

Nicolaisen, I. (1995). Persons and non-persons: Disability and personhood among the Punam Bah of Central Borneo. In B. Ingstad & S. R. Whyte (Eds.), *Disability and culture* (pp. 38–55). Berkeley: University of California Press.

Oaks, L. (2001). *Smoking and pregnancy: The politics of fetal protection.* New Brunswick, NJ: Rutgers University Press.

Ochs, E., & Capps, L. (2001). *Living narrative: Creating lives in everyday storytelling.* Cambridge, MA: Harvard University Press.

Oliver, M. (1990). *The Politics of disablement.* London: Macmillan.

Olsen, C., Cross, P., Gensburg, L., & Hughes, J. (1996). The effects of prenatal diagnosis, population aging, and changing fertility rates on the live birth prevalence of Down syndrome in New York State, 1983–1992. *Prenatal Diagnosis, 16*, 991–1002.

O'Sullivan, P., Mahoney, G., & Robinson, C. (1992). Perceptions of pediatricians' helpfulness: A national study of mothers of young disabled children. *Developmental Medicine and Child Neurology, 34*, 1064–1071.

Overboe, J. (1999). "Difference in itself": Validating disabled people's lived experience. *Body and Society, 5*(4), 17–29.

Parens, E., & Asch, A. (Eds.) *Prenatal testing and disability rights.* Washington, DC: Georgetown University Press.

Paterson, K., & Hughes, B. (1999). Disability studies and phenomenology: The carnal politics of everyday life. *Disability & Society,* 14(5), 597–610.

Petchesky, R. (1987). Fetal images: The power of visual culture in the politics of reproduction. *Feminist Studies, 13*(2), 263–292.

Pfeiffer, D. (1999). The categorization and control of people with disabilities. *Disability and Rehabilitation, 21*(3), 106–107.

———. (2002). The philosophical foundations of disability studies. *Disability Studies Quarterly, 22*(2), 3–23.

Phillips, M. (1990). Damaged goods: Oral narratives of the experience of disability in American culture. *Social Science & Medicine, 30*(8), 849–857.

Polaneczky, R. (1998, March). The surprising news. *Redbook*, 103-131.

Pollitt, K. (1998). Fetal rights: A new assault on feminism. In R. Weitz (Ed.), *The politics of women's bodies: Sexuality, appearance and behavior* (p. xx). New York: Oxford University Press.

Polloway, E., Patton, J., Smith, J. D., & Smith, T. (1996). Historic changes in mental retardation and developmental disabilities. *Education and Training in Mental Retardation and Developmental Disabilities, 31*(1), 3–12.

Poplaawski, N., & Gillet, G. (1991). Ethics and embryos. *Journal of Medical Ethics, 17*, 62–69.

Press, N., Browner, C., Tran, T., Morton, C., & LeMaster, B. (1998). Provisional normalcy and "perfect babies": Pregnant women's attitudes toward disability in the context of prenatal testing. In S. Franklin & H. Ragoné (Eds.), *Reproducing reproduction: Kinship, power, and technological innovation* (pp. 46–65). Philadelphia: University of Pennsylvania Press.

Purdy, L. (1996). *Reproducing persons: Issues in feminist bioethics.* Ithaca: Cornell University Press.

Putnam, M. (2005). Conceptualizing disability: Developing a framework of political disability identity. *Journal of Disability Policy Studies, 16*(3), 188–198.

Quine, L., & Pahl, F. (1986). First diagnosis of severe mental handicap: Characteristics of unsatisfactory encounters between doctors and parents. *Social Science and Medicine, 22,* 53–62.

Quine, L., & Rutter, D. R. (1994). First diagnosis of severe mental and physical disability: A study of doctor-parent communication. *Journal of Psychology and Psychiatry and Allied Disciplines, 35*(7), 1273–1287.

Ragoné, H. (1994). *Surrogate motherhood: Conception in the heart.* Boulder: Westview Press.

———. (1999). The gift of life: Surrogate motherhood, gamete donation, and constructions of altruism.

Rapp, R. (1997). Real-time fetus: The role of the sonogram in the age of monitored reproduction. In G. Downey & J. Dumit (Eds.), *Cyborgs and citadels: Anthropological interventions in emerging sciences and technologies* (pp. 31–48). Santa Fe: School of American Research Press.

———. (1999a). Forward. In L. Layne (Ed.), *Transformative motherhood, On giving and getting in a consumer culture* (pp. xi–xix). New York: New York University Press.

———. (1999b.) *Testing women, Testing the fetus: The social impact of amniocentesis in America.* New York: Routledge.

Read, J. (1998). Conductive education and the politics of disablement. *Disability and Society, 13*(2), 279–293.

———. (2000). *Disability, the family and society: Listening to mothers.* Buckingham: Open University Press.

Riccitiello, R., & Adler, J. (1997, Spring/Summer). 'Your baby has a problem.' *Newsweek* [Special issue], 46–50.

Rice, N. (2006). "Reining in" special education: Constructions of "special education." In *New York Times* editorials, 1975–2004. *Disability Studies Quarterly, 26*(2). Retrieved November 12, 2007, from www.dsq-sds.org.

Ricoeur, P. (1981). *Hermeneutics and the human sciences.* Cambridge: Cambridge University Press.

Roberts, D. (1991). Punishing drug addicts who have babies: Women of color, equality, and the right of privacy. *Harvard Law Review, 104,* 124–155.

Rosaldo, R. (1993). *Culture and truth: The remaking of social analysis.* Boston: Beacon Press.

Rose, A. (1997). "Who causes the blind to see": Disability and quality of religious life. *Disability & Society, 12*(3), 395–405.

Ross, G., Lipper, E., & Auld, P. (1985). Consistency and change in the development of premature infants weighing less than 1,501 grams at birth. *Pediatrics, 76*(6), 885– 891.

Rothman, B. K. (1986). *The tentative pregnancy: Prenatal diagnosis and the future of motherhood.* New York: Viking/Penguin.

——. (1989). *Recreating motherhood.* New York: WW Norton.

——. (1994). Beyond mothers and fathers: Ideology in a patriarchal society. In E. N. Glenn, G. Chang, & L. R. Forcey (Eds.), *Mothering: Ideology, Experience, and Agency* (pp. 139–157). New York and London: Routledge.

Rothschild, J. (2005). *The dream of the perfect child.* Bloomington: Indiana University Press.

Rowland, R. (1992). *Living laboratories: Women and reproductive technologies.* Bloomington: Indiana University Press.

Rush, B. (2003). Interdependent living: A healthy and healing lifestyle. Retrieved June 13, 2003, from http://www.allenshea.com/interdependent.html.

Sachs, J. S. (1997). Is something wrong? *Parenting, 11*(5), 110–119.

Scheer, J. (1994). Culture and disability: An anthropological point of view. In E. Trickett, R. Watts, & D. Birman (Eds.), *Human diversity* (pp. 244–260). San Francisco: Jossey-Bass.

Scheer, J., & Groce, N. (1988). Impairment as a human constant: Cross-cultural and historical perspectives on variation. *Journal of Social Issues, 44*(1), 23–37.

Scheper-Hughes, N. (1990). Difference and danger: the cultural dynamics of childhood stigma, rejection, and rescue. *The Cleft Palate Journal, 27*(3), 301–306.

——. (1992). *Death without weeping: The violence of everyday life in Brazil.* Berkeley: University of California Press.

Schmidt, M., & Moore, L. J. (1998). Constructing a "good catch," picking a winner. In R. Davis-Floyd & J. Dumit (Eds.), *Cyborg babies: From techno-sex to techno-tots* (pp. 21–39). New York and London: Routledge.

Schultz, S. (2000). Letter. *MUMS National Parent-to-Parent Newsletter, 80,* 12.

Schur, D. (1994). Letter. *MUMS National Parent-to-Parent Newsletter, 58,* 10.

Schwarz, M. T. (1997). Snakes in the ladies' room: Navajo views on personhood and effect. *American Ethnologist, 24*(3), 602–627.

Scotch, R. (1988). Disability as the basis for a social movement: Advocacy and the politics of definition. *Journal of Social Issues, 44*(1), 159–172.

Shakespeare, T. (1994). Cultural representations of disabled people: Dustbins for disavowal? *Disability and Society, 9*(3), 283–299.

——. (1998). Eugenics, genetics and disability equality. *Disability and Society, 13*(5), 665– 681.

——. (2005). Disability studies today and tomorrow. *Sociology of Health and Illness, 27*(1), 138–148.

——. (2006). *Disability rights and wrongs.* London: Routledge.

Shakespeare, T., & Watson, N. (1997). Defending the social model. *Disability and Society, 12*(2), 293–300.

Sheldon, A., Traustadottir, R., Beresford, P., Boxall, K., & Oliver, M. (2007). Review symposium: Disability rights and wrongs? *Disability and Society*, *22*(2), 209–234.

Shore, R. (1997). *Rethinking the brain: New insights into early development.* New York: Families and Work Institute.

Shuttleworth, R. (2002). Defusing the adverse context of disability and desirability as a practice of the self for men with cerebral palsy. In M. Corker & T. Shakespeare (Eds.), *Disability/postmodernity: Embodying disability theory* (pp. 112–126). London: Continuum.

Shuttleworth, R., & Kasnitz, D. (2004). Stigma, community, ethnography: Joan Ablon's contribution to the anthropology of impairment-disability. *Medical Anthropology Quarterly*, *18*(2), 139–161.

Simeonsson, R., Lollar, D., Hollowell, J., & Adams, M. (2000). Revision of the International Classification of Impairments, Disabilities, and Handicaps: Developmental issues. *Journal of Clinical Epidemiology*, *53*(2), 113–124.

Singer, P. (1993). *Practical ethics*, 2nd ed. New York: Cambridge University Press.

——. (1995). *Rethinking life and death: The collapse of traditional ethics.* New York: St. Martin's Press.

——. (2007). A convenient truth [Op-Ed], *New York Times*, January 26, 2007.

Singh, I. (2004). Doing their jobs: Mothering with Ritalin in a culture of mother-blame. *Social Science & Medicine*, *59*, 1193–1205.

Sloper, P., & Turner, S. (1993). Determinants of parental satisfaction with disclosure of disability. *Developmental Medicine and Child Neurology*, *35*, 816–825.

Solnit, J. A., & Stark, M. H. (1961). Mourning and the birth of a defective child. *Psychoanalytic Study of the Child*, *16*, 523–527.

Stabile, C. A. (1992). Shooting the mother: Fetal photography and the politics of disappearance. *Camera Obscura*, *28*, 179–205.

Stahl, S. (1983). Personal experience stories. In R. Dorson (Ed.), *Handbook of American folklore* (pp. 268–276). Bloomington: Indiana University Press.

Stanton, E. C. (1891). The matriarchate or mother-age. *National Bulletin*, *1*, 1–7.

Stein, D., Brailowsky, S., & Will, B. (1995). *Brain repair.* New York: Oxford University Press.

Steinbock, B., & McClamrock, R. (1994). When is birth unfair to the child? *Hastings Center Report*, *34*(6), 15–21.

Stern, A. M. (2002). Beauty is not always better: Perfect babies and the tyranny of paediatric norms. *Patterns of Prejudice*, *36*(1), 68–78.

Strathern, M. (1992). *Reproducing the future: Anthropology, kinship, and the new reproductive technologies.* New York: Routledge.

Suda, S. (2000). Letter. *MUMS National Parent-to-Parent Newsletter*, *80*, 12.

Summers, L. (2004). Alien or activist: A woman in search of a big life. In S. Klein & J. Kemp (Eds.), *Reflections from a different journey: What adults with disabilities wish all parents knew* (pp. 117–121). New York: McGraw-Hill.

Taussig, K-S., Rapp, R., & Heath, D. (2003). Flexible eugenics: Technologies of the self in the age of genetics in A. Goodman, D. Heath, & M. S. Lindee (Eds.), *Genetic/nature/culture* (pp. 58–76). Berkeley: University of California Press.

Taylor, J. (1998). Image of contradiction: Obstetrical ultrasound in American culture. In S. Franklin & H. Ragoné (Eds.), *Reproducing reproduction: Kinship, power, and technological innovation* (pp. 17–45). Philadelphia: University of Pennsylvania Press.

Tembe, F. (2002). Education of children with mental handicap in Mozambique. *Disability World (web-zine), 12*. Retrieved May 19, 2008, from http://www.disabilityworld.org/01-03_02/children/education.shtml.

Thelen, E. (1995). Motor development: A new synthesis. *American Psychologist, 59*(2), 79–95.

Thomas, C., & Corker, M. (2002). A journey around the social model. In M. Corker & T. Shakespeare (Eds.), *Disability/postmodernity: Embodying disability theory* (pp. 18–31). London: Continuum.

Thomson, R. G. (1997). *Extraordinary bodies: Figuring physical disability in American culture and literature*. New York: Columbia University Press.

———. (2004). Integrating disability, transforming feminist theory. In B. Smith & B. Hutchison (Eds.), *Gendering disability* (pp. 73–103). New Brunswick, NJ: Rutgers University Press.

Traustadottir, R. (1991). Mothers who care: Gender, disability and family life. *Journal of Family Life, 12*(2), 211–228.

Tregaskis, C. (2002). Social model theory: The story so far.... *Disability & Society, 17*(4), 457–470.

Tremain, S. (2002). On the subject of impairment. In M. Corker & T. Shakespeare (Eds.), *Disability/postmodernity: Embodying disability theory* (pp. 32–47). London: Continuum.

Tremain, S. (ed.) (2005). *Foucault and the government of disability*. Ann Arbor: University of Michigan Press.

Tronto, J. (1993). *Moral boundaries: A political argument for an ethic of care*. New York: Routledge.

Valle, J., Connor, D., & Reid, K. (2006). IDEA at 30: Looking back, facing forward—a disability studies perspective. *Disability Studies Quarterly, 26*(2). Available online at www.dsq-sds.org. Retrieved November 12, 2007.

Van Riper, M. (2007). Families of children with Down syndrome: Responding to "a change in plans" with resilience. *Journal of Pediatric Nursing, 22*(2), 116–128.

Vermeulen, E. (2004). Dealing with doubt: Making decisions in a neonatal ward in The Netherlands. *Social Science & Medicine, 59*, 2071–2085.

Victorian Infant Collaborative Study Group. (1991). Eight-year outcome in infants with birth weight of 500 to 999 grams: Continuing regional study of 1979 and 1980 births. *Journal of Pediatrics, 1118*(5), 761–767.

Wang, C. (1992). Culture, meaning and disability: Injury prevention campaigns and the production of stigma. *Social Science & Medicine, 35*(9), 1093–1102.

Wasia, T. (2002). Letter. *Matchmaker: MUMS National Parent-to-Parent Network Newsletter 90*, 12.

Watson, S. (2002). Letter. *Matchmaker: MUMS National Parent-to-Parent Network Newsletter, 88*, 12.

Watts, J. L., & Saigal, S. (2006). Outcome of extreme prematurity: As information increases so do the dilemmas. *Archives of Disease in Childhood, Fetal and Neonatal Edition, 91*, F221–F225.

Wayman, K., Lynch, E., & Hanson, M. (1990). Home-based early childhood services: Cultural sensitivity in a family systems approach. *Topics in Early Childhood Special Education, 10*(4), 56–75.

Webster, A., Hand, C., Franey, J., & Hingly, P. (1999). Disability and inclusive education: A United Kingdom perspective. *Disability Studies Quarterly, 19*(4), 346–353.

Weiss, M. (1994.) *Conditional love: Parent's attitudes toward handicapped children.* Westport, CT: Bergin and Garvey.

——. (1997). Territorial isolation and physical deformity: Israeli parents' reaction to disabled children. *Disability and Society, 12*(2), 259–272.

——. 1998. Ethical reflections: Taking a walk on the wild side. In N. Scheper-Hughes & C. Sargent (Eds.), *Small wars: The cultural politics of childhood* (pp. 149–162). Berkeley: University of California Press.

Wendell, S. (1996). *The rejected body: Feminist philosophical reflections on disability.* New York: Routledge.

Whyte, S. R. (1995). Disability between discourse and experience. In B. Ingstad & S. R. Whyte (Eds.), *Disability and culture* (pp. 267–291). Berkeley: University of California Press.

Whyte, S. R., & Ingstad, B. (1995). Disability and culture: An overview. In B. Ingstad & S. R. Whyte (Eds.), *Disability and culture* (pp. 3–37). Berkeley: University of California Press.

Wilson-Costello, D., Friedman, H., Minich, N., Fanoroff, A., & Hack, M. (2005). Improved survival rates with increased neurodevelopmental disability for extremely low birth weight infants in the 1990s. *Pediatrics, 115*(4), 997–1003.

Zeman, A. (1997). Persistent vegetative state. *Lancet, 350*, 795–799.

Zola, K. (1985). Depictions of disability—metaphor, message and medium in the media: A research and political agenda. *Social Science Journal, 22*, 5–17.

Zull, J. (2002). *The art of changing the brain.* Sterling, VA: Stylus Publishing.

Index

early intervention 4, 13, 88, 103–4,
107, 117–18, 130, 174, 177, 181
Early Intervention Coordinating
Council 88, 103
early intervention program 88, 103,
181
early intervention services: access to
180; eligibility for 107
early intervention system, delay
required to warrant public funds
117
earned disabilities 31
egg donation 49
Eisenberg, A. et al 25
eligibility for early intervention
services 104
emotional burden of diagnostic
uncertainty 123
emplotment 108–16; mothers' vs.
doctors' 111–116 process 110;
within stories 118
eugenics 16, 72
euthanasia 50, 56
exchangeability 158–66
exercising 18
exogenous pulmonary surfactant 84
expectations during pregnancy 23, 41
extra-corporeal membrane oxygenation
111

Family Planning Advocates of New
York State 55
father's role in birth outcome 28
fear of disability, use by pro-choice
activists 54
feeblemindedness, prevention of 16
feminism: and devaluation of disabled
people 147; and fetus personhood
54, 58; and the issue of personhood
54; and mother-blame 45; and
reproductive choice 45
feminist movement: and women's
accountability 22, 45; and fear of
disability 42
feminist disability scholar 172, 197
Ferguson, P. 65, 68, 240n

fetal personhood 53, 54, 60, 61, 243n
fetus support 70
Finkbine, Sherry 54
Frank, A. 182
Frank., G. 74
functional determinists 206

Galton, F. 72
Ganienkeh Territory 1
Garrison, Amy 223; on hope 118, 135
General Business Law 159
genetic defect, as cause of disability 21
Geronimus, A. 38
gestational age of viability 60
gestational surrogacy 49, 154
"getting a lemon" 156–60
gift rhetoric 152
Ginsburg, F. 3, 36, 108; and Rapp,
R. 37
Goffman, E. 74
Goldenring, J. 51
Graber, Marilyn 223
Graham, Tina 26, 224; on being
blessed 168; on compassion 169;
on devalued motherhood 75; on
diet 20; on having more children
159; on unconditional love 150
growth attenuation treatment 174

Hack, M. 83
Hagstrom, Bonnie 224
Hahn, H. 183
Haiti 92
Hamburg, D. 137
Hamilton, Lorraine 224; on child as
blessing 151; on her reactions to
her child 166; on prenatal testing
43; on special kids for special
parents 80
Hanson, Francine 31, 225; on prenatal
care 31
Haraway, D. 38
hardships in parenting a disabled child
81
Harmon, Karen 225
Harris, G. 50, 51

reproductive choice: and fear of disability 43; feminist responses 45
reproductive strategies 38
reproductive technologies 10, 16, 17, 128, 154
responsibility, in gendered terms 21
Rett Syndrome 150
Revised Gesell Developmental Schedules 104
rhetoric of the gift 167
Richards, P. 205
right to life 60
right-to-life movement 55
risk, biomedical concept of 128
rites of passage 59
Rivera, Elena 233
Rivers, Denise 233; on attitudes to other children 169; on child's future attitudes 35; on choices 35; on coping 157; on diagnosis 123; on doctors' knowledge 101; on job loss 210; on medical staff 39, 40; on prenatal care 30
Roberts, D. 36
Robertson, J. 36
Robertson, Laura 234; on doctors' knowledge 98; on prenatal care 30
Romano, Becky 234; on acceptance of child's disability 70; on attitudes to other children 169; on child evaluation 119; on child's appearance 201; on doctors' attitudes 162; on God 144; on medical examination of her child 63; on personal growth 165; on predictions 126
Rothman, B.K. 58, 86, 87, 154
Rubenstein, Linda 234; on prenatal care 37
Rush, B. 213

sale of reproductive body parts 154
Sanders, Julie 235; on medical staff 39, 40; on personhood of her child 164

Sawyer, Jane 235; on abandoned celebrations 59; on daughter's birth 49; on first reactions to her child 164; on her child as a real baby 61; on her child's difference 202; on love of a disabled child 167; on pride as a mother 76
Saxton, M. 46
Scheer, J. 50
Scheer, J. and Groce, N. 15
Scheper-Hughes, N. 92, 152, 166
Schiavo, Terri 54
Schur, Diane, on her son as giver 145
Seattle Children's Hospital 174
selective abortion 2, 41, 45, 128, 158
selective embryo reduction 49
self-blame 31
self-consciousness 54
Sellers, Keisha, on her child's personhood 61
sentience 54
severe fetal abnormalities, as reason for abortion 55
Shakespeare, T. 192, 196, 213, 245n
shopping for babies 158
Shuttleworth, R. 2, 194
sickle cell anemia 55
Singer, P. 176
Singh, I. 197
Smith, Phyllis 19, 235
social model of disability 182–4, 189, 194–5, 198, 214; critiques of 194–204, 213
social valuation 70
sociality vs. individualism 51
Somich, Sonya 26, 236; on labeling 65
Songye 51
sonograms 55
Southern Africa 52
spastic diplegia 65, 132
spasticity 132
special education model 176
special kids for special parents 32, 77–84, 144, 210
special mothers, God's support 77